T0382874

The Economics of Venture Capital Firm Operations in India

This book studies diverse categories of venture capital (VC) firms in India based on their ownership type (domestic versus foreign), stage of investment (early versus growth stage), and VC investment team composition (entrepreneurial experience versus investing experience). For each category of VC firms, the nuances in their investment, portfolio involvement, and exit strategies are separately analysed. Employing the framework of information asymmetry, the book studies how different categories of VC firms rely on distinct mechanisms such as deal syndication and domain specialization to address the ensuing adverse selection and agency risks. It also delves into the macro context by assessing whether the emergence of VC in India has been driven by 'pull' or 'push' factors. This is accomplished by analysing in depth the supply and demand of VC funds. Finally, it critically reviews the existing policies of entrepreneurial finance and arrives at recommendations for future directions of the same.

Kshitija Joshi is General Manager, Group Data and Analytics, at the Aditya Birla Group, Bengaluru. She was, until recently, a member of the faculty of Economics at the National Institute of Advanced Studies, Indian Institute of Science, Bengaluru. She has worked across sectors – government, industry, and academia – with a focus on data-driven economic policy research.

The Economics of Venture Capital Firm Operations in India

Kshitija Joshi

CAMBRIDGE
UNIVERSITY PRESS

University Printing House, Cambridge CB2 8BS, United Kingdom

One Liberty Plaza, 20th Floor, New York, NY 10006, USA

477 Williamstown Road, Port Melbourne, VIC 3207, Australia

314–321, 3rd Floor, Plot 3, Splendor Forum, Jasola District Centre, New Delhi–110025, India

79 Anson Road, #06–04/06, Singapore 079906

Cambridge University Press is part of the University of Cambridge.

It furthers the University's mission by disseminating knowledge in the pursuit of education, learning and research at the highest international levels of excellence.

www.cambridge.org
Information on this title: www.cambridge.org/9781108836340

© Kshitija Joshi 2020

First published 2020

Printed in India by Nutech Print Services, New Delhi 110020

A catalogue record for this publication is available from the British Library

ISBN 978-1-108-83634-0 Hardback

Contents

Tables

Figures

Acknowledgements

To start with, I would like to express my sincere gratitude to my PhD supervisor and then department chairman (Department of Management Studies, Indian Institute of Science [IISc], Bangalore), Professor M. H. Bala Subrahmanya. If not for him, I would have never become interested in the domain of venture capital (VC). I sincerely admire his trust in his students, patience, attention to detail, and his penchant for perfection. He has been a great pillar of support throughout my PhD journey. It was primarily his idea that I should work on converting my PhD thesis into a book. Without that nudge, this book would perhaps never have seen the light of the day. Above all, his ethics and value system are something that I will respect all my life irrespective of wherever I am. I consider myself extremely fortunate to have worked under his supervision. I would also like to thank Professor Chiranjit Mukhopadhyay for enabling me to appreciate the nuances in statistics. His timely feedback on various aspects of my work has added a lot of value to my thesis.

I am also grateful to Professor Shailesh Nayak, Director of National Institute of Advanced Studies (NIAS), Bangalore, for his unwavering support to me during my tenure as a faculty member at the institute where this book took shape. I also thank Professor Narendar Pani, other faculty, and staff at NIAS for their help. My gratitude is due towards my IISc ex-colleagues Krishna Satyanarayana, Muralidharan Loganathan, K Ganeshraman, Deepak Chandrasekhar, Vindhyalakshmi Arkalgud, Pratheeba Vimalnath, and Sharada Balsubramaniam for many insightful discussions that shaped my PhD thesis, other publications, and this book. My close friends Sumedha Bajar and Mrunalini Deshpande from NIAS kept me in good spirits throughout the course of this book. Thanks are certainly due to my current organization, Group Data and Analytics Cell at the Aditya Birla Group, for being patient and encouraging while I had to spend many hours working on the manuscript proofs.

Above all, I am grateful to my family. It was my husband, Amey, who encouraged me to quit my corporate job and actively pursue my PhD. My young son, Mihir, has been really accommodating all these years which has enabled me to focus on my academic interests. Moreover, I would like to thank my parents-in-law who came down to Bangalore and took care of my home so that I could solely concentrate on my work. I am also grateful to my parents for their support.

Lastly, I would like to thank Aniruddha De and Anwesha Rana from Cambridge University Press for their efforts. Any errors that remain are mine.

1

Introduction

Preamble

Venture capital (VC) is regarded as one of the most important financial innovations of the twentieth century. It has emerged as an important source of funding in modern times in particular, because it finances those companies that might not have received funding otherwise (Schwienbacher 2009). It has played a key role in the emergence of new economy industries, resulting in high economic growth (Dossani and Kenney 2002). Some of the world's most visible companies today, such as Intel, Apple, Yahoo, Google, Sun Microsystems, Facebook, or Cisco, would not have probably existed without VC support (Gompers and Lerner 1999). VC has been extremely successful in contributing to the development of innovation, and converting innovation into profitable technologies (Schwienbacher 2009). VC-led innovations are also known to have significant spillover effects on the rest of the economy (Van Pottelsberghe and Romain 2004). In fact, the aggregate impact of the companies funded by VC has been found to be far more important than the size of the VC market itself (Schwienbacher 2009). VC has had a significantly positive impact on short-term as well as long-term employment (Wasmer and Weil 2000).

VC as a source of financial intermediation primarily evolved in the United States. Among others, the advancements in the electronics industry and computer technology in the Silicon Valley are believed to have been the major catalysts contributing to the formalization of the VC industry there (Gompers and Lerner 2004). Later, in the 1990s, the VC industry spread to other parts of the world – Europe, Israel, Taiwan, and the other emerging economies in Asia. In India, VC as a source of funding to be reckoned with emerged only during 2006–7 onwards (Bain Consulting 2012).

Despite its late beginnings, the growth trajectory of the Indian VC industry has been particularly steep. As of the present time, there are more than 900 VC firms operating in India (Venture Intelligence 2019). India has emerged among the most favoured destinations for the allocation of global VC funds, and in 2019 ranked fourth in terms of global VC investments, after US, UK, and China (Ernst and Young 2014). VC has funded more than 10,000 deals since 2005 (Venture Intelligence 2019), and almost all unicorns operating in India as of 2019 have been VC funded (Bain Consulting 2012). Several multinational corporations (MNCs) such as Intel, Qualcomm, SAP, Cisco, and Cipla have set up India-focused funds (Planning Commission 2012). Microsoft, Google, Bosch, Merck, Airbus, and Amazon have set up their own business accelerators to leverage the innovative technologies developed by the Indian start-ups. Moreover, the effort of transnational corporate houses have been supplemented by other Indian industrial conglomerates as well. Accordingly, many domestic business groups such as Reliance, Tata, the Aditya Birla group, TVS, Godrej, Patni, Wipro, and Infosys have established their own asset management arms. The VC backed ventures are known to lead the non-VC backed ones in all the major parameters of economic performance – sales, profitability, wages, exports, foreign exchange earnings, and research and development (R&D) investments (India Venture Capital Association 2011). It has been estimated that venture capitalists in India have the potential to create 2,500 successful new ventures over the next decade (Planning Commission 2012). These ventures are, in turn, expected to create 40 million jobs and generate USD 200 billion in revenues.

It can thus be said beyond doubt that VC has played a very important role in the promotion of entrepreneurial ventures in the Indian economy. Yet it is still not clear how the Indian VC firms operate, and what specific roles they play in supporting as well as growing new ventures in the economy. It is in this context that it is important to take up this study.

Definitions and Concepts

At the outset, it is important to define the major concepts that have been used in this empirical study. This section briefly explains some such concepts that have been extensively used here.

What Is Venture Capital (VC)?

Venture capitalists (VCs) are financial intermediaries between investors and entrepreneurs. However, unlike other conventional financial mediators (namely banks and stock markets), VCs primarily focus on funding newly emerging products, services, technologies, and business models that are potentially ineligible for financing by the traditional sources. The peculiar profile of the VC-funded projects (namely emerging domains, nascent technologies, unstructured business and revenue models, intangible assets, absence of cash flow) give rise to significant informational asymmetries between the investors and the investee firms (Sahlman 1990; Amit, Glosten, and Muller 1990, 1993; Amit, Brander, and Zott, 1998). Consequently, the presence of such high level of information asymmetry often makes it difficult for these start-ups to raise loan financing from banks. Moreover, the presence of a low equity base and the absence of cash flow make it unsustainable for them to support debt finance from banks. Also, most banks are known to be risk averse and unlikely to lend in the absence of tangible collateral. This is exactly the opposite of what is needed for funding start-ups, especially in the technology domains.

Owing to the underlying information asymmetry, investments in VC-funded businesses are deemed to be extremely risky. To overcome these risks, VC is not merely a financing arrangement but rather an overall partnership with the investee firm wherein the VCs get involved in all aspects of the venture, namely hiring critical human resources, business development, marketing, planning, and strategy. The Planning Commission (2005) defines VC as 'a special kind of financing arrangement; wherein the provision of finance is customized to the needs of the receiver and the skills of the provider and requires close, ongoing face-to-face interaction, i.e., it is not an arms-length transaction with standardized templates for contracts and lender-borrower relationships'.

Thus, VCs essentially invest their funds in start-ups for which they obtain an equity position in the company. However, unlike public equity, these shares are highly illiquid, and thus the VCs need to hold them for several years prior to selling them. Moreover, there exists no ready market for disposing these shares. Furthermore, since most of the investee companies do not generate positive cash flows during the initial years, they do not pay out dividends as well. In fact, the VCs themselves need to create appropriate opportunities for exiting these investments at a suitable time (Schwienbacher 2009).

Stages in VC Financing

The VCs may choose to provide funding for certain selective stages in a venture's lifecycle, or alternatively provide funding throughout. VC funding is often a relay race, with different VCs specializing in diverse stages of investment. Stage specialization is necessitated by the fact that the *niche* risks encountered by each firm are distinctly different for each subsequent stage. The Planning Commission (2005) identifies the following stages of development of investee firms, during which the VCs generally provide capital:

Seed financing: to the technologist/entrepreneur to prove a concept;
Start-up financing: for product development and initial marketing to a few customers;

First stage financing: to initiate commercial production and marketing;
Second stage financing: for expansion to scale;
Later stage financing: for expansion of an enterprise that is already profitable;
Bridge/Mezzanine financing: as a preparation for going public or for buyout/takeover.

Financing at a very early stage is, however, seldom provided by venture funds, and it often comes from friends and family. It also comes from angel investors who may comprise either private individuals, trusts, or even official agencies that provide low-cost seed capital. Of late, in India, several business incubators have been established within the academic set-ups of universities and research institutes with an aim of providing seed-financing and mentoring nascent ventures (Planning Commission 2012). Later stage funding usually comes from the private equity (PE) firms.[1]

The VC Cycle

At this point, it is important to understand the modalities of VC. For this, we need to first understand the VC set-up. The VC set-up is made up of three entities – the limited partners or LPs (providers of funds), the general partners or GPs (investors of funds), and the investee companies. Usually, LPs refer to the group of institutional investors such as pension funds and insurance companies, or other entities such as foundations, corporations, and individual angel investors. The GPs are the fund managers, comprising finance professionals or erstwhile entrepreneurs. The investee companies are the seekers of capital (fledging firms) with ventures in domains that are mostly ineligible for funding from conventional sources. The VC cycle depicting the flow of funds between various entities in the VC set-up has been shown in Figure 1.1.

The GPs, as fund managers, set up an asset management company that pools capital from the LPs having surplus deployable funds and distributes it among seekers of capital, namely entrepreneurs. Most of these funds are close-ended ones, usually having a lifetime of ten years. The entire lifecycle, from fund-raising to exits (from investee companies), must be completed within this period, and the funds returned to the respective LPs (Gompers and Lerner 2004).

The GPs seek their return through capital appreciation on their investments. However, unlike stock market investors, they cannot sell off their portfolio at any

---

[1]   In India there are no formal definitions of VC and PE, although generally it is agreed that investments lower than USD 5 million in companies less than five years old fall under the purview of VC and everything else be classified as PE.

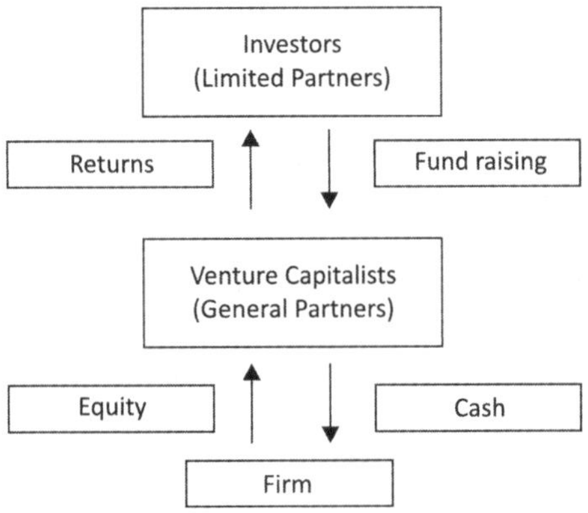

Figure 1.1 The venture capital cycle
Source: Gompers and Lerner (2004).

point of time in the open market, as a readily available market for VC investments most often does not exist. In fact, the VCs need to create liquidation opportunities for their investments when they mature. For their investments, the GPs are usually paid a fixed management fee annually for managing the VC funds. Over and above that, they have a variable component in terms of a specified proportion of the fund's profits. The fixed portion is usually about 1.5 to 3 per cent of the committed capital, or the net asset value and the variable proportion is usually about 20 per cent of the fund profits (Gompers and Lerner 2004). Generally, VC firms look for a return of five to ten times the original investment, but the absolute level of returns depends on several factors, such as the industry and market structure, the stage of investment, and the investment horizon.

Historical Evolution of Venture Capital

VC as a source of financial intermediation has always existed in the world in some form or the other. The decision by Spain's Ferdinand and Isabella to finance Christopher Columbus's voyage of exploration can be considered one of the earliest and the most profitable investments in the history of VC (Megginson 2004). The funding of the East India Company by the merchants in Great Britain could be stated as another such historical example (Brenner 2003).

However, in its current form, VC has been a predominantly American financial innovation (Megginson 2004). Prior to World War II, the source of risk capital for entrepreneurs was either the government (or government-sponsored institutions) or informal investors. However, after World War II, a set of financial intermediaries in the form of VCs emerged on the scene, whose sole activity was investing in fledgling firms that could potentially achieve a rapid growth with a concomitant capital appreciation (Dossani and Kenney 2002).

Since, the VC industry first emerged in the US and then spread to rest of the world, it is important to understand the underlying conditions that led to its emergence there, and the factors which have contributed to its sustained growth since then. In general, there are three factors that may be considered vital to the success of the VC industry, namely a conducive entrepreneurial climate, a robust exit scenario, and a supportive policy regime.

The US as an economy scores high on each of the three prerequisites of the success of the VC industry. To start with, the US government invested heavily in university-based research from its early days. On the one hand, such cash flows into the top engineering universities (Stanford, Berkeley, the Massachusetts Institute of Technology [MIT], and many others) allowed for rapid research improvements in semiconductors and their applications (in computers, radios, phones, and televisions), and on the other, public funding provided a buffer against failure, which encouraged these universities to undertake further riskier research projects (Anjum 2014). These universities, in turn, provided a steady supply of technology entrepreneurs to the Silicon Valley (Dossani and Kenney 2002). In fact, some of the most well-known VC-funded companies on the planet such as Microsoft, HP, Google, Sun Microsystems, Cisco, Oracle, Intel, and Facebook are known to have been originated by the alumni of such illustrious universities located in the vicinity of the Silicon Valley.

The Silicon Valley is not just a stand-alone hub of entrepreneurs, but rather an entire ecosystem constituting VCs, law and accounting firms, and universities and research centers. As such, job mobility was one of the most significant attributes of the technology professionals in the Silicon Valley, resulting in a constant reshuffling of talent and ideas. This constant churn of knowledge led to a quick failure of obsolete ideas, followed by the rapid emergence of better ones. Such a process, akin to the Schumpeterian *creative destruction* has, over time, contributed to an increasing pool of technology entrepreneurs, which has, in turn, been the key contributor for the success of the VC industry in the US.

After the VC industry became institutionalized in the US, it began to emerge in Europe. Initial VC activity occurred in the late 1970s in the UK and the early 1980s in continental Europe. The VC managers from the US who had moved to Europe in search of profitable investment opportunities were instrumental in setting up the initial VC firms there. In its earlier days, the European VC industry was heavily dominated by banks and corporations; however, over time, the US VC firms started playing a dominant role in this market. In general, compared to the US, the European VC industry is regarded to be more conservative and risk-averse, with a much lower focus on early-stage deals and technology-sector investments (rather, consumer industry and energy sectors are more prominent there). Of late, Europe has become a major hub for start-ups in the CleanTech and FinTech space – a majority of which are VC funded.

VC in Asia

After the development of the VC industry in the US and its spread to Europe, the industry gradually emerged in Asia during the mid to late 1980s. Among the Asian economies, Israel, China, and India present compelling case studies. China, India, and Israel rank the highest among the Asian economies (in fourth, fifth, and sixth positions respectively) in terms of worldwide deployment of VC funds (Ernst and Young 2014). Moreover, Tel Aviv, Beijing, and Bengaluru are reckoned among the top ten start-up capitals of the world (Anjum 2014).

Among these, Israel's story is particularly intriguing. Senor and Singer (2009) have investigated the trillion-dollar question: 'How is it that Israel – a country of 7.1 million people, surrounded by enemies, in a constant state of war since its founding, with no natural resources – produces more start-up companies than large, peaceful and stable nations like Japan, India, Korea, China, Canada and UK?' According to the authors, the most significant contributing factor for this phenomenon is the presence of a resilient entrepreneurial culture. Israel specializes in high-growth technology entrepreneurship aimed at commercializing radically innovative ideas. Culturally too, there is a lot of social prestige associated with entrepreneurship, and that prompts many young Israelis to launch high-technology start-ups. Moreover, a business failure is not perceived as a stigma; rather, it counts as an important *experience* on the curriculum vitae (Senor and Singer 2009).

The Israeli government created a government-funded organization, Yozma (meaning initiative), in the early 1990s. Yozma essentially was a fund-of-funds, which received USD 100 million from the government. It invested USD 8 million in ten funds, which had to be augmented with USD 12 million each from foreign VC firms. These sibling funds have formed the backbone of the Israeli VC industry (Dossani and Kenney 2002). After this initial thrust from the government, public support became less significant (by the late 1990s) and the institution of VC became self-sustainable based on private sources of funds alone. These ten Yozma funds created between 1992 and 1997 were later bought out or privatized, and today manage nearly USD 3 billion of capital and support hundreds of new Israeli companies (Senor and Singer 2009).

Right from their inception, exits had never been a bottleneck for VC-funded Israeli start-ups. They were never constrained to list on the Tel Aviv stock market alone, and as such, have been listing on the National Association of Securities Dealers Automated Quotations (NASDAQ) since the 1980s (Dossani and Kenney 2002). As a nation, Israel has more start-ups listed on NASDAQ than those from Europe, Korea, Japan, Singapore, China, and India combined (Senor and Singer 2009). Acquisitions by larger companies in the US is another prominent channel of exiting the VC-funded companies in Israel. In fact, this is the key reason that explains why, despite its innovation-focused entrepreneurship, Israel does not have big brands (Anjum 2014).

Among the worldwide historical origins of VC, China's story is particularly interesting since China is primarily a communist country while VC may be regarded a through-and-through capitalist innovation. However, over time, China has emerged as the topmost destination for VC investments in Asia (Ernst and Young 2014). More intriguing is the part that this feat has been attained in a matter of just one decade (Anjum 2014). To get an insight into this conundrum, we feel that it is important to study the origins and growth of the Chinese VC industry.

Historically, the emergence of VC in China may be attributed to both *pull* and *push* forces. While *pull* forces are the ones arising from the attractiveness of China as the prominent investment destination, *push* forces are the ones that direct more capital to China – mainly owing to its better performance in sheer relative terms. Prima facie, it appears that at least initially it was the push factors that played an important role in the Chinese context (Dauterive and Fok 2004). In the years following the dotcom bust in the US, the VCs there were reluctant to support technology firms in the Silicon Valley, and instead, looked eastwards for other profitable destinations. China, with its robust growth rates, availability of talent pool, and increasing openness to trade was seen as a potentially viable opportunity then. This also corresponded with the accession of China to the World Trade Organization (WTO) in 2001. In fact, this was viewed as a signal that China was soon going to be an integral participant in the global marketplace in the twenty-first century.

Although initially it was the *push* forces that dominated, the *pull* factors soon took over, guided by a number of positives that worked in China's favour. Compared to America (with 254 million internet users), China has over 632 million internet users (that is, over 44 per cent of the Chinese population), and as of 2013, there were about 700 million active smartphones in China (TechCrunch 2014). Thus, it should not be surprising that most Chinese start-ups are based in the mobile-led technologies and Internet-led consumer businesses (Anjum 2014). The talent pool available in China has been one of the most important factors that has worked in China's favour.

Figure 1.2 shows a map representing the ranking of global cities by the number of VC-funded companies hosted by them.

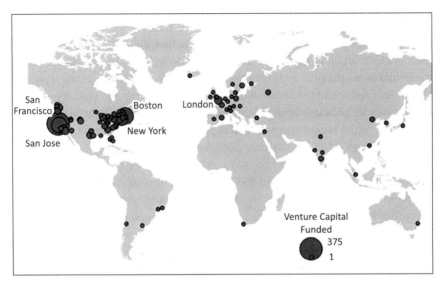

Figure 1.2   Global concentration of VC funded companies
Source: SeedTable.com (2013).

In Figure 1.2, the bigger the size of the dot, the greater is the concentration of VC-funded companies. Quite naturally, San Francisco, San Jose, Boston, and New York have the highest concentrations. Among other cities, London now ranks at the very top tier of VC-funded start-up cities, while Toronto and Vancouver in Canada; Berlin, Paris, Amsterdam, Dublin, Madrid, and Barcelona in Europe; Tel Aviv in the Middle East; Bangalore, New Delhi, and Mumbai in India; Beijing and Shanghai in China; Singapore and Sydney in the Asia Pacific region; and Buenos Aires and Rio de Janeiro in South America – each has significant clusters of start-up activity (SeedTable 2013).

To summarize, we have observed that the world over, there have been three essential prerequisites contributing to the origin and sustained development of the VC industry, namely positive entrepreneurial climate (including entrepreneurial-VC ecosystem), ease of exit from VC-funded companies (particularly in terms of exiting via the initial public offering [IPO] route), and regulatory policies that facilitate the supply and the demand sides of the VC markets. Across all countries, the government has invariably played a significant role in nurturing the VC industry, – although the nature of its intervention varies with the stage of development. During the initial phases, the government's role is more direct (in terms of making seed-capital available), while at the later stages it is more facilitative in nature (establishing conducive environment for VC investments).

Venture Capital in India

Having discussed at length the progress of VC across the world, it is now time to discuss its evolution in India. We start this section by providing a background of the Indian socio-political and economic scenario that prompted the emergence of VC. This is followed by a discussion about evolution of the VC industry in India and the relevant policies impacting the same. Finally, we throw light on the current state of VC in the Indian economy and highlight the major challenges ahead.

Since Independence, democratic polity and a socialistic ideology have been the cornerstones of the Indian economy. Although, historically, India has had a rich culture of private enterprise, the idea of 'building business to sell' was still a relatively new concept. In fact, most of the older businesses were built with the purpose of bequeathing them to the next generation (Planning Commission 2012).

In the early years, despite facing severe resource constraints, the Indian government had exhibited the vision to invest in education, which resulted in the establishment of prestigious engineering and business schools in the form of Indian Institutes of Technology (wherein the curriculum was modelled on the lines of the prestigious MIT in the US) and Indian Institutes of Management. The main aim of these institutions was to make India self-reliant in terms of technical and managerial skills (Dossani and Kenney 2002). However, job opportunities in India failed to keep pace with the quantum of technical personnel graduating out of these schools, and soon many students were obligated to migrate overseas in search of better employment opportunities. Those who stayed in India were employed in either government jobs, large conglomerates, or family businesses. Thus, a large pool of capable engineers and scientists were available in India who were substantially underpaid (Dossani and Kenney 2002).

India's financial system was quite sophisticated compared to the other emerging economies of that period (Dossani and Kenney 2002). Historically, the country had a deep network of banks – most of them state-controlled. However, a large section of these bank managers were not proficient finance professionals; rather, they were civil servants with a background in bureaucracy. This culminated in a risk-averse lending culture within the banking system.

Socially, there was a large stigma associated with business failure, which deterred educated professionals from taking on risks by starting new ventures. Moreover, with the guarantee of lifetime employment provided by the government-owned organizations, such risks were further deemed unnecessary. To add to that, most financial intermediaries were either hesitant or were legally prohibited from providing capital to the fledgling entrepreneurial firms – particularly those that were technology based (Dossani and Kenney 2002). To sum up, despite having a talented pool of technology personnel and a robust financial system, technology entrepreneurship and entrepreneurial funding had not yet emerged in India till the mid-1980s.

It was against this backdrop that the information technology (IT) industry evolved in India. By then, the industry had already made its presence felt in the US. In fact, during the decade of the 1980s, the world witnessed a severe shortage of software programmers (Dossani and Kenney 2002). Incidentally, around the same time, Indian private software firms such as Wipro, HCL, and Tata Consultancy Services had started exhibiting their programming prowess. Buoyed by this, the Indian government began to liberalize the computer and software industry by encouraging software exports (Evans 1992). Meanwhile, multinational firms in this domain such as Texas Instruments and IBM had established their offices in India. India also had a number of successful overseas IT entrepreneurs who had migrated there during the earlier decades. As such, this provided a conduit through which the Indian engineers could build strong networks in the Silicon Valley and learn state-of-art global computing. Meanwhile, outsourcing, and consequently off-site contract programming, also picked up. Around the same time, illustrious Indian entrepreneurs such as Kanwal Rekhi, Vinod Khosla, and Suhas Patil had become established names in the Silicon Valley (Dossani and Kenney 2002). These and many more entrepreneurs were extremely keen on leveraging the talent pool in India.

To sum up, by the end of the 1980s, India had most of the preconditions for creation of a vibrant VC industry in India – relatively well-established stock market, growing IT industry that could provide a steady stream of high growth firms, skilled talent pool, and a cadre of successful Silicon Valley entrepreneurs keen on leveraging this pool. It was against this backdrop that the institution of VC emerged on the Indian scene.

The opening up of the economy post 1991 brought many foreign VC firms to India. However, the Indian VC sector received a further boost in its true sense during the severe recession encountered in the developed economies worldwide post 2007. It has been widely believed that the credit meltdown in the developed economies (particularly the US and the Eurozone) was the principal factor that drove VC funds worldwide to scour for other prospective investment destinations. These were then directed to the emerging economies such as India (and China) that exhibited strong resilience in the face of severe recession in the western world (Bain Consulting 2011, 2012). For India, coincidentally, this trend corresponded with high debt costs (high interest rates owing to high inflation) and choppy equity markets, thus making VC a potentially attractive source of funding from the point of view of Indian entrepreneurs (Bain Consulting 2011, 2012). Consequently, huge inflows of VC were reported in India post 2007. Studies reveal both 'pull' and 'push' forces have been responsible for the emergence of the VC ecosystem in India (Joshi and Satyanarayana 2014), and as of 2019, there were about 980 VC firms operating in India (Venture Intelligence 2019).

Growth and Current Status of the Indian VC Industry

At this stage, it is important to delve into the growth and current status of the VC industry in India.

Number of VC Firms

From Figure 1.3, it can be seen that the number of VC firms in India have grown exponentially from just 8 in the pre-1992 period to about 908 at the end of 2018.

In fact, the most rapid growth has been witnessed post 2002, that is, after the Securities and Exchange Board of India (SEBI) took charge as the central regulatory authority for VC firms operating in India.

Growth of VC Investments

As the number of VC firms operating in India increased, the cumulative VC investments increased as well – by more than five times from that of USD 2.6 billion in 2006 to USD 24.02 billion at the end of 2018, reaching a high of USD 35.84 billion in mid-2018 (Figure 1.4).

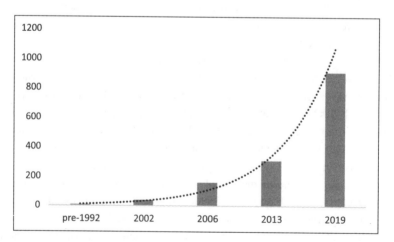

Figure 1.3   Number of VC firms

Source: Venture Intelligence (2019).

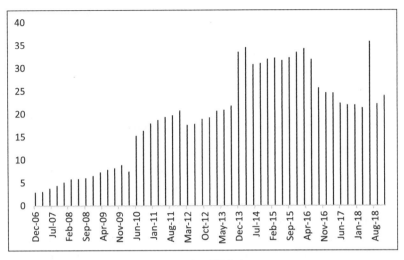

Figure 1.4 Cumulative VC investments (in USD bn)
Source: SEBI (2019).

VC-Funded Companies and Deals

Figure 1.5 presents the growth trajectory of VC-funded companies and deals. *Companies* are the primary business entities funded by the VCs. However, each

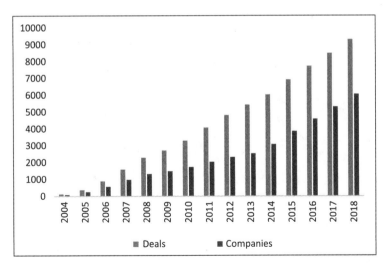

Figure 1.5 VC funded companies and deals
Source: Venture Intelligence (2019).

company can receive funding during multiple stages of its lifecycle either from the same VC firm or different VC firms. We have defined each stage of funding as a separate *deal*.

The number of VC-funded companies and deals have gone up from 92 to 6,062 and 133 to 9,318 between 2004 and 2018 respectively.

Sector-wise Break-up of VC and PE Deals

Having looked at the growth of VC firms, VC-funded companies, and the VC investments, it will be interesting to analyse the sector-wise break-up of VC investments. Accordingly, Figure 1.6 presents the sector-wise break-up of VC/PE deals.

From Figure 1.6, the bias in VC funding towards IT, banking, financial services and insurance (BFSI), and life sciences domains is quite obvious – with about 62 per cent of the deals coming from these three sectors alone. The data used for Figure 1.6 comprise both VC and PE deals. If we were to look at VC deals alone (which are mostly early-stage investments), the bias in favour of these sectors would be even more prominent. The other sectors that have received a relatively higher share of PE funding in particular are manufacturing, energy (mostly comprising clean technology), education and media.

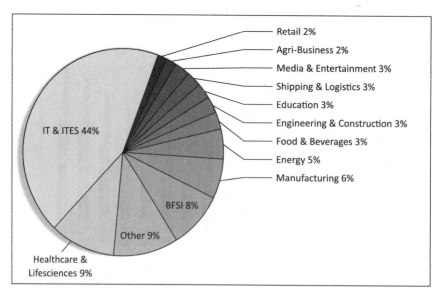

Figure 1.6 Sector-wise break-up of VC and PE deals
Source: Venture Intelligence (2019).

Distribution of Aggregate VC Investments across Domestic and Foreign VC Firms

It is further interesting to look at the break-up of aggregate VC investments across domestic and foreign VC firms. Accordingly, Figure 1.7 presents the break-up of the cumulative VC investments across such VC Firms (for all sectors taken together).

At an aggregate level, about 72 per cent of the cumulative investments have been made by foreign VC firms, while about 28 per cent have been made by the domestic VC firms. The actual role of foreign funds in the Indian VC sector is understated in these computations. Although the domestic VC firms raise overseas funds, in definitional terms, these still qualify as investments made by domestic VC investors. Moreover, a large proportion of foreign VC funds bypass the SEBI route and are invested via the foreign direct investment (FDI) route. Figure 1.7 captures only those funds that have come in via the SEBI registration route. According to various reports, more than 80 per cent of the VC funds invested in India have been raised overseas (Deloitte 2012; Ernst and Young 2014).

Distribution of Deals by Stage of Funding

It is further interesting to view the break-up of deals by their stage of funding. Figure 1.8 shows the same. Only about 33 per cent of the total VC-funded deals (between 2004 and 2013) are early-stage ones. Early-stage deals have been defined based on the data provided by Venture Intelligence (definition – investment amount less

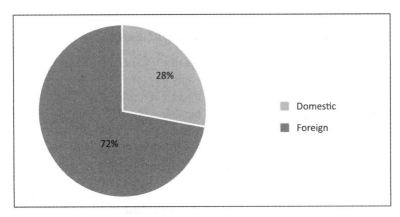

Figure 1.7 Distribution of aggregate VC investments across domestic and foreign VC Firms

Source: SEBI (2019).

Note: Since investments by foreign VC firms are restricted in the real estate sector according to FDI norms, the same have been excluded from the computations in this figure.

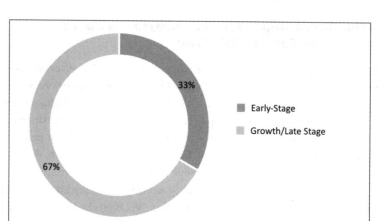

Figure 1.8 Distribution of deals by stage of funding
Source: Venture Intelligence (2019).

than USD 5 million in companies less than five years old, which are not offshoots of larger conglomerates).

It must be noted that the proportion in Figure 1.8 has been computed in terms of the number of deals. If this proportion was to be computed in terms of the funding amount, it would have been even smaller, since the relative funding size of early-stage deals is relatively much lower (we do not have the funding amount details available to us to compute the same).

Funded Companies versus Successful Exits

Successful exits have been defined as those via the IPO and mergers and acquisitions (M&A) route. Since a successful exit is the only way for a VC firm to earn its return on investment, it is important to analyse the exit scenario.

Figure 1.9 shows the changes in the number of funded companies and exits over time. From the figure, it can be seen clearly that successful exits have lagged behind by a significant margin. Although about 10,000 companies have been funded (between 2004 and 2018), only about 1,201 successful exits have been witnessed.

Distribution of VC Firms by Cities in India

Finally, it is also important to understand how the VC firms are distributed across the cities in India. Figure 1.10 presents the same.

The VC firms are not uniformly distributed across cities. Rather, there is a clear cluster formation with about 93 per cent of the VC firms coming from just three

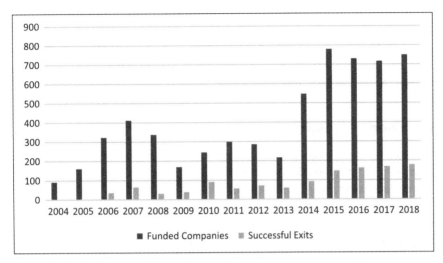

Figure 1.9 Funded companies and successful exits

Source: Venture Intelligence (2019).

Note: Only IPO and M&A exits have been considered here.

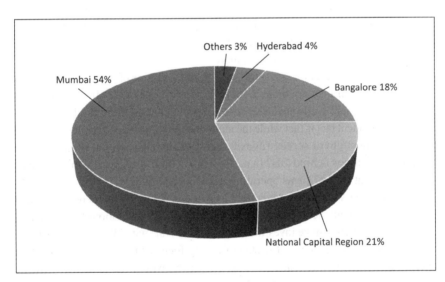

Figure 1.10 Distribution of VC firms across Indian cities

Source: Venture Intelligence (2019).

Indian city clusters, namely the National Capital Region (New Delhi, Gurgaon, Noida), Mumbai, and Bangalore. It must be pointed out that the importance of Bangalore as a primary VC-entrepreneurial hub is understated in Figure 1.10.

Many VC firms that have registered offices in other cities also have secondary offices in Bangalore (for example, SeedFund, Nexus Partners, Norwest Venture partners). Moreover, most of the foreign VC firms that have relatively much larger fund sizes compared to the domestic ones are located here (for example, Sequoia Capital, Accel Ventures, ICICI Ventures).

Pertinent Questions

Based on the discussion about the Indian VC-entrepreneurial ecosystem, policies relevant to VC operations in India, and the current status of the Indian VC industry, several interesting issues can be raised.

To start with, it would be interesting to understand the factors responsible for the meteoric rise of India's VC industry. In particular, what underlying dynamics have worked in its favour to make it one of the most sought after nations in the world for deploying VC funds – was this sudden change caused by *push* factors alone or have *pull* forces also played an important role here?

Even within India, the spread of VC has not been uniform; rather, the VC firms have exhibited a tendency to be geographically clustered. But what could be the underlying reasons for the same? What would it take to make this phenomenon more broad-based? In fact, should the government policies focus on further enhancing the depth of the VC ecosystem in the prevailing geographies or should resources be expended to make this ecosystem more broad-based?

Further, why is it that foreign funds have been the engine of growth of the Indian VC industry? Will they continue to do so in the future as well? If not, then what policy measures are warranted to ensure a smooth flow of these funds?

Another evident fact is that while the number of VC-funded companies has grown rapidly, the quantum of successful exits significantly lags behind. What could be the possible reasons behind this? In particular, are there any specific impediments to the exits that the VC firms operating in India encounter?

Although the VC-funded deals have grown exponentially, is there a sufficient understanding about the micro-aspects related to VC firm operations? In particular, how do the VC firms make investment decisions to start with? Would these aspects of decision-making differ by the stage-funding focus of the VC firms? Would it differ across foreign and domestic VCs? Moreover, would the same differ by the differences in the investing team background?

Then again, to what extent do the VCs operating in India get involved in their respective portfolio companies? Do they take on a monitoring role alone or do they also provide a significant value addition? In particular, can the Indian VC firms be classified into distinct clusters in terms of their decision-making strategies? Finally, what kind of VC firms are likely to witness a greater proportion of successful exits?

Since none of the above questions have been empirically probed in the context of Indian VC firms to the best of our knowledge, it would be appropriate to examine them in the form of an empirical research study. The current study presents such an attempt.

Chapter Schemata

This book is organized into seven chapters. The second chapter consists of a detailed review of literature related to our study. In this regard, we have reviewed literature pertaining to both the macro and micro aspects of VC investing. While the former pertains to the VC ecosystem at large, the latter relates to the decision-making aspects, specifically the ones governing VC investment decisions, their portfolio involvement intensity, and their exit strategies. Chapter 3 presents the objectives of the study, its scope, and the methods of analyses in granular detail. Chapter 4 analyses the supply side and Chapter the demand side of the Indian VC ecosystem. Chapter 6 investigates the investment decisions of the VC firms. In particular we probe the nature of latent signals that guide the VC firms in making investment decisions in light of the prevailing information asymmetry between them and the investee companies. Chapter 7 examines the intensity of involvement of the VC firms in their funded ventures. We are interested in assessing how these VC firms gain control over the ensuing agency risks therein. Chapter 8 looks into the exit related strategies used by the Indian VC firms. Here, we are interested in detailing out the underlying factors that ultimately result in successful exits from the investee ventures. Finally, Chapter 9 summarizes the major findings of the study and discusses its managerial and policy implications.

2

Ecosystem and Strategic Decision Making

The aim of this chapter is to present a comprehensive survey of the most significant studies in the domain of venture capital (VC). The latter may be classified into two broad streams – first, those that delve into the *ecosystem related aspects* of the VC industry and, second, those that probe the *micro-level decision-making processes* of the individual VC firms *per se*. While the former visualizes the VC ecosystem as a macro entity, the latter discuss the underlying risks and other challenges encountered by the individual VC firms in their micro-level decision-making processes.

Since the motivation of this study is gaining an insight into both these aspects, our review of the literature encompasses both these dimensions. To start with, we begin with an overview of the VC ecosystem as an integrated whole. We then move on to review literature that focuses on the individual VC firm as a micro-entity.

The VC Ecosystem

The VC ecosystem may be viewed as a conventional supply–demand framework (Poterba 1989). The limited partners (LPs), namely fund providers, and general partners (GPs), namely fund managers, constitute the *supply* side of this ecosystem, whereas the investee firms comprise the *demand* side. The supply (Ss) and the demand (Dd) sides of the VC ecosystem are each, in turn, affected by a set of *systematic* and *non-systematic* influences. Systematic influences refer to the overall macro environment and policy level factors that affect all the concerned economic agents in the system in a more or less uniform manner. The non-systematic influences are the micro aspects of these economic entities that, in turn, influence their performance. Each of these has been discussed in detail in the following sections.

Supply Side of the VC Ecosystem

As noted, the supply side of the VC ecosystem is affected by both systematic and non-systematic factors. At a global level, the systematic influences govern the overall quantum of VC funds allocated to any economy. In general, the LPs are inclined to allocate more VC to better-performing economies. The non-systematic influences refer to the attributes that affect the fund-raising potential of the individual GPs. These in particular depend on the success rates of their historical investments and the relative expertise of the individual VC fund managers.

Systematic Influences on the Supply of VC

A high rate of growth of gross domestic product (GDP) is a strong indicator of robustness of the economy. In general, LPs are willing to allocate more VC funds to economies with a robust GDP growth (Gompers and Lerner 1999; Bonini and Alkan 2006, 2010; Cherif and Gazdar 2011). In fact, this has been advanced as the rationale behind the huge flow of VC funds to China and India since 2007–8, that is, the years following the recession in the United States (US) (Bain Consulting 2012).

Interest rates on government bonds are a proxy for the risk-free interest rate. Consequently, an increase in this rate increases the opportunity cost for the LPs from allocating their funds to VC vis-à-vis other competing investment alternatives. This, in turn, will reduce the supply of VC funds unless the LPs are duly compensated in the form of higher returns from their investments in investee firms (Gompers and Lerner 1999; Bonini and Alkan 2009).

Robustness of stock markets is a precondition for success of the VC industry. The returns on any VC investment are conditional on a successful exit. Among all the exit channels available to a VC fund manager, initial public offer (IPO) has been found to be the most profitable (Black and Gilson 1999; Cochrane 2005). Thus, naturally, the role of strong stock markets becomes quite imperative. In fact, NASDAQ in the US and Neuer Markt in Europe have played a very important role in developing a vibrant VC industry there (Fiedler and Hellman 2001; Gompers and Lerner 2004). These markets (also known as over-the-counter exchanges) have less stringent listing criteria (in terms of a track record of profitability) compared to the conventional stock exchanges, and have thus facilitated the listing of VC-funded firms. Studies have also found a significant relationship between the number of VC-backed IPOs and new fund-raising by the GPs in the following year (Black and Gilson 1999).

Government policies that have either direct or indirect influence on the VC market are quite vital too. Among these, policies pertaining to taxation are of particular importance. Capital gains taxes directly affect the incentives of the LPs/GPs as they are mandated to pay taxes on the capital appreciation for the companies they invest in. When the capital gains taxes are lowered, the LPs/GPs need to look for a relatively lower expected rate of return on their VC investments (Poterba 1989; Gompers and Lerner 1999; Bonini and Alkan 2009). This implies that at the same expected rates of return as earlier, more VC funds become available in the market. The other set of policies are those that lift the existing restrictions on corporate and government entities to invest in VC. Also, the policies pertaining to the relative simplicity of bankruptcy procedures are quite imperative. It is well understood that about 90 per cent of the VC-funded businesses tend to fail. Under such circumstances, if the bankruptcy procedures are not simple enough to manoeuvre through, it can present itself as a major deterrent to the investors.

Above all, socio-economic and political factors play a key role in determining the course of the VC industry in any economy. Factors such as high level of corruption, political instability, conflicts and crime, poor socio-economic conditions resulting in social unrest, poor economic freedom, and poor assignment of property rights are some of the critical factors that deter the supply of VC funds (Bonini and Alkan 2006; Cherif and Gazder 2011). In general, the VC industry is found to be vibrant in economies that perform better on these attributes.

Non-systematic Influences on the Supply of Venture Capital

Non-systematic factors are those that determine the fundraising potential of the individual fund managers, namely GPs, and are mainly based on their erstwhile performance and reputation (Gompers and Lerner 2004). Earnings multiples on exited deals are indicative of the performance of the GPs, and is often used as a key metric in the assessment of past performance. Accordingly, the value of equity held by GPs in the firms which have gone public in the immediate past has been found to be important in influencing the size of fundraising (Gompers and Lerner 2004). Past reputation also affects the size of the funds raised. Older and larger GPs have higher probabilities of raising larger funds (Gompers and Lerner 2004). It has also been found that more capital is allocated to GPs that provide strategic/management advice in addition to the provision of mere financial capital. In fact, strategic/management role played by the GPs is found to be of greater importance in fundraising compared to marketing or administrative roles. In addition, fundraising is greater among funds with higher returns and performance fees and lower fixed management fees (Cumming, Fleming, and Schwienbache 2005).

Demand Side of the VC Ecosystem

To reiterate, the demand for VC arises from the fledgling entrepreneurial ventures. Thus, in order to gain an insight into the nature of influences affecting the demand side, we need to probe the attributes related to the start-up ecosystem. Moreover, it is imperative to point out here that the start-ups do not emerge on a stand-alone basis, but rather develop in the form of clusters. The venture capitalists (VCs) and start-up clusters are closely co-located, as they draw upon mutual synergies from one another. The following section investigates the factors that result in the emergence of such start-up clusters.

Factors Influencing the Demand for VC

Macro parameters influencing the start-up ecosystem can be divided into three categories, namely macroeconomic indicators, government policies, and regional start-up ecosystem related factors. Reynolds (1993) and Reynolds and Storey (1993) have identified agglomeration and urbanization as vital determinants of start-up establishment rates in a region. In general, start-ups do not emerge on a stand-alone basis but rather as a part of the larger ecosystem. In fact, the presence of a *critical minimum mass* specialized in a particular domain plays an important role in the establishment, sustenance, and survival of start-ups, particularly in the high-technology domains. Start-up clusters are known to facilitate the absorption of external knowledge and thus result in significant positive externalities in the form of knowledge *spillovers*.[1] High-tech clusters allow employees of various start-ups to network with one another and make it easier for the firms to gain access to specialized suppliers, scientific knowledge, and technological expertise indigenous to the area (Stough, Haynes, and Campbell 1998; Beaudry and Swann 2001; Dumais, Ellison, and Glaeser 2002; Rosenthal and Strange 2005; Pe'er and Vertinsky 2006; Wennberg and Lindquist 2010).

Entrepreneurial spawning is perhaps the most important and yet the most understated element responsible for the evolution of start-up clusters (Mason 2007). In fact, the origin of most technology clusters can be traced to a few individuals who leave their parent firms in order to start their own ventures with the aim of commercializing their novel technological ideas (Mason 2007). These pioneering entrepreneurs serve as role models for others who similarly quit their parent organizations, thus generating further spin-offs. This process of 'entrepreneurial spawning' ultimately culminates in the overall upgradation of the regional economy (Castilla et al. 2000). In a majority of clusters world over, a small number of key organizations have been found to be the source of a disproportionate number of multiple entrepreneurs (Langford, Wood, and Ross 2002; Neck et al. 2004; Dahl, Pedersen, and Dalujm 2005).

---

[1] Silicon Valley, Boston Route 128, and the Cambridge region in the United Kingdom are well-known clusters of high-tech start-ups.

The nature of technology itself has a significant role to play in the emergence of start-up clusters. It is important to understand that not all technologies, but rather only the ones that are truly disruptive that have the potential to result in high-tech clusters (Kenney and von Burg 1999). Further, the nature of technology needs to be such that it has the potential to result in a continuous flow of profitable opportunities. The growth trajectory of the new technology is also important. Technologies that provide scope for multiple applications often turn out to be the most dominant ones (Mason 2007). A prominent example of this is the comparison between semiconductors (enabling technology for nearly every important electronic innovation) and mini-computers (a product segment in the computer industry). A study by Kenney and von Burg (1999) in this regard points out how the latter stagnated while the former grew rapidly owing to its much wider range of applications.

Human capital is by far the most important resource for the knowledge-based economy (Drucker 2014) and has rightly been identified as the most important predictor of entrepreneurial firm formation and entrepreneurial absorptive capacity (Davidsson and Honig 2003; Acs and Armington 2006; Qian, Acs, and Stough 2012). Moreover, informal ties among human resources provide market or technological intelligence, allowing companies to make superior decisions as to which technologies to adopt or, at times, discontinue. Bahrami and Evans (1995) envision employee churn as a 'recycling mechanism' that helps preserve the value of assets committed to failed enterprises. Other studies point out that most clusters fail since they cannot reach the level of labour market flexibility and social networks as in Silicon Valley (Saxenian 1994; Casper 2007).

Studies about high-tech clusters in emerging economies have mainly focused on India, China, and Taiwan. Apart from the influences previously discussed, a few other factors seem to be instrumental in the development of clusters therein. The most notable among these has been the role played by the returnee entrepreneurs (Kenney, Breznitz, and Murphree 2013). These first-generation returnee immigrants, with their valuable overseas work experience, entrepreneurial skills, access to global networks, and VC, have been identified as the prime agents in the high-tech cluster formation process (Saxenian 2002; Chacko 2007).

Furthermore, MNCs have been key drivers of high-tech cluster formation in emerging economies. Although these economies have always served as offshore locations to western MNCs, over the past decade or so a different pattern has emerged (Gereffi 2005). While earlier, MNCs offshored only labour-intensive, standardized manufacturing processes (Gereffi 2005), of late, they have been found to offshore more advanced functions, including software and product development (Patibandla and Petersen 2002). These MNCs have played an important role in cluster formation, particularly by customizing local institutions and business practices in accordance with their sourcing needs and based on their experience in other local business contexts. The resultant specialized resources and service capabilities attract follower MNCs with similar sourcing needs (Manning 2008).

Having delved into the literature pertaining to the macro parameters that influence the VC-entrepreneurial ecosystem, we shall now discuss the factors that impact the decision-making processes of the individual VC fund managers. But for this, it is important to first put into perspective the key challenges encountered by the former, understand the rationale for the very existence of VCs as a separate source of finance, and see how the same differs from the conventional financial intermediaries.

Why Do VC Firms Exist: An Economic Rationale

The *new economy* ventures are known to significantly differ from the conventional small and medium enterprises in many aspects. Among others, nascent technologies, domains and business models, and, most importantly, intangibility of assets are the mainstay of such new-age firms. The main differentiating factor in terms of financing these two types of firms is the acute level of information asymmetry possessed by the former. In fact, VCs exist as they are known to possess the *niche* in selecting and monitoring projects with a high level of information asymmetry (Chan 1983; Sahlman 1990; Amit, Glosten, and Muller 1990, 1993; Macintosh 1994; Amit, Brander, and Zott 1998).

Information asymmetry results in two distinct types of risks: adverse selection[2] and agency risks[3]. In general, such risks are usually managed by the use of either 'collateral' or 'reputation'. However, the types of ventures that show up for VC funding seem to lack both. They lack 'collateral' as most of their assets are intangible (held in the form of intellectual property). They also lack 'reputation' as these ventures often have no historical track record. Consequently, the incidence of market failure is known to be particularly severe in this domain of entrepreneurial finance. Over time, VC financing has emerged as an effective solution to tackle this kind of market failure (Barry et al. 1990; Fried and Hisrich 1994).

Information asymmetry results in imperfect markets and the presence of VCs enables the markets to move towards perfection (Wright and Robbie 1998). VCs make this possible by bringing in strong supply as well as demand side benefits to the market. Supply side benefits imply a greater supply of funds from the institutional

---

[2] Risks from *hidden information* (entrepreneurs possess certain information not known to the VCs).

[3] Risks from *hidden actions* (entrepreneurs can take certain actions not observable by the VCs).

investors into the VC market. Demand side benefits imply a greater demand for VC funds from the entrepreneurs.

Supply Side Benefits

VCs have a distinct advantage over other investors in terms of collecting, analysing, processing, and utilizing information pertaining to new economy ventures. Their *niche* specialization also enables them to make better decisions. VCs play an important role as collectors of information. They gather information usually at a much lower cost than what other investors would incur had they collected it directly (Chan 1983; Sahlman 1990; Fried and Hisrich 1994). Since they gather information on behalf of many investors, they possess economies of scale, and as they invest in many ventures, they encounter significant economies of scope (through their established network of referral sources, accountants, attorneys, recruiters, and other service providers). Moreover, they benefit from their learning curve. Information collected in the context of one venture can be useful in the context of another (especially if they belong to the same industry). All these factors significantly reduce the information-gathering costs for a VC (Barry et al. 1990).

In fact, the fund providers regard VCs not merely as information-gathering agents but also decision-making agents. The contracts between the former and the VCs are designed in a manner such that it grants the latter complete decision-making authority (Sahlman 1990). This could be because VCs can make better investment decisions than their investors owing to their *niche* abilities of dealing with imperfect information. In fact, it has been observed that capital markets attach great value to the post-investment activities of a VC, assuming that VCs are better at overseeing and guiding new enterprises than the investors (Barry et al. 1990; Megginson and Weiss 1991).

Due to these factors, the very presence of VCs brings more investment funds into the entrepreneurial finance market.

Demand Side Benefits

Entrepreneurs find VC to be a more viable source of finance compared to the other financial intermediaries. The stock markets provide just financial capital; however, VCs additionally provide business advice, contacts, and reputational capital to the new ventures (Sahlman 1990). Confidentiality of proprietary business information is another demand side benefit that the VCs bring to the market. Public listing requires the entrepreneur to make public the information that would have been otherwise closely guarded. Often, this information is exclusive and a source of potential economic rents to the entrepreneur, and public disclosure of such vital information may prove to be quite dear to the firm (Campbell 1979; Fried and Hisrich 1994; Yosha 1995).

Most importantly, public equity might not be a feasible option at all for most new economy entrepreneurs. Public equity markets usually warrant a minimum scale of business operations. However, since most new economy ventures get started on a much smaller scale, the quantum of capital needed by them is often much lower than what is required to achieve the minimum efficient scale in the public equity markets (Fama and Jensen 1983a, 1983b; Fried and Hisrich 1994). Moreover, public equity is associated with high fixed information and contracting costs. By reducing these costs, the VCs can provide a source of outside equity to the entrepreneur. In fact, for most new economy entrepreneurs, VCs represent not only the best, but also the only source of equity (Fried and Hisrich 1994).

Sources of Entrepreneurial Finance and the Role of VCs

Banks and stock markets are the conventional sources of entrepreneurial finance. Bank lending is in the form of loans (non-tradable debt) wherein the investor invests in a project for a certain period and gets fixed returns on a periodic basis. The periodic payments made by the borrower comprise both principal and interest components, such that over a specified number of years the loan is paid off in full. There could be different variants of bank loans wherein just the interest is paid initially and the principal only at a later stage. Since a pre-determined fixed return to a lender is assured, bank loans are regarded to be the least risky across the entire spectrum of investments. In the event of default, bank lenders usually have the first claim over the liquidated assets of a venture.

Stock markets make use of financial instruments in the form of both debt and equity. Similar to a bank loan, the debtors are assured of a fixed return on a periodic basis. However, its additional advantage over bank loans is that the debt instrument is tradable, and the investors can exit their debt by selling the debt instrument in the stock market. In the event of liquidation, the debtors' stake in the venture's assets comes right after the banks' claims. Equity refers to a kind of ownership in the company. The equity holders do not get a fixed return on their investments; however, they do have a share in the profits of a venture. Typically, equity holders would be the last to be paid off in case of liquidation. But they would also be the first claimants over the profits of a venture. Equity is traded in the market, and equity holders can exit their investments by trading their equity on the stock markets. Thus, loans and debt instruments are aimed at protecting the investors against downside risk, whereas equity instruments enable them to exploit the upside potential.

Just like equity, VC investment instruments also constitute an ownership in the venture, but with a significant difference. There exists no readily available market to trade the equity and exit the venture. Thus, it is known as 'private' equity. The entity holding private equity has, on the one hand, a large share in the profits of the venture but, on the other, cannot exit the venture easily in the event of business failure. Moreover, since the assets of the new economy ventures financed by VCs are mostly intangible in nature, they are expected to yield very little value on liquidation (Gompers and Lerner 1999).

However, all these distinctions between VC and the other sources of finance are merely at an operational level. At a more conceptual level, it is the information asymmetry (of VC-funded projects) and the risks emanating from it that differentiate VC finance from bank or public equity investments (Scholtens 1999). The information asymmetry for bank lending, compared to VC financing, is much lower as the projects are relatively well structured, whereby the risks across the various life stages of the project are more or less known. Lessons learned by competitors from poor investments are shared between banks by the central bank of the country. Moreover, the non-performing assets are audited, and periodic reports are available in the public domain. Besides, the overall risk to the banking system is always lower due to the presence of a regulator in the form of the central bank of a country. This results in a greater likelihood of a bailout in the event of a bank failure. Banks also make use of strategies such as debt securitization to reduce risks. Therefore, they face lower non-systemic as well as systemic risks. The non-systemic risks are those that can be reduced by portfolio diversification. Systemic risks for banks are also lower, as they are shielded from external pressures by the regulator.

The extent of information asymmetry for public equity investments, compared to VC financing, is much lower too, as most of the critical information, particularly that regarding the company financials, is available in the public domain. The resulting risks are also much lower, as the 'non-systemic' risks can be minimized by portfolio diversification. Thus, it is only the systemic component of risk that the investors have to hedge against.

On the other hand, VC investments encounter a significant magnitude of systemic and non-systemic risks (Rea 1989). Unlike the banks and stock markets, VCs are unable to reduce the non-systemic risks by optimally diversifying their portfolio. For them, diversification is neither *possible* nor *feasible*. Let us understand why this is so. VCs derive their *niche* from their ability to deal with information asymmetry. One of the ways in which this is achieved is by specializing in a particular domain – by sector, industry, or the stage of lending. Specialized domain knowledge is known to reduce risks arising from adverse selection (Barney 1991; Manigart, Joos, and de Vos 1994; Norton and Tenenbaum 1993). However, higher the degree of specialization, greater the risks arising from the lack of portfolio diversification.

Thus, the VCs essentially trade off the risks arising from adverse selection with those arising due to the lack of diversification. Consequently, non-systemic risks are endemic in the portfolio composition of the VCs. Diversification is also not feasible in the case of VC investments. In a public equity portfolio, diversification is possible as the magnitude of investment in each individual venture as an overall proportion of the portfolio is quite small. VC investments are relatively larger in magnitude, and thus only limited diversification is possible (Robinson 1988).

The conventional sources of funding also differ from VCs in terms of their level of involvement in the funded venture. To reduce the magnitude of agency risks, a VC firm needs to be an 'active' source of finance (Elango et al. 1995; Sapienza, Manigart, and Vermeir 1996). Hence, the VCs not only provide finance, but also participate at a more strategic level in the overall functioning of the investee venture administration, finance, marketing and sales, risk management, recruitment, product development, and so on. Thus, compared to VC, banks and stock markets are considered relatively 'passive' sources of finance.

Information Asymmetry Risks and Risk Mitigation Strategies

As noted, information asymmetry results in two distinct types of risks – adverse selection and agency risks. This section aims at a more detailed discussion of these risks.

Adverse Selection Risks and Risk Mitigation Strategies

Typically, ventures that are ineligible for financing by the conventional financial intermediaries show up for VC funding. Since the riskiest projects tend to get self-selected for VC financing, the problem of adverse selection arises quite naturally. The VCs are known to overcome the risks arising from adverse selection by putting in place several risk mitigation mechanisms, namely specialization, syndication, and intensive screening of investments (during the pre-investment phase).

Specialization

Domain specialization enables the VCs to clearly weed out the riskiest projects, thus reducing the intensity of the adverse selection problem. As such, VC firms are not 'generalists'. In fact, they tend to specialize by industry (such as biotechnology or information technology), life stage of the venture (early, growth, late), geography, or even the funding size (Ruhnka and Young 1991; Gupta and Sapienza 1992). The *resource-based* view propounds that specialization equips the VC firm with idiosyncratic or tacit knowledge about a domain, which, in turn, enables them to adjudge the risks appropriately. In fact, it is this tacit knowledge that enables the VC firm to derive its niche competitive advantage (Barney 1991; Barney, Wright, and Ketchen 2001; Newbert 2007).

However, from the finance theory perspective, a specialized portfolio is necessarily non-diversified. Thus, the risk of the portfolio held by a VC firm will be at least as high as the average risk across all the individual investments in its portfolio (Norton and Tenenbaum 1993; Manigart, Joos, and de Vos 1994). The more the VC portfolio is focused or specialized in a specific investment domain, the more are the outcomes of the investments correlated to each other (since systemic components impact all the investments in a uniform manner) and hence higher the risk (Manigart et al. 2002).

Syndication of Investments

Different VCs coming together and jointly investing in a single deal is known as syndication. Usually, VCs are more comfortable with a deal when other VCs with similar experience are willing to invest as well (Lerner 1994). The rationale behind syndication is that if multiple entities review risk, it might be possible to reach closer to the 'true' estimate of risk. This consequently leads to a superior selection of investments (Sah and Stiglitz 1984). Another venture capitalist's decision to invest is an important signal that influences the lead investor's decision to invest (Gompers and Lerner 1999). Also, syndication can help in spreading the risk across multiple entities, thus providing the motivation to the VCs to consider those investment projects that would not have got considered earlier (Barry 1994).

Syndication not only helps in spreading risks, but also brings together more expertise and support that is warranted to add value to the venture (Gompers and Lerner 2004). Thus, syndication may help in alleviating agency risks as well. Above all, syndication with a known VC firm is one of the important ways of achieving 'certification' and 'reputation' for a relatively new VC firm (Gompers and Lerner 2004). Reputation and certification, in turn, enable a new VC firm to gain access to better entrepreneurial ventures in the future, thus reducing the intensity of the adverse selection problem in upcoming projects too. For foreign VCs spreading their wings to Asian economies, syndication with the local VCs proves to be an important strategy of handling the information asymmetry risks associated with geographic distance and cultural differences (Dai, Jo, and Kassicieh 2012).

However, it must be understood that not all VCs view syndication favourably. In the event of conflicts of interest among co-investing VCs, syndication might result in negative synergies (Gompers 1996; Gompers and Lerner 2004). After having financed the first round of investment, the VC firm is aware of the 'true' value of investment. Hence, it may use this information advantage to serve its own interests. Thus, it may have the incentive to misrepresent the true value to the second round of investors (Lerner 1994). If the VC firm believes that the investee firm's prospects are attractive, it may reserve very few shares to outsiders even when having more investors may be advantageous to the investee firm. On the other hand, if the VC firm is troubled by the firm's prospects, it may reduce its stake in the next stage of financing and try to get more capital from outsiders. Either of the outcomes is less efficient from the point of view of the investee firm (Gompers and Lerner 2004).

Intense Screening of Investments (during Pre-Investment Stage)

Intense screening and evaluation allow the VCs to gain a substantial amount of information prior to investing and this helps in significantly reducing the magnitude of the adverse selection problem (Fried and Hisrich 1994). The screening of investments can be broken up into broadly two dimensions – the 'criteria' and the 'process' – used by the VCs to evaluate potential investments. In general, VCs differ in the screening criteria they use to select ventures based on the type of industry, stage of development, geographic location, and the stage of investment.

Agency Risks and Risk Mitigation Strategies

Agency risks occur due to the presence of the classic principal–agent problem. The entrepreneurs are privy to certain information that is unavailable to the VCs. Besides, not all actions of an entrepreneur are observable. Thus, entrepreneurs can take actions that may be potentially detrimental to the interests of the VC. Typically, the entrepreneurs are usually committed to only a single venture, whereas a VC manages an entire portfolio of investment projects. This often results in conflicts over the amount to invest in a venture. Since the entrepreneurs only have limited liability in using VC funds, they may want the VC firm to continue to invest even long after the project has ceased to be viable (Barry 1994). Further, entrepreneurs may do this intentionally, as the venture brings in additional private benefits to the entrepreneur. Even unintentionally, entrepreneurs can overstate the upside potential from the project as they are unable to assess the true project potential themselves (Barry 1994). Kaplan and Stromberg (2000) have summarized the main areas of conflicts of interest between VCs and entrepreneurs as follows:

1. Agent (entrepreneur) does not exert enough amount of 'costly' effort.
2. Agent takes up actions that yield private benefits and not necessarily monetary benefits.
3. Agent spends resources on perks and stealing.
4. Agent holds up investors by threatening to leave a project.

VCs tackle the problems resulting from agency risks by either incentivizing the entrepreneurs or by taking coercive actions against them. To achieve the same, VCs take recourse to contracting, monitoring, and staging of investments. Each of these will be discussed in detail in the following sections.

Contracting

Contracts between the VCs and entrepreneurs are a well-researched area in VC literature. Contracts are an important tool in the hands of a VC to guard against opportunism by entrepreneurs. These contracts, which are important at various levels, usually pertain to cash flow rights, voting rights, board rights, liquidation rights, and other control rights. Cash flow rights, voting rights, control rights, and future financings are often made contingent on observable measures of financial and non-financial performance. Control rights are designed to provide complete control to the VC in case of poor venture performance. However, if the venture performs extremely well, the VCs have the option to retain cash flow rights and relinquish most of their control and liquidation rights. Non-competing clauses and vesting provisions aim at mitigating the potential hold-up problems between the entrepreneurs and investors. Exit related contracts aim at minimizing the friction during the period of VC exits.

Stringent contracts are necessary to reduce the variability of the firm's returns; however, doing so might also decrease the average returns, since now the entrepreneurs become more risk averse. Therefore, the contracts should be designed such that the entrepreneurs are also incentivized to deliver on the upside (Pruthi, Wright, and Lockett 2003). Thus, compensation of the entrepreneurs is an important aspect contained in most of the contracts. Entrepreneurs receive a rather modest salary, and a major part of their compensation comes from the performance of the venture (Barry 1994). They generally own a dominant equity interest and benefit directly from value creation (Barry 1994). Usually, the degree of dilution of the entrepreneur's ownership interest is directly tied to performance, such that the entrepreneurs receive a larger fraction of a more successful venture. The contracts also give enough power to the VCs to fire or demote an ineffective manager.

Most importantly, the contracts ensure that VCs always have seniority over cash flows. VCs want to protect themselves against downside risks if things do not go well. However, they also wish to benefit from the upside potential if the venture turns out to be promising (Schwienbacher 2009). These aspects are taken care of by share purchase agreements. The most common feature of a share purchase agreement is the convertible preferred stock. The preferred stock gives the venture capitalist a superior claim to cash flow and to distributions from liquidation in the event the venture is unsuccessful. The conversion feature also provides participation on the upside. The conversion price is commonly a function of performance, so that if a venture is unsuccessful, the venture capitalist stands a better chance of recovering the investment. At the same time, the increased conversion price following good performance increases the incentives to the entrepreneur (Barry 1994).

Monitoring of Investee Firms

Intensive monitoring is one of the ways to keep in check opportunistic behaviour of the entrepreneurs, that is, agency problems. At a theoretical level, it has been argued that agency problems result from the existence of incomplete contracts (Fama and Jensen 1983a). If contracts were complete, agency problems would have been irrelevant. Thus, close monitoring by the venture capitalist is needed to resolve the gaps left by the contracts. The intensity of monitoring may vary from just informal meetings with the entrepreneurs to having formal reporting requirements (on financial and other activities) and ranging up to the VC presence on the board of directors of the company.

Agency costs and the intensity of monitoring are closely related. Higher agency costs make intense monitoring necessary. Monitoring is expected to be the highest in early stage ventures (Gorman and Sahlman 1989; Sapienza 1992; Gompers and Lerner 1999). These ventures often have no performance history and hence information asymmetries are high, resulting in high agency risks. They face not only high agency risks, but also high business risks. They confront considerable managerial, market, and technological challenges. Being less developed as an organization, they require significant non-cash resources from outside. Thus, they face a high risk of management failure. VCs believe that they can better control the business risk associated with early-stage investing by remaining in close contact with the venture and thus monitoring is expected to be intense in the early-stage investments (Rosenstein et al. 1993; Ruhnka and Young 1987, 1991; Barney, Hannan, and Burton 1989). Similarly, high-tech firms and those with very high research and development (R&D) intensities require close monitoring (Gompers and Lerner 1999). In general, the presence of intangible assets results in high agency costs. As assets become more tangible, VCs can recover more of their investment in liquidation, and expected losses due to inefficient continuation are reduced. This reduces the need to monitor tightly.

The involvement of a VC with an investee firms also varies based on the conditions faced by the investee firm. The representation of the VCs on the boards of investee firms is most intensive at times when the need for oversight is greater. The replacement of the top manager of the company coincides with organizational crisis and heightens the need for monitoring. It has been found that VCs are more likely to join or be added to the boards of private companies in periods when the chief executive officer (CEO) of the company changes (Lerner 1995; Gompers and Lerner 1999).

However, the monitoring role of the VCs should not be interpreted as that of an overseer or a regulator, but rather as that of a value-added service provider (Deakins, O'Neill, and Mileham 2000). Empirical studies have shown that VCs significantly reduce the time-to-market for a product. Also, VC-funded firms are faster to professionalize by designing employee compensation plans – like stock options, recruiting senior management – by bringing CEOs from outside the firm, and by assisting with acquisitions by facilitating strategic relationships with other companies (Hellman and Puri 2000, 2002; Kaplan and Stromberg 2001).

However, monitoring efforts also involve significant opportunity costs. There is a point when the costs of addressing agency problems exceed the benefits. It is until that point that the VC firms will support the investees.

Staging of Investments

Staged capital infusions may be regarded as one of the most potent control mechanisms a venture capitalist can employ to lessen the impact of the moral hazard problem (Gompers and Lerner 1999). In fact, staged capital commitment has been identified as one of the most important features of the venture capitalist–entrepreneur contracts. To start with, the venture capitalist commits only a fraction of the capital needed for the ultimate development of the project. Subsequent financing is then tied to the successful completion of the intermediate objectives (Sahlman 1988). In staged financing, the VCs essentially buy a call option on further investment and the entrepreneurs are given powerful incentives to perform.

Staging of investments creates an abandonment option for the venture capitalist and thus increases the value of investment for the venture capitalist. Staged capital commitments keep the entrepreneur focused on the task at hand and may motivate a rapid pace of activity on his part. Further, the entrepreneur's decision to accept such a contract is an important signal of his commitment to the venture. Entrepreneurs know that if they mislead the VCs in the beginning, they may be 'found out' before additional funds are committed. It provides information about the entrepreneur's belief in his estimate about the time and costs involved to develop the relevant stages of the project (Barry 1994).

Gompers (1996) relates the intensity of monitoring to staging. He measures the intensity of monitoring by the length of time between two subsequent capital infusions. A shorter period between two stages of financing implies that a venture capitalist has yet to develop complete trust in the venture and hence is also a proxy for a greater degree of monitoring.

Risks and Signaling

In addition to the risks arising from information asymmetry, the VCs encounter other distinct types of risks as well:

1. Risks due to 'liability of newness' – arising from undeveloped or underdeveloped products, markets, services, technologies, and business models (Stinchcombe 1965).
2. Technical risks – arising from obsolescence of technology before the product comes to market.
3. Competitive risks – that a competitor may come up with the same product earlier.
4. Managerial risks – arising from poor management.
5. Financial risks – that a fund may run out of money faster than expected.
6. Liquidity risks – that the market may not be liquid enough to exit an investment at the appropriate time.

However, since the primary focus of this study is on the assessment of information asymmetry risks, we focus our investigation of literature around the aspects concerning the same.

The presence of a high level of information asymmetry makes it rather unfeasible to arrive at potential risk estimates about a prospective deal. Consequently, the VCs are known to extensively rely on tacit *signals* for arriving at appropriate risk assessments. Based on the literature, we have classified these signals into three distinct categories – those obtained from entrepreneurial and founding team characteristics, VC firm and deal related characteristics, and those obtained from the macroeconomic and policy environment.

Signals Obtained from Entrepreneurial Characteristics

Founder or founding team related attributes are often viewed as a proxy of creditworthiness in the absence of tangible performance data on the investee firm (Hsu 2007). Accordingly, managerial and entrepreneurial expertise are critical investment parameters extensively discussed in the literature. In fact, a '"B" grade idea with an "A" grade entrepreneur may be preferred over an "A" grade idea with a "B" grade entrepreneur' (Hsu 2007). Empirical studies have identified entrepreneurial personality and experience to be more important than product, market, and financial considerations in the funding decisions (MacMillan, Siegel, and Narasimha 1986).

The specifics of the kind of human capital possessed by the entrepreneur and the managerial team seem to be an important factor in the risk assessment.

VCs prefer investing in teams with industry experience and a mixed educational background, for example, engineering and management (Goslin and Barge 1986; Dixon 1991; Franke et al. 2008). An entrepreneur with a doctoral degree has been found to be closely associated with a high incidence of VC funding, particularly in the IT sector (Hsu 2007).

Entrepreneurs with a demonstrated track record of setting up successful start-ups in the past are an important signal for risk assessment of a venture (Hsu 2007). The incidence of successful funding from other VCs in the past is another factor considered to be important by the VCs. Similarly, entrepreneurs with a high level of social capital are important (Hsu 2007; Bygrave and Timmons 1992; Shane and Stuart 2002). Social capital implies the ability of the entrepreneurs to recruit talented executive officers and technical staff from their own network. It also means contacts with other VCs and the ability to leverage their network. Both these factors are not only signals about the entrepreneurial skills, but are expected to substantially reduce the involvement by the venture capitalist in the new venture. Since the opportunity cost of VC resources is high, these factors are critical in funding.

Signals Obtained from VC Firm and Deal Characteristics

Stage of investment, industry/sector, and size of investment of the investee firm are important indicators of risk. Usually, ventures in the earlier stages of investment and those coming from high-tech sectors have the highest level of information asymmetry associated with them. Consequently, the adverse selection and agency risks are the highest in such cases.

The domain of specialization of the VC firm is among the most important guiding factors in its investment decisions. Each VC firm consciously maps the domain of the potential new deal with its own specialized domain. We have already seen that VC firms are specialists who specialize by life-stage of the venture, funding size, sector or geography (Ruhnka and Young 1991; Gupta and Sapienza 1992). Thus, in general, any potential project whose profile does not match with the specialization domain of the VC firm is deemed to be risky and hence not considered viable for funding.

Syndication or co-investing with other VC firms is another important signal of potential risk. Presence of a co-investor is usually regarded as a positive signal (Sah and Stiglitz 1986; Barry 1994; Gompers and Lerner 1999; Dai, Jo, Kassicieh 2012). However, at times, it is also viewed at negatively, especially in the event of conflicts of interest among the co-investing VCs (Lerner 1994; Gompers 1996; Gompers and Lerner 2004).

Geographical proximity between the venture capitalist and the investee firm is another potential indicator of riskiness. It is a proxy for the extent of monitoring that is possible. Since monitoring is critical for reducing agency risks, lesser geographical distance is typically associated with lower risk (Sapienza 1992; Lerner 1995; Sapienza, Manigart, and Vermeir 1996; Manigart et al. 2000; Sapienza, de Clercq, and Sandberg 2005; Cumming and Dai 2010). Geographical distance not only impacts the agency risks but those emanating from adverse selection as well. In the VC industry, the information on investment opportunities is not public. Rather, it is only discretely available through organizational networks. A high geographic distance reduces the effectiveness of these channels and thus affects the ability of the VCs to access high quality investment opportunities (Cumming and Dai 2010).

Synergies between the proposed venture and the existing portfolio of VC investments are regarded to be quite important in estimating risks. The proposed new venture may either compete with the existing ventures in the venture capitalist's portfolio or may complement it. In either way, this would create significant synergies. In case of competing deals, there may be economies of scale and scope to be leveraged and risks reduced. However, these might also result in a mutual conflict of interest or end up in the cannibalization of one another's market share. In case of complementarities, the deals may potentially add significant value to each other, thus reducing the overall risk from both investments. In fact, it has been pointed out in the literature that at certain times the new venture would not have got selected on a stand-alone basis if not for the synergies it has with the rest of the portfolio (Chesbrough 2002; Petty and Gruber 2011).

Signals Obtained from the Macroeconomic Environment and Government Policies

Expectations about the current and future macroeconomic environment are critical for VCs. An economic boom goes hand in hand with the liquidity of the markets and hence directly affects the ease of exit. Since exit is the only way for a venture capitalist to realize its return on investment, the venture capitalist closely assesses the factors that are coincidental with exit. Early-stage investments are usually not affected by illiquid markets, as the exit horizon is long into the future. However, late-stage investments desire a quick exit via an initial public offer (IPO) and hence are more interested in a liquid market (Schwienbacher 2005, 2009; Cumming and Johan 2010).

The other area that is of importance to VCs is favourable government policies pertaining to VC investments in general, particularly those relating to the taxation (Poterba 1989; Gompers and Lerner 1999) and the ones that facilitate exits (Anjum 2014).

VC Lifecycle and Decision-Making

The three critical decisions in a VC firm's lifecycle are as follows:

1. Entry – investment in fledgling companies;
2. Involvement in portfolio companies – intense monitoring (and value-add)
3. Exit – exiting the investee firms via appropriate exit routes.

At each of these life stages, the VC firm encounters information asymmetry risks and makes a conscious attempt to gain control over the same. Usually, during the first lifecycle stage, namely investments, the VC firm needs to encounter adverse selection risks, whereas during the latter two phases (portfolio involvement and exits) it needs to encounter agency risks.

Accordingly, the aim of this section is to understand each of these lifecycle stages in further detail.

VC 'Entry' Decisions: Whom to Fund?

VC-backed new businesses have shown to achieve higher survival rates than non-VC-backed ones (Timmons and Spinelli 1994). This is attained by their special expertise in successively weeding out bad investment proposals. Hence, the project evaluation process of VCs has received much attention by the research community in entrepreneurship and finance (Franke et al. 2006).

Fried and Hisrich (1994) describe the sequential decision-making process used by the venture capitalist in funding ventures. This process was arrived at based on their face-to-face interaction with several VCs in the US. The flow chart proposed by them is given in Figure 2.1. The authors describe the evaluation process to comprise a number of sequential steps with different aspects of the proposal being reviewed at each subsequent stage. Let us briefly describe the various stages of the evaluation process. Each VC firm follows certain guidelines within which it operates. The firm-specific criteria analyse whether the proposal meets these primary guidelines. These typically refer to the investment size, industry or sector, geographic location of the investment, and the stage of financing.

The firm-specific screen eliminates proposals that clearly do not meet these criteria. The proposals that pass through the firm-specific screen move to the next stage – generic screen. This stage involves a rigorous appraisal of the various investment criteria. The first phase evaluation comprises multiple 'reference checks' across the VC firm's (and the investee company's) existing vendors, attorneys, accountants, bankers, customers (existing and potential), and competitors. The objective of the second phase is to understand the major obstacles to the investment and arrive at a plan to overcome them. The closing stage follows.

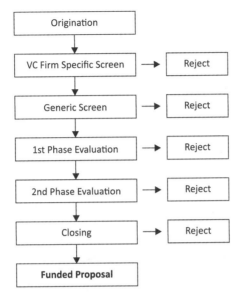

Figure 2.1   Investment evaluation process
Source: Fried and Hisrich (1984).

Moving on from the venture evaluation process to the venture evaluation criteria, literature indicates that VCs emphasize on the following:

1. The venture's management team
2. The market
3. The product or service
4. The venture's financial potential

Each of these constructs has been broken down into multiple factors by researchers (Tyebjee and Bruno 1984; MacMillan, Siegel, and Narasimha 1985; Hall and Hofer 1993; Ray 1991; Ray and Turpin 1993; Rah, Jung, and Lee 1994). However, certain results have stood the test of time. In terms of the management team, studies indicate that VCs prefer investing in teams with industry experience and which can draw on a mixed educational background (Goslin and Barge 1986; Franke et al. 2008). In terms of the venture's target market, the literature suggests that VCs prefer market opportunities of considerable size and with high growth rates, as these provide the conditions for strong revenue growth and high levels of value creation (Tyebjee and Bruno 1984). With regard to a venture's product offering, research shows that VCs apply evaluation criteria such as innovativeness of the offering, its competitive advantage, patents, and the level of customer loyalty for the potential product (Khan 1987). In terms of the venture's financial potential, the literature identifies criteria such as expected rate of return and expected risks (Macmillan, Siegel, and Narasimha 1985). Not only the rate of return per se but also the absolute value of return is important for the VCs (Tyebjee and Bruno, 1984).

VC 'Involvement' Decisions: How Intense Should the Involvement Be in the Funded Venture?

The extent to which the VC firm gets involved with the new venture arises from the need for monitoring. Monitoring is one of the most important ways of dealing with the ensuing agency risks. However, monitoring need not necessarily be only in terms of the venture capitalist playing the role of an overseer or regulator. In fact, in most cases, the VC professionals provide significant value-added services to the investee firm (Deakins, O'Neill, and Mileham 2000). Such assistance provided by the venture capitalist is important, as it ultimately makes the venture a win-win situation. The fact that VCs add value may be seen from the fact that in the long run, VC-backed IPOs consistently outperform the non-VC-backed ones (Gompers and Lerner 2004).

The VCs usually complement the new venture in terms of providing it with the professional expertise that it lacks. Typically, technology companies need non-technology inputs from investors and vice versa. In large investments, investors probably assist only in strategy development; however, in small ventures, the venture capitalist may need to get involved at a hands-on level. In general, it is believed that the key to value addition lies in identifying the weakest link prior to investment (Annamalai 2010).

Broadly, the VCs are seen to add value to the new venture in three ways (Hellman and Puri 2002):

1. Reputation: The VCs bring reputation to a relatively new venture. Of course, this is partly driven by the fact that success to the new venture also brings reputation to the venture capitalist.
2. Professionalism: The VCs bring in professionalism to the new firm by putting in place HR policies, compensation structures, accounting, audit, and other operational processes.
3. Time to market: VCs enable the firms to bring products to market faster.

In addition to these, the VC firm is often responsible for putting in place a framework of corporate governance for the new venture. The extent of VC firm participation in corporate governance may be proxied by the representation of the VC firm on the governing board of the new ventures – both in terms of the number of representatives and the years of service (Jain 2001). It has been observed that VCs take long-term board positions in ventures and usually assist them in half of their corporate lives prior to the IPO (Barry et al. 1990). The influence of the board on the venture is the maximum in the period preceding the IPO when major financial, operational, and strategic decisions need to be taken to prepare for a public offering.

Other studies analyse the circumstances under which VCs add the most value (Sapienza 1992). It has been found that the value of venture capitalist involvement varies with circumstances. VCs are seen to add the most value in uncertain circumstances resulting from inherent volatility and instability of the external environment. Also, the most effective VCs are those who maintain frequent, open communication while minimizing conflicts. Contrary to the belief that VCs add the most value at the early stage of the venture, opportunities exist for adding value in all venture stages.

VC 'Exit' Decisions: When and How to Exit a Funded Venture?

Exiting the funded venture is the final stage in the VC's investment lifecycle. The exit stage is considered so important that the potential for exit is one of the primary driving factors affecting the entry decision itself. Most ventures do not generate any cash flows during the initial years, and hence the payment of dividends to investors is often not possible. Thus, exit is the only way for a venture capitalist to realize its return on investment (RoI).

VCs are not long-term investors and would thus have the incentive to exit at the most profitable opportunity without unnecessary delay. Moreover, exit is the signal of VC quality. Such a signal is important for successful follow-on fund-raising by the GPs. A successful exit enables the venture capitalist to reallocate funds across other investments. Above all, a credible threat of exit may minimize a potential moral hazard problem and prompt the entrepreneur to exert more effort (Cumming 2010).

Broadly, there are five different kinds of exit options available to the venture capitalist (Schwienbacher 2009): IPO,[4] trade sale (mergers and acquisition [M&A]),[5] management buy-out (re-purchase),[6] re-financing (secondary sale),[7] and liquidation (write-off).[8]

---

[4] The company achieves a stock market listing so that the venture capitalist can sell its shares in the public.

[5] The sale of the investee company to another company.

[6] The venture capitalist sells back its shares to the entrepreneur.

[7] The venture capitalist's stocks are purchased by another institutional investor (for example, another upstream venture capitalist).

[8] The company files for bankruptcy.

Agency Risks and VC Exits

The risks resulting from information asymmetry are quite pertinent, even during the final stage of the VC lifecycle, namely exit from investee companies. At this stage, there exists significant asymmetry between the sellers of the given firm's equity and its potential buyers (Cumming and Macintosh 2003b). In general, the sellers have greater access to information about the entrepreneurial firm in terms of its *true* quality. Moreover, they have an enhanced ability to evaluate that information owing to their lengthy involvement with the firm and also have superior understanding of the *space* in which the firm is operating in (namely its industrial environment, number of competitors and their *niche* skills, and so on). Some buyers are relatedly less well positioned to resolve these information asymmetries compared to others, consequently reducing the price at which the venture capitalist's interest is sold (Cumming and Macintosh 2001). In general, greater information risk results in a heavier discounting of the investee firm's future cash flows. Thus, the buyers who are less able to resolve these information asymmetries will pay less for the venture capitalist's interest in the entrepreneurial firm than buyers who are better positioned to do so. Thus, in general, the VC firm as a seller would prefer to select the buyer who is best able to resolve information asymmetries (Cumming and Macintosh 2003a).

In this regard, the potential buyers in an IPO and M&A are known to best resolve information asymmetries (Cumming and Macintosh 2001, 2003a). This can be seen from the fact that the internal rates of return (IRR) on IPOs and M&As are typically the highest compared to other exit routes (Cumming and Johan 2010). This finding has been noted in several empirical studies in the context of VC exits in a number of countries including the US, Canada, United Kingdom, and in Europe (Cumming and Macintosh 2003a, 2003b; Cochrane 2005; Nikoskelainen and Wright 2007). Thus, in general, there exists a pecking order in terms of the profitability of exits. It has been shown empirically, that the exits are shown to exhibit the following rank order in the decreasing order of their profitability: IPOs, M&As, re-financing, re-purchase, and write-offs (Cumming and Macintosh 2003a, 2003b).

Summary

In this chapter, we have attempted to review the literature in the domain of VC. The literature encompasses both the macro aspects and the micro dimensions of the VC industry. While the former investigates the relevant studies pertaining to the supply and demand sides of the VC ecosystem, the latter explores the decision-making strategies of the VC firms during their investment lifecycle using the theoretical lens of information asymmetry and agency theories.

3

Context and Methods

The aim of this chapter is to outline the objectives and scope of the study and discuss in detail the data, definitions, and the profile of the sample venture capital (VC) firms.

The Objectives

The objectives for this study can be divided into two aspects: First, the macro-level objectives concerning the supply and demand aspects of the VC ecosystem. Second, those related to the micro-level decision-making strategies of the VC firms (fund managers).

Macro-level Objectives

Based on the macro aspects of the VC ecosystem, we derive the first three objectives:

1. To determine the *systematic* and *non-systematic* influences governing the supply side of the Indian VC ecosystem.
2. To understand the *systematic* influences governing the demand side of the VC ecosystem (with specific emphasis on the development of the VC start-up geographic clusters).
3. To derive policy implications for promoting VC funding for the growth of start-ups and new economy ventures in India.

Micro-level Objectives

Based on the micro aspects pertaining to the decision-making strategies of VC fund managers, we derive the next five objectives:

1. To probe the *investment decisions* of the Indian VC firms in the light of the ensuing adverse selection risks. Our aim is to understand the nature of tacit

signals (and tangible factors) that enable the VC fund managers to establish control over the magnitude of such risks.

2. To understand the determinants of the *intensity of involvement* of the VC fund managers in the investee firms, particularly from the viewpoint of addressing the agency risks.

3. To examine the determinants of *successful exits* for Indian investee firms. To further study how these are related to the magnitude of the underlying agency risks.

4. To derive managerial implications for the VC fund managers and entrepreneurs based on the analysis. For the former, we propose to outline the factors that *similar* peers regard important in assessing potential risks from prospective deals. For the latter, we provide pointers about the specific segments of VC fund managers they need to approach in order to enhance their chances of successful funding.

5. To derive policy implications based on the above with the aim of addressing the major areas of friction encountered by the VC fund managers while investing in India.

Scope of the Study

The scope of this study has been defined in the light of the objectives discussed. To start with, our study is confined to the VC operations and investments in the Indian economy. It covers both the domestic and foreign VC firms that invest in India. Our sample also covers a few VC firms that are principally based abroad (that is, have no registered office in India) and yet invest in India. Of late, local venture capitalists (VCs) can invest in overseas deals as well. However, such overseas deals are not covered in the scope of this study.

We restrict our study to the funded ventures since the year 2006. In 2002, the Securities and Exchange Board of India (SEBI) was made the nodal regulator for all VCs in India. Quite naturally, any meaningful analysis pertinent to the VCs can be made only after that. However, since most of the data about the aggregate VC investments are available only post 2005, in our analysis we have chosen 2005 as the cut-off year.

Our study covers both SEBI-registered and non-registered VC firms. It must be noted here that while it is mandatory for all domestic VC firms to be registered with SEBI, the foreign VC firms can bypass this procedure and invest in India via the foreign direct investment (FDI) channel, namely the automatic approval route of the Reserve Bank of India (RBI). While registering with SEBI has its advantages, it also imposes asset-side regulations with substantial restrictions on the nature of investments to be made (Ernst and Young 2014), consequently, resulting in many

VC firms bypassing the SEBI route. Other VC firms have invested in India via the Mauritius registry route (to take advantage of the Double Tax Avoidance Treaty). To sum up, most foreign VC firms have preferred to circumvent the SEBI route (Desai 2002; Rastogi 2008) and invest in India via other channels. Owing to these reasons, in our research we have decided to cover both the VC fund managers registered with SEBI and those that have gained an entry into India via the other routes mentioned.

Regarding the geographic location of the VC fund managers, we have covered VC firms across all the major cities in India – Bangalore, Chennai, Hyderabad, Mumbai, Pune, Kolkata, and the National Capital Region (NCR).[1] About 95 per cent of the VC firms investing in India (as of 2014) operate out of these seven cities (Venture Intelligence 2019). We also contacted the VC firms located in Ahmedabad and Jaipur but failed to get a successful response.

Regarding the funding stage focus, our sample covers VC fund managers that are early, growth, and late stage investors. We believe that the nature of attributes considered by the early-stage VC firms in decision-making are likely to be quite different from those used by the later stage ones. Thus, in order to address the same, we have purposefully chosen to cover VC firms across all investment stages in our sample. To further increase the variability, we have consciously included in our sample VC firms with a social sector focus and those that are offshoots of larger corporate entities. Further, we also include VC firms that have *erstwhile* entrepreneurs on their investing team. Moreover, since the primary objective of our study was to evaluate the VC decision-making strategies, we needed to include in our sample only those VC firms that possessed reasonable investing (and portfolio management) experience. Accordingly, we consider only those VC firms that have funded at least four deals historically.

Further, we cover the various aspects of the relationships between the VC firms (fund managers or general partners) and the entrepreneurs (investee firms). However, we do not cover factors governing the affiliations between the VC fund providers (limited partners) and the fund managers (general partners).

For evaluating the decision-making strategies of the VC firms, we do not perform a deal-level analysis. Rather, the unit of analysis for this study will be an individual VC firm. The primary reason for this is the unavailability of detailed data at the deal level. It must be noted that the VC fund managers and entrepreneurs are bound by strict contracts whereby it is unlawful to divulge the proprietary deal-level data to third parties. In case deal-level data becomes available in the future, it can serve as a significant extension of this study.

---

[1] The National Capital Region (NCR) refers to New Delhi, Gurgaon, Noida, and Faridabad.

Data and Definitions

This section describes the major data sources and the definitions of key variables used in the context of this study.

Data Sources

This study is based on both primary and secondary data. Detailed information about the sources of data has been given later.

While the primary data used for this study have been collected on the basis of semi-structured questionnaires and face-to-face/telephonic interviews, the secondary data have been collected from multiple sources. Variables directly pertaining to the profile of the specific VC firms have been sourced from the Venture Intelligence database. This database provides access to the data directory of the VC and private equity (PE) firms operating in India. Further, it also makes available deal-level data for the VC- and PE-funded companies in India. In particular, it provides the details about each deal in terms of the company name, sector of investment, financing stage, city, region, month and year of investment, presence of co-investors, nature of ownership of the investor (domestic or foreign VC firm), and the type and timing of exit. From Venture Intelligence, we first sourced the deal-level data, which have then been aggregated for each VC firm to compute the variables, such as the number of historical deals and exits. Other information (such as the sector/domain focus of the VC firm, stage focus, background of the managing partners – erstwhile entrepreneur or not, SEBI registration, VC fund type – social or corporate) was obtained from either the Venture Intelligence database or from the respective company websites (after confirming with the concerned executives). The data on the aggregate VC funds raised and cumulative VC investments were obtained from SEBI. The data on funds raised by individual VC fund managers were obtained from Venture Intelligence.

Definitions

For the purpose of this study, the VC firms in our sample have been categorized into three distinct segments: one, based on the stage of funding (early, growth, and late stage focus), two, based on ownership type (domestic or foreign VC), and, three, based on the VC investing team background (VC firm professionals with erstwhile entrepreneurial experience versus not). In the first category, the early-stage VC firms comprise funds that focus on seed stage and Series A funding (less than USD 5 million and companies less than five years old), the growth-stage VC firms are those that focus mainly on Series B funding (USD 5 million to USD 20 million and companies more than five years old), and the late-stage VC firms are those focus on Series C funding or higher (greater than USD 20 million). These definitions have been taken from the Venture Intelligence database. In the second category, we have *domestic VC firms* and *foreign firms* (those that are wholly owned subsidiaries of foreign VC fund managers). It must be pointed out that although domestic VC firms raise funds abroad, they have still been classified as *domestic* as long as their country of origin and destination of investments is India. With respect to the VC investing team background, even if a single member among the senior partners/principals of the firm is known to have prior founding experience, we classify the firm as one that has *erstwhile* entrepreneurs on its investing team.

In addition to the ones discussed, we have a few other VC segments as well. Corporate VC firms are defined as those that are offshoots of larger corporate entities, investment banks, or retail banks. Government VC firms represent VC funds floated by Indian governments (central and state) or by public sector banks. VC firms with high-technology focus have been defined as those whose primary focus of investments is information technology (IT), information technology enabled services (ITES), and biotechnology and life sciences domains. Social sector VC firms are either the ones registered as impact funds with SEBI or the ones that have a strong social sector focus in their investments.

Based on the deal-level data available from the Venture Intelligence database, a few other variables were created. *Number of historically funded deals* was created by aggregating the number of deals funded by the VC firm between the period 2006 and 2013. *Number of historical exits* was created by taking a sum of historical initial public offering (IPO) and mergers and acquisitions (M&A) exits at the VC firm level (note: information about exits via other routes was not available to us). *Proportion of syndicated deals* was created by taking the ratio of deals (with presence of co-investor) to the aggregate number of funded deals. *Age of the VC firm* was computed by taking the difference between year 2014 and the year in which the VC firm established its operations in India.

Segmentation Rationale

For the purpose of analysis, the VC firms in our sample have been divided into three broad segments: stage-focus based (early-stage versus growth/late-stage focused); ownership-pattern based (namely domestic versus foreign); and composition of their investment team (namely erstwhile entrepreneurs versus investors). The rationale for this segmentation has been explained here.

Typically, the early-stage ventures are regarded as informationally opaque (Schertler and Tykvova 2011). Moreover, this problem is particularly severe if these ventures belong to high-technology domains (Dai, Jo, and Kassicieh 2012).

Naturally, latent signals become quite important in early-stage investment decisions. Understanding early-stage investing decisions has been one of the important underlying themes of the conventional VC literature. As early-stage VC investing has not been studied for India so far, we decided to further analyse this segment. In this regard, since no formal definitions about the investment stages are available as yet for India, we defined the same based on the self-reported information obtained from the investment professionals belonging to each VC firm.

The presence of foreign VC firms in the Asian markets in general and India and China in particular have grown in leaps and bounds over the past one and a half decades. About 70 per cent of the VC funding in the Asian markets comes from firms of foreign origin (Dai, Jo, and Kassicieh 2012). Given the geographical distance and the cultural differences between the countries of origin and the investment destinations, the magnitude of information asymmetry risks is bound to be particularly severe (Schertler and Tykvova 2011; Dai, Jo, and Kassicieh 2012). Hence, we believe it is important to assess the signals used by the foreign VC firms while investing in distant markets such as India. Further, it might be particularly interesting to analyse how these differ from the ones used by their domestic counterparts. The specific definition of foreign VC firms was obtained from the Venture Intelligence (2019) database.

One of the emerging streams of literature in the VC domain is the composition of the top management teams (TMTs) of the VC firms, and how it influences their VC portfolio composition. Among these, of interest is the past educational and entrepreneurial background of the VC professionals (Patzelt, zu Knyphausen-Aufseß, and Fischer 2009; Zarutskie 2010). Drawing from the resource-based theory, prior background confers significant tacit knowledge on the fund managers that enables them to make better VC investing decisions (Barney 1991; Peteraf 1993). Hence, we decided to further explore this and accordingly segmented the VC firms in our sample into two categories – one in which the TMT has past founding experience and the other where the TMT possesses financial investing experience alone. In our context, TMT implies senior VC professionals (managing directors, senior partners, principal, and so on) with significant investing and portfolio management responsibilities. For the purposes of our definition, even if a single member in the TMT possessed prior founding experience, we deemed the VC firm as having a TMT with erstwhile founding experience, else otherwise. The information pertaining to the erstwhile background of the TMT was obtained by reviewing the profile of senior professionals belonging to each VC firm from the respective VC firm websites and professional networking websites such as Linkedin.com. This was corroborated with the professionals themselves during the course of our discussions.

The composition of the broad segments in our sample is as follows: by funding stage focus – about 37 per cent of the VC firms in our sample have an early-stage focus, 29 per cent have a growth-stage focus, and 34 per cent have a later-stage focus. For the purpose of analysis and sharper results, we have grouped together VC firms with growth- and later-stage focus. Thus, in aggregate, about 63 per cent of the VC firms have a growth- or later-stage focus. By ownership type, about 60 per cent of the VC firms in our sample are of domestic origin, whereas the rest 40 per cent is of foreign origin, that is, they are offshoots of larger foreign VC firms or other foreign corporate entities. By VC firm TMT composition, about 26 per cent of the VC firms have erstwhile founders on their TMTs, whereas the rest 74 per cent have TMTs with financial investing experience alone (these are typically finance professionals from business schools [in India or overseas] with prior investing or portfolio management experience).

Methodology

Objectives 1 and 2 were analysed based on secondary data. Objectives 4 and 5 were analysed using ex post facto exploratory research methods. Primary data used in this analysis were collected using semi-structured questionnaires and face-to-face/telephonic interviews with executives from seventy-two active VC fund managers operating in India during the period between June 2013 and May 2014. One professional was interviewed per VC firm. Follow-up interviews were requested to seek further clarity wherever required. The VC firms in our sample cover fifteen out of the top twenty VC firms in India, in terms of the number of funded VC deals. These seventy-two firms have collectively funded more than 70 per cent of the VC deals during the period between 2010 and 2014 (Venture Intelligence 2019).

The primary unit of analysis for this study is an individual VC firm (fund manager), the required information about which was collected from one professional per firm. We believe this response to be quite representative (of the overall VC firm investing ideology) since in most cases the person interviewed by us held a senior position in the organization, such as principal, managing partner, or vice-president. Thus, all these professionals played a very critical role in deciding the fate of and further managing the prospective deal.

We used two questionnaires for this study – one each for studying objectives 1 (signals and factors used by VC firms in arriving at investment decisions) and 2 (intensity of involvement in the funded company). Both these questionnaires were administered at the same point in time. An insight into the items in these questionnaires has been discussed in the following sections (a copy of these questionnaires has been attached in the appendices to Chapters 6 and 7).

Questionnaire 1 Description: Objective 1 (VC Investment Decisions)

The purpose of this questionnaire was to understand the nature of tacit signals and tangible attributes used by the VC firms at the time of making investment decisions. This questionnaire has five sections – the first four measure the tacit signals and the last one concerns the tangible attributes.

The first four sections comprise items about signals pertaining to the *entrepreneur and founding team, VC firm and deal, macroeconomic environment and policy attributes*, and finally those that matter in the *Indian economic, political, social, and cultural milieu*. Section five covers questions pertaining to the business model, product/service/market characteristics, competitive landscape, and financial and cost related characteristics. There are fifty-four items (questions) in all. In this questionnaire, the aim was to assess how *favourably* a VC fund manager views a hypothetical deal given that it demonstrates the *said* characteristic as mentioned in the *item*. Accordingly, the respondents were asked to rate on a Likert scale how favourably they view the attribute from the viewpoint of funding the prospective deal (5: Extremely Favourable, 4: Highly Favourable, 3: Moderately Favourable, 2: Not Favourable, and 1: Extremely Unfavourable).

Questionnaire 2 Description: Objective 2 (VC Decisions – Intensity of Involvement)

The purpose of this questionnaire was to understand the intensity of involvement of the VC firm executives in the investee firm. Accordingly, the questionnaire is divided into six sections based on the nature of involvement – HR related, business operations, marketing and business development, financial activities, business strategy, and crisis situations. There is a total of forty-five items across these sections. Each item refers to a specific micro-aspect of involvement. The respondent is asked to rate each item on a 5-point Likert scale ranging from 1 to 5, where 1 indicates least intensely involved and 5 indicates most intensely involved.

Profile and Characteristics of Sample VC Firms

This section describes the profile and characteristics of the VC firms in our sample here. We examine the univariate profile of the sample firms with respect to their characteristics such as geographical location in India, VC age (number of years of operation in India), number of historically funded deals and exits, funding stage focus (early, growth, late), ownership pattern (domestic or foreign, corporate or government-owned), technology focus (high technology domain versus otherwise), regulatory pattern (SEBI-registered versus not), and the composition of the VC firm's TMT (prior founding background versus prior financial investing experience).

Geographic Location

Figure 3.1 presents the distribution of VC firms across geographic locations in India.

Out of the total sample of seventy VCs, about 40 per cent of the VC firms belong to Mumbai/Pune, 33 per cent to Bangalore, 16 per cent to the National Capital Region, and 9 per cent to other Indian cities (Hyderabad, Chennai, Kolkata, and Lucknow). About 3 per cent of the VC firms are located overseas with no registered office in India. The geographical distribution of VC firms in our sample is more or less comparable with their actual distribution in the master database (namely Venture Intelligence data directory comprising all VC firms operating in India). Both in the sample and the master database, about 90 per cent of the VC firms are in just three major geographic hubs – Mumbai, Bangalore, and NCR.

VC Age: Number of Years of Operation in India

Figure 3.2 shows the distribution of the VC age, that is, the number of years of operation in India (as of January 2014) for the VC firms in our sample. From Figure 3.2, it may be noted that VC as a source of funding is still at its nascent stages in

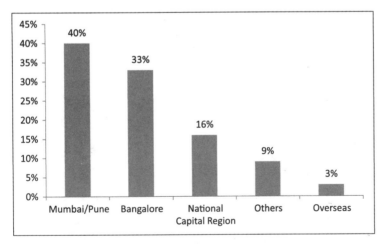

Figure 3.1 Geographic locations of VC fund managers in India

Source: Primary data collected by the author.

Note: NCR covers New Delhi, Gurgaon, and Noida.

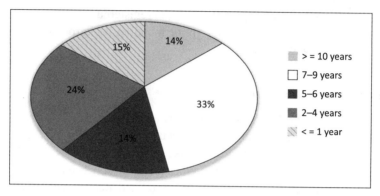

Figure 3.2 Number of years of operation in India
Source: Primary data collected by the author.

India. More than 50 per cent the VC firms have begun operations post 2007 (that is, number of years of operation less than or equal to six years).

This trend of a sudden boom in the Indian VC industry post 2007 may be primarily attributed to the recessionary tendencies in the western world which redirected the flow of VC funds to the emerging economies with relatively better macroeconomic credentials (Bain Consulting 2011, 2012).

Historical Deals and Exits

Figures 3.3 and 3.4 present the number of historical deals and exits (between 2006 and 2013) for the VC firms operating in India.

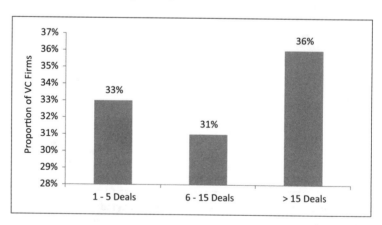

Figure 3.3 Historical deals
Source: Primary data collected by the author.

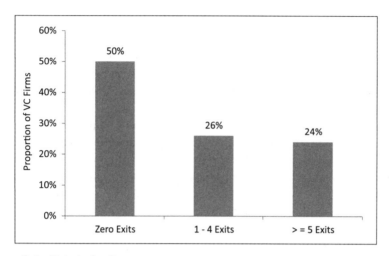

Figure 3.4   Historical exits

Source: Primary data collected by the author.

The bar graph in Figure 3.3 shows the proportion of VC firms with 1–5 deals, 6–15 deals, and > 15 deals respectively. The bar graph in Figure 3.4 shows the proportion of VC firms with 1–4 exits, 5 or more exits, and no exits respectively.

Based on the sample dataset (from which Figures 3.3 and 3.4 have been derived), we understand that the VC firms have funded on an average eighteen deals during the period 2006–13. Similarly, they have witnessed on an average four exits for the deals funded by them during the same period. Please note that we have included only the exits via IPO and M&A routes here (since only the data on these two exit routes was available to us).

From Figures 3.3 and 3.4, it can be further deciphered that the distribution of the funded deals and, moreover, the exits across VC firms is not uniform. Particularly worth noting is that about 50 per cent of the VC firms in our sample are yet to experience a single viable exit. This observation can be explained in the following manner. To start with, it is well understood that the exits scenario for the Indian VC firms has been fairly grim so far (Bain Consulting 2012, 2013). To be more specific, exits via the IPO route have not really been a viable exit option for most technology start-ups in India, primarily owing to the stringent listing criteria of the Indian stock markets (Planning Commission 2012). Moreover, unlike in other countries (such as Israel or China), start-ups in India are not allowed to list overseas prior to listing on Indian exchanges (Planning Commission 2012).

The relatively low proportion of exits may be further attributed to certain other causes as well. To start with, most of the funded deals during the 2006–08 time frame have been executed at unrealistically high initial valuations (Bain Consulting

2012). During this period, the influx of VC funds was high and relative availability of viable deals low. This had the effect of too much money chasing too few deals, resulting in the inflation of their *true* values (Bain Consulting 2012). Unrealistic initial valuations warrant even higher returns (from exits) in absolute terms. Since such returns are relatively difficult to come by, it translates to a lower number of viable exits (Bain Consulting 2012).

Moreover, as seen in Figure 3.2, a relatively significant proportion of the VC firms in India are still quite young (about 39 per cent of them have been set up since 2010). The typical period of stay in an investee firm for a VC fund manager ranges from four to six years (Gompers and Lerner 2004). Consequently, for a large proportion of deals, the complete cycle from investment to exit is not yet complete. Naturally, this would reflect in the low proportion of exits. For the mature deals, the depressed condition of the stock markets in India seem to have played a major role in further delaying exits (Bain Consulting 2011, 2012, 2013).

Stage and Technology Focus

Figures 3.5 and 3.6 present the stage and technology sector focus of the VC firms in our sample.

About 37 per cent of the VC firms in our sample focus on investing in early-stage ventures alone. Although in India there are no official definitions about the VC investment stages as yet, there exists a broad agreement among VC professionals and policymakers about the key parameters regarding these definitions. Typically, any investments in the range of USD 250,000 to 5 million in unlisted companies

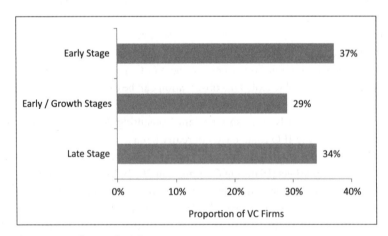

Figure 3.5 Stage focus of VC firms

Source: Primary data collected by the author.

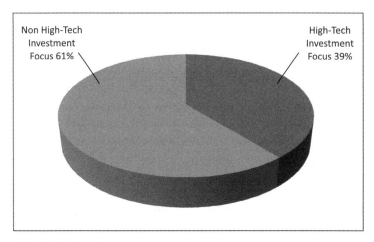

Figure 3.6 Technology focus

Source: Primary data collected by the author.

with an annual turnover of less than USD 8 million are classified as early-stage investments (Planning Commission 2012). The first and second rounds of institutional investments in a company less than five years old and one which is not part of a larger business entity and has an annual turnover of less than USD 4.5 million are also termed as early-stage investment (Venture Intelligence 2019).

Investments in the range of USD 5 to 15 million constituting third/fourth rounds of institutional funding in companies that are five to ten years old are classified as growth-stage investments (Venture Intelligence 2019). Investments in excess of USD 15 million in much older companies constituting higher rounds of investments are classified as late-stage investments (Venture Intelligence 2019). However, it must be pointed out here that these definitions are at best approximate, and there may exist significant variations from deal to deal.

Owing to the absence of a standardized definition of investing stages (by the funding size), we preferred to collect the information pertaining to the funding stage focus directly from the VC firms themselves. For this, we asked the VC firms to state whether they considered themselves as early-, growth-, or late-stage investors (based on the deals funded by them so far). Thus, the funding stage definitions (in the context of our research study) are purely based on what has been self-reported by the sample VC firms. Based on the same, about 37 per cent of the VC firms in our sample invest in early-stage companies alone, 29 per cent in both early- and growth-stage firms, and 34 per cent focus only in late-stage companies.

About 39 per cent of the VC firms in our sample focus on investing in high-technology domains. *High-technology domains* refer to sectors which use technology intensely – either directly or as a major enabler, such as IT and ITeS, biotechnology and life sciences, Internet-backed businesses, mobile value-added services, and cloud computing. Our definition of *high-tech* includes both product and services companies. The *non-high-tech* domains, on the other hand, refer to the more conventional brick and mortar businesses, such as manufacturing, agro-based ventures, real estate, infrastructure, and healthcare (hospital or pharmacy chains).

To specifically define whether the concerned VC firm (from our sample) exhibited a high-tech focus or not, we carefully analysed its portfolio companies. If more than 80 per cent of the companies in its portfolio belonged to the high-tech domains (as defined earlier), the concerned VC firm was deemed to exhibit a *high-tech* investment focus. These definitions were further verified with the concerned VC firm professionals during the course of our interactions with them.

Composition of TMT of the VC Firms

Figure 3.7 presents the distribution of VC firms based on the composition of their TMTs. .

We found that these TMTs comprised two broad categories of professionals: (*a*) erstwhile entrepreneurs and (*b*) professionals with prior financial investing experience (either in VC, investment banking, or any other finance domains)

For the purpose of this study, even if a single member on the VC senior management team (principal/partner/managing director) possessed erstwhile founding experience, the VC firm TMT was deemed to possess *prior founding experience*. Based on this definition, about 26 per cent of the VC firms in our sample were classified as *TMTs with prior founding experience*.

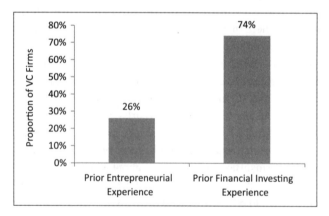

Figure 3.7 Composition of top management team of the VC firm

Source: Primary data collected by the author.

Here, our conjecture is that investors with prior founding background would tend to view the investment potential of the prospective deals quite differently compared to those with financial investing experience alone (based on our initial set of discussions with VC firms). Similarly, the portfolio management strategies devised by the former are likely to differ as well. Since we are interested in empirically testing this proposition later in the thesis, we decided to classify the sample VC firms accordingly.

Ownership Pattern of VC Firms

Figures 3.8, 3.9, and 3.10 present the ownership pattern of VC firms. While Figure 3.8 shows the ownership across foreign and domestic VCs, Figure 3.9 shows the same for corporate and non-corporate VCs, and Figure 3.10 shows it for government-owned VCs.

About 40 per cent of the VC firms included in our sample are of foreign origin, that is, they are offshoots of larger VC entities from other countries (mostly the United States and Singapore). About 60 per cent of the VC firms are of domestic origin, that is, started by Indian entities (government, corporate, and private or VC arms of other financial institutions operating in India). It must be pointed out here that although 60 per cent of the fund managers are of domestic origin, a vast majority of them raise VC funds overseas as well. Yet these have been classified as *domestic* investors since their geography of registration and the destination of investments is in India.

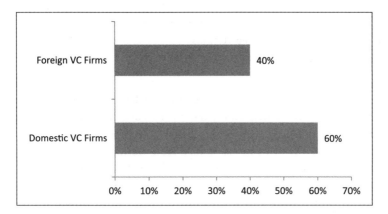

Figure 3.8 Domestic versus Foreign VCs
Source: Primary data collected by the author.

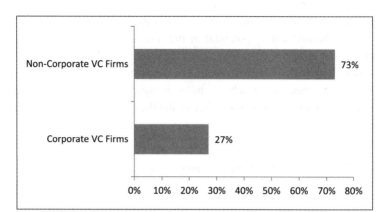

Figure 3.9   Corporate VCs
Source: Primary data collected by the author.

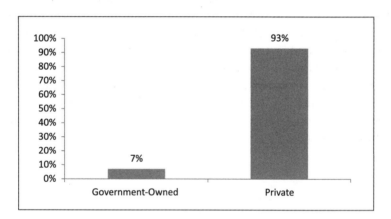

Figure 3.10   Government-owned VC firms
Source: Primary data collected by the author.

Corporate VC firms refer to the VC arms of larger corporate entities (both multinational and domestic), banks, and other financial organizations. About 27 per cent of the firms in our sample are classified as corporate VC firms. Just about 7 per cent of the VC firms in our sample are government owned. Government-owned VC firms are those that have been established by public sector banks, state finance corporations, or central/state governments directly.

To summarize, it can be said that most VC firms in our sample are domestic, private, non-corporate VC firms.

Regulatory Pattern of VC Fund Managers

Figure 3.11 presents the regulatory details of the VC firms with respect to their registration with SEBI, which is the central regulatory authority for all VC funds operating in India.

In our sample, about 39 per cent of the VC firms are registered with SEBI, while 61 per cent of them are not registered with SEBI.

While it is mandatory for all domestic funds to be registered with SEBI, the foreign VC funds may choose to bypass the SEBI route and enter India via the automatic approval route of the RBI or the Foreign Investment Promotion Board (Desai 2012).

However, in our sample, not all domestic VC funds are registered with SEBI. This could be due to the following reason: The funding for certain categories of domestic VC firms could potentially emanate from *non-pooled* sources (where funds directly belong to the primary investors themselves or other informal sources such as friends and family, and not necessarily *pooled* from other secondary investors or limited partners). Since only the VC firms relying on *pooled* sources of funds need to be registered with SEBI, the VC firms relying on *non-pooled* sources are found to bypass this route (Planning Commission 2012).

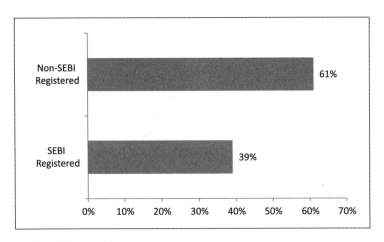

Figure 3.11   SEBI registration

Source: SEBI (2015).

4

Fund Raising
Systematic and Non-systematic Influences

Introduction

The aim of this chapter is to analyse the supply (Ss) side of the VC ecosystem in India. On the supply side, the limited partners (LPs) and the general partners (GPs) constitute the key players governing the flow of VC funds. Among these, the LPs are the fund providers that determine the aggregate quantum of VC funds allocated to India. The GPs are the fund managers who raise these funds and invest them in fledgling investee companies (Gompers and Lerner 2004). In general, the flow of aggregate VC funds is impacted by the macro fundamentals of the economy and the conducive policy environment (Cumming and Macintosh 2006; Bonini and Alkan 2009; Cherif and Gazdar 2011). On the other hand, the fund-raising potential of the individual VC fund managers is the function of their historical reputation and performance (Gompers and Lerner 1999). The former set of factors are referred to as *systematic influences* since they tend to affect all the VC fund managers in a uniform manner. The latter set of factors are the *non-systematic influences* since these vary based on the reputation and performance of each fund manager.

In this chapter, we first examine the *systematic* influences on aggregate fund-raising. We then probe the role played by the *non-systematic* influences in determining the fund-raising potential of the VC fund managers.

Supply of VC Funds

The aim of this section is to lay out a plan for in-depth analyses pertaining to the supply side of the VC ecosystem.

Conceptual Framework on the Factors Influencing the Supply of VC Funds

A broad structure for analysing the supply of VC funds has been given in Figure 4.1. The key hypotheses based on the same have been outlined here.

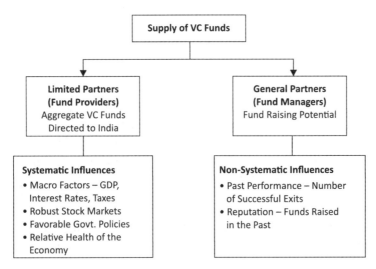

Figure 4.1   Systematic and non-systematic influences on supply of VC funds

Source: Author.

Proposed Hypotheses

Hypothesis 1: Higher growth of real gross domestic product (GDP) positively influences aggregate fund-raising (in general, more funds are directed to growing economies).

Hypothesis 2: Higher interest rates on risk-free assets negatively influence aggregate VC fund-raising (since the opportunity cost of allocated funds to VC as a conduit of investing funds increases).

Hypothesis 3: Robustness of the stock markets positively influences aggregate fund-raising (since initial public offering [IPO] is known to be the most profitable channel of exiting VC investments).

Hypothesis 4: Relative performance of the Indian economy vis-à-vis other potential VC investment destinations will positively affect aggregate fund-raising (since the return on VC investments is expected to be higher in better performing economies).

Hypothesis 5: Better historical performance significantly affects the fund-raising potential of individual VC fund managers (greater number of successful exits in the past and higher earnings multiples are strong indicators of positive historical performance).

Hypothesis 6: Past reputation of the fund managers positively affects their fund-raising potential (number and quantum of funds raised in the past is a positive indicator of reputation).

Sample, Data, and Methods of Analysis

The sources of data for the variables used in this analysis have been presented in Table 4.1.

This analysis is based on two set of samples: first, for aggregate VC fund-raising and, second, for funds raised by individual VC fund managers (GPs). Based on the same, we have built two sets of regression models – the former assesses the role of systematic influences on fund-raising at an aggregate level while the latter analyses the fund-raising potential of the fund managers (GPs).

For the model on aggregate fund-raising, we have quarterly time series observations from December 2006 to March 2014, for domestic and foreign VC firms separately. These data were obtained from the Securities and Exchange Board of India (SEBI). Since SEBI does not directly publish data pertaining to aggregate fund-raising, we have used the available information on cumulative VC investments as a suitable proxy for the same.

The data pertaining to funds raised by the individual VC fund managers (GPs) were obtained from the Venture Intelligence database. However, it must be noted here that the same is not exhaustive, as a large section of GPs are known to keep their fund-raising details strictly confidential. Although in principle this information is available with SEBI, their Memoranda of Understanding (MoUs) with the respective fund managers restricts them from sharing it with third parties. Thus, we have included in our sample only the details available in the public domain.

Discussion of Results

This section discusses two sets of models. To start with, we discuss the model results on aggregate fund-raising. This is followed by the discussion about models on the fund-raising potential of individual VC fund managers.

Models of Aggregate VC Fund-Raising

To reiterate, our primary conjecture is that systematic influences determine the quantum of aggregate fund-raising. For this regression model, the dependent variable is the *growth* of aggregate VC funds raised (first difference of the natural

Table 4.1 Variable definitions and data sources

Variable Name	Abbreviation	Data Source	Details
Aggregate VC Funds Raised (Dependent Variable)	Agg_VC_Funds	SEBI – Handbook of Statistics	Quarterly Time-series Data on Cumulative VC Investments by Domestic and Foreign VC Firms
Funds Raised by Each VC Fund Manager (Dependent Variable)	VC Fund, PE Fund	Venture Intelligence	Cross Section Data on Funds Raised Based on Publicly Available Data
Gross Domestic Product	GDP	RBI – Handbook of Statistics on the Indian Economy	Quarterly Estimates of Gross Domestic Product (at Market Prices) (at Constant Prices) New Series (Base : 2004–5)
Wholesale Price Index	WPI	EPW – Research Foudation Database	WPI – All Commodities WPI (Base 2004–5 = 100)
Index of Industrial Production	IIP	RBI – Handbook of Statistics on the Indian Economy	IIP – General Index (Base Year: 2004–5)
Aggregate Bank Deposits	DEPOSITS	RBI – Handbook of Statistics on the Indian Economy	Aggregate Deposits of Scheduled Commercial Banks
Non-Food Credit	CREDIT	RBI – Handbook of Statistics on the Indian Economy	Non-Food Credit Outstanding
Market Capitalization	MCAP	RBI – Handbook of Statistics on the Indian Economy	Market Capitalization – BSE And All-India
BSE Index (Market Returns)	BSE Returns	RBI – Handbook of Statistics on the Indian Economy	BSE 100 Index (Base: 1983–4 = 58)
Exchange Rate	X Rate	RBI – Handbook of Statistics on the Indian Economy	Exchange Rate of the Indian Rupee vis-à-vis US Dollar
Effective Federal Funds Rate	FedRate	Fed Reserve of St. Louis – Board of Governors of the Federal Reserve System (US)	Average of Daily Figures

Contd

Contd

Variable Name	Abbreviation	Data Source	Details
London Interbank Offered Rate	LIBOR	Fed Reserve of St. Louis – ICE Benchmark Administration Limited (IBA)	Average of Daily Figures
Reference Interest Rate – India	MIBOR	RBI – Handbook of Statistics on the Indian Economy	Weighted Average Call Money Rates
Real Gross Domestic Product – USA	GDP – US	Fed Reserve of St. Louis – US. Bureau of Economic Analysis	Seasonally Adjusted Annual Rate
Consumer Price Index – USA	CPI – US	Fed Reserve of St. Louis – US. Bureau of Labor Statistics	Consumer Price Index for All Urban Consumers: All Items
Historical Deals (Past 5 years)	Deals5	Venture Intelligence	Computed for Each GP Based on Historical Deals Data
Successful past exits (Last 5 years)	Exits5	Venture Intelligence	Computed for Each GP Based on Historical Deals Data
Number of Start-Ups	StartUps	Venture Intelligence	Cumulative VC-funded Start-Ups per Quarter
Historical Funds Raised	Funds5	Venture Intelligence	Funds (in USD Mn) Raised during the Past 5 Years for Each GP

Source: Author.

logarithm of the original variable). The first differencing was done in order to de-trend the series appropriately.

The independent variables may be classified into two types: one, those that represent the *pull* factors and, two, those that characterize *push* aspects. The variables depicting *pull* forces are the ones representing the macro fundamentals of the Indian economy, namely GDP growth, IIP[1] growth, WPI[2] growth (inflation rate), MIBOR[3] (proxy for interest rate) deposit growth and credit[4] growth. Further, we compute other variables such as BSE[5] returns (first difference of natural logs of BSE index values), market capitalization to GDP ratio, credit/GDP ratio, and deposit/GDP ratio. We have also used the data on the number of early stage start-ups in India as a proxy for the scale of the prevailing VC-entrepreneurial ecosystem. The variables representing the *push* forces are the ones pertaining to the macro fundamentals of the other developed economies (which constitute the main source of VC funds flow to India) – Federal funds rate/LIBOR[6] (interest rate proxies), the United States' (US) GDP growth, and the US inflation rate. It must be noted here that we have used US macro data as a representative for the developed economies, since about 70 per cent (Venture Intelligence 2019; Preqin 2014) of the foreign venture capitalists (VCs) operating in India are known to be of US origin. Additionally, we have created other variables to capture the relative differences in the macroeconomic attributes between India and the US namely difference between interest rates (FedRate minus MIBOR), difference between GDP growth rates (India GDP growth minus US GDP growth), and difference in inflation rates (India inflation rate minus US inflation rate).

We have considered the lagged values of independent variables since these macro level variables are expected to affect the dependent variable with a time lag. Our dataset for this model is comprised of fifty-two quarterly observations in all – twenty-six each for the aggregate VC funds raised by domestic and foreign firms. Since the quantum of funds raised by the foreign VC firms is much higher in magnitude compared to their domestic counterparts, we have created a control variable to represent the funds from foreign VC firms accordingly.

The regression results have been presented in Table 4.2. We have used ordinary least squares (OLS) regression as the modelling technique here. (We understand that, ideally, time series techniques such as vector auto-regression would have

---

[1] Index of industrial production.
[2] Wholesale price index.
[3] Mumbai inter-bank offered rate.
[4] Non-food credit.
[5] Bombay Stock Exchange.
[6] London inter-bank offered rate.

proved more appropriate in this regard. However, the paucity of data points [just twenty-six each for domestic and foreign VC firms] have barred us from doing so.) The models were built using SPSS 21.0.0.0. In the model results, we report the adjusted R^2, T-values for each coefficient, model F-statistic from ANOVA and the variance inflation factor (VIF). It may be observed that in both the models, model F-statistic is significant. The multi-collinearity is under control, since the VIF values are below 10 (Hair et al. 2015; Kennedy 1992; Marquardt 1970).

The regression equation for the model on aggregate VC fund-raising can be stated as:

Aggregate VC Funds Raised (YoY Growth) $= \beta_0 + \beta_1$ Absolute Macrofundamentals$_{India}$ $+ \beta_2$ Robust Stock Market Performance$_{India}$ $+ \beta_2$ Start-Ups$_{growth}$ $+ \beta_3$ Relative Macrofundamentals$_{India}$ $+ \beta_4$ Indicator Foreign VC Funds   ... (4.1)

Note: Absolute Macrofundamentals$_{India}$ (GDP growth, IIP growth, interest rates, inflation rate); Robust Stock Market Performance$_{India}$ (market returns – BSE and NSE, market capitalization/GDP ratio); Relative Macrofundamentals$_{India}$ (India minus US GDP growth rate, MIBOR minus Federal funds rate; Indicator Foreign VC Funds (foreign VC funds minus VC funds registered in India and overseas).

As observed from Table 4.2, the macro fundamentals of the Indian economy, both absolute and in relative terms (vis-à-vis the US), have played a vital role in determining the rate of growth of aggregate VC fund-raising. Among these, GDP is regarded as the most reliable metric of economic growth. Difference in the relative GDP growth rates of India and the US seems to be an important determinant of aggregate fund-raising in India. The US is considered to be the world leader in VC investments (Gompers and Lerner 2004; Bain Consulting 2011, 2012, 2013). With the US growth slowing down considerably in the latter half of the last decade, the fund providers (LPs) needed to look for newer investment destinations. Thus, the lower growth of the US GDP could have potentially resulted in directing higher flow of VC funds to India. Various industry reports about the global VC scenario have time and again emphasized this fact (Bain Consulting 2011, 2012, 2013; Ernst and Young 2014).

Not only the overall GDP, but the IIP growth in particular shows up as an important indicator of aggregate VC fund-raising. This result should not be surprising since, of late, the majority of private equity (PE) investments have been directed towards sectors such as infrastructure (utilities and energy), telecom, and real estate (Bain Consulting 2014; Venture Intelligence 2019). Since the linkages between these segments with the overall industrial sector are expected to be relatively strong, the performance of the Indian industry is seen to emerge as an important determinant of the flow of VC funds. In our opinion, this finding is extremely important as it underlines the vitality of the industrial sector for India.

It has been widely believed that regulatory bottlenecks to investments in sectors such as infrastructure, energy, and telecom can prove to be a major deterrent to the emergence of India among the topmost destinations for VC investments in the future (Bain Consulting 2011, 2012, 2013). Moreover, of late, India's GDP growth has been primarily led by the service sector with IIP showing a negative or only a marginally positive growth. This is a cause for concern as it is likely to have severe consequences not only for VC fund-raising but for the overall economy in general (Bala Subrahmanya 2014; Joshi and Bala Subrahmanya 2014).

Table 4.2 Regression model results: aggregate fund-raising

Model Variables	Dependent Variable: Aggregate VC Fund-Raising (Growth)					
	Model 1 Coefficients			Model 2 Coefficients		
	Model 1 Coefficients	P-Value	VIF	Model 2 Coefficients	P-Value	VIF
Constant	-0.101	0.348		0.144	0.086	
Inflation Rate India (Lag 1)	-2.657	0.011	2.016	-2.735	0.005	1.899
Difference – India and US GDP Growth Rates (Lag2)	0.038	0.001	1.881			
MIBOR (Lag1)	0.029	0.036	2.147			
Indicator Variable – Foreign VC	0.074	0.054	1	0.074	0.044	1
Indicator Variable – Year 2008	0.391	0	1.287			
Number of Start-Ups Growth (Lag1)				0.354	0.009	3.352
Index of Industrial Production				1.209	0.051	3.721
	Model 1 Statistics			Model 2 Statistics		
Number of Observations	52			52		
Adjusted R^2	0.572			0.61		
F-Statistic	14.61 with 5 and 46 Degrees of Freedom. P-Value = 0.000			20.51 with 4 and 47 Degrees of Freedom. P-Value – 0.000		

Source: Author.

Note: Separate models were built in order to overcome potential multi-collinearity issues resulting from the inclusion of all variables in the same model.

High interest rates in India have been another important factor that seem to have influenced the growth of aggregate VC fund-raising. Prima facie, this direction of influence may appear counter-intuitive – the growth of aggregate VC funds is positively related to MIBOR (compared to a negative relationship in general as suggested in the literature). Ideally, higher interest rates would tend to reduce the flow of funds into the VC sector since it increases the relative opportunity costs associated with VC investments. However, it must be understood that this is the supply-side explanation. Looking at the same from the demand side, high interest rates make VC funding relatively cheaper for entrepreneurs compared to the other sources of debt and thus increase their relative appetite for VC funds. This is possibly what may have happened in the Indian context. This conjecture has been supported by several industry reports which propound that high debt costs (owing to higher inflation) combined with depressed capital markets have been some of the key drivers that led to the emergence of VC as an attractive funding source compared to other alternatives (Bain Consulting 2012). In fact, the high interest rate regime in India could have potentially paved the way for the gradual emergence of the VC–start-up ecosystem here.

Among the ecosystem related variables, the high rate of growth of Indian start-ups seems to have attracted more VC funds here. In fact, the start-up ecosystem in India has been steadily evolving during this period (Bala Subrahmanya 2015). Thanks to the policy focus, both academia- and industry-backed incubators have been making their presence felt (Ministry of MSME 2013). Not only the domestic corporates (Wipro, Infosys, Godrej, TATA) but also the multinationals operating in India (Amazon, Google, Intel, Microsoft) have set up their own VC financing arms. Bangalore has steadily emerged as the start-up capital of India (Pullen 2013). Thus, this evolution of the start-up ecosystem seems to have played an imperative role in directing VC funds to India.

High inflation raises doubts about the stability of the economy and hence is considered to be a deterrent to the flow of VC funds. The model results confirm this.

Among the indicator variables, the fund-raising potential of the foreign VCs has been found to be significantly higher compared to the domestic firms. This is quite expected, given the depth of their experience in VC investing across the world (Bain Consulting 2011, 2012, 2013, 2014). Quite interestingly, the foreign VC firms also faced considerably fewer restrictions compared to their Indian counterparts while investing across sectors and were correspondingly somewhat freer from complex tax and legal burdens (Bain Consulting 2011, 2013). Naturally, all these factors seem to have positively contributed the flow of foreign VC funds.

Further, fund-raising has been found to be higher particularly during all quarters of the year 2008 compared to other periods in our sample. The year 2008 coincides with some of the worst crisis periods for the developed economies in particular (Bain Consulting 2011). This could have potentially led to the diversion of funds to some of the better performing economies such as India.

However, it must be pointed out that none of the direct stock market related variables (such as BSE returns) emerged significant in the models. We believe that this could be because IPO has not been the chosen route of exit for most of the VC-funded companies in India. In fact, only about 8 per cent of the total exits have been via the IPO route (Venture Intelligence 2019). The possible reason for this could be the stringent listing criteria for start-ups on Indian stock exchanges (Desai 2002). Unless we have stock markets analogous to the NASDAQ (in the US) and Neuer Markt (in Europe) with relative ease of listing, IPO cannot be the choice of exit route for Indian VC-funded companies. However, in the recent past (in 2012), an attempt has been made by the Indian authorities in this regard with the setting up of trading portals for small and medium enterprises (SME) on the BSE and the NSE. Nevertheless, they have yet to gain traction (Ministry of MSME 2013). Moreover, very recently (in June 2015), SEBI has instituted a set of alternative listing requirements that ease the listing procedures for start-ups belonging to the technology domains.

Thus, to conclude the discussion on aggregate VC fund-raising models, we believe that relatively better macroeconomic fundamentals of the Indian economy during the last decade coupled with the gradual evolution of the Indian start-up ecosystem have been instrumental in determining the aggregate supply of VC funds. In summary, the rapid evolution of the VC industry in India cannot be attributed to *push* factors alone; rather, *pull* forces too seem to have played quite an imperative role in this regard.

Models Determining the Fund-Raising Potential of the VC Fund Managers

The objective of building these models is to assess the role of micro factors (such as performance and reputation) in determining the fund-raising potential of the GPs. We have built two separate models in this regard – one each for PE and VC funds. The reason for building separate models was two-fold.

First, the overall quantum of fund size is much higher for PE funds compared to that of the VC funds. This may be attributed to the fact that the PE funds mainly invest in growth and later-stage ventures (where the funding sizes are relatively larger). They are also more prone to investing in core fundamental sectors of the economy (such as infrastructure, real estate, and manufacturing) which again warrant higher funding sizes. As against this, the VC funds focus on emerging and nascent domains and on early-stage ventures, where the relative funding sizes are much lower. According to Venture Intelligence (2019), the average deal size for a VC deal is about USD 3.46 million while that for a PE deal is about USD 21 million. Thus, we believe, combining the two samples (on PE and VC) will not be appropriate as the sheer quantum of PE funds are likely to overpower the minor variations in the volume of VC funds. This may be a potential deterrent in getting sharper results.

Second, our conjecture is that, compared to VC fund-raising, PE fund-raising is likely to depend more on the overall state of the economy rather than the historical reputation and performance parameters of the individual fund managers (GPs). The reason for the same is that core sectors (that the PE investments are focused on) are likely to be more directly influenced by the state of the macroeconomy compared to the VC investments, where the focus is on niche domains.

Our dataset is comprised of 109 and 44 observations on the PE and VC funds respectively from the period 2006 to 2013. Please note that the level of aggregation for this dataset is the VC/PE *funds raised* and not the fund manager (GP) per se. Typically, each fund manager (GP) raises multiple funds from time to time. Thus, if a particular fund manager (GP) has raised two separate funds in this period, it will show up as two separate observations in our analysis dataset. For the independent variables, we created appropriate proxies for measuring the historical *performance* and *reputation*. It must be pointed out at the outset that any data pertaining to the financials of exited deals are not available in the Indian context. Thus, we had to forego the usage of any variables that directly measure the financial performance on the exited deals. This led us to create other proxies depicting reputation. For this, we have created variables such as: Deals5 (number of deals funded during past five years), Exits5 (number of *successful* exits in the past five years), Funds5 (volume of funds raised during the past five years), age of the fund manager (difference between the year of establishment of the GP in India and the year current fund was raised), and an indicator variable that states whether the current fund is the *maiden* fund for that fund manager (GP). Of these, Exits5 is a proxy for historical performance while all others are proxies for reputation. Among exits, we considered only those via IPO and mergers and acquisitions (M&A) routes since only the data on the same is available to us. Further, we also created indicator variables for VC fund manager type (government, corporate, and private), foreign VC, and geographical location of the fund manager in India.

While the fund-raising potential depends on the reputation and performance of the fund managers, it is also determined in parallel by the overall macroeconomic performance of the economy during the period under consideration. Thus, as control variables, we have imputed the information pertaining to the macro fundamentals corresponding to the time period in which the concerned VC/PE fund was raised.

The T-test results clearly show that there exist significant differences among almost all the model variables with respect to both means and variances. This supports the hypotheses that the samples on the VC and the PE funds are essentially different in terms of their scale and variation and thus should not be combined together while building regression models (Table 4.3).

Table 4.3 Fund-raising potential of PE and VC fund managers

		Model variables: results from T-tests			
	Type of Fund	Mean Value	Computed T-Value	P-Value	Test Results for Homogeneity of Variances
Fund Size (USD Mn)	PE	210.91	6.484	0	F-Statistic 23.09, P-Value 0.000
	VC	79.21			Conclusion: Unequal Variances
Age of the Fund Manager (at the Time of Fund Raising)	PE	4.39	0.0224	0.982	F-Statistic 0.0810, P-Value 0.776
	VC	4.37			Conclusion: Equal Variances
Funds Raised in Past 5 Years (USD Mn)	PE	94.62	3.958	0	F-Statistic 27.407, P-Value 0.000
	VC	18.24			Conclusion: Unequal Variances
Number of Successful Exits (in Past 5 Years)	PE	5.7	2.351	0.02	F-Statistic 10.917, P-Value 0.001
	VC	2.78			Conclusion: Unequal Variances
Number of Funded Deals (in Past 5 Years)	PE	2.47	-2.98	0.004	F-Statistic 27.824, P-Value 0.000
	VC				Conclusion: Unequal Variances
		8.63			

Source: Author.

The regression equation for the models on fund-raising potential can be expressed as:

VC/PE Funds Raised by VC Fund Managers $= \beta_0 + \beta_1$ Historical Reputation $+ \beta_2$ Historical Performance $+ \beta_3$ VC Fund Type$_{\text{Indicator Variable}} + \beta_4$ Relative and Absolute Macroeconomic conditions

Note: Historical Reputation and Performance (funds raised, deals funded, successful exits over past five years); VC Fund Type (VC fund raised by Indian government, foreign fund)

Table 4.4 presents the OLS regression model results for the models on VC and PE fund-raising by the respective fund managers (GPs). The models were built using SPSS 21.0.0.0. In the model results, we report the adjusted R^2, T-values for each coefficient, model F-statistic from ANOVA, and the variance inflation factor (VIF). It may be observed that in both the models, model F-statistic is significant.

The multi-collinearity is under control, since the VIF values are below 10 (Hair et al. 2015; Kennedy 1992; Marquardt 1970; Neter, Wasserman, and Kutner 1989).

Table 4.4 Regression results: fund-raising potential of general partners

Model Variables	Model 1: VC Fund-Raising			Model 2: PE Fund-Raising		
	Dependent Variable: Funds Raised by VC Fund Managers			Dependent Variable: Funds Raised by PE Fund Managers		
	Model 1 Coefficients	P-Value	VIF	Model 2 Coefficients	P-Value	VIF
Constant	-20.937	0.37		203.455	0	
Number of Successful Exits (in Past 5 Years)	6.204	0.005	1.06	3.97	0.026	1.857
Funds Raised in Past 5 Years (USD Mn)	0.952	0	1.121	0.208	0.029	1.338
Number of Funded Deals (in Past 5 Years)				5.076	0.084	1.278
Indicator Variable – Government GP Fund	-41.85	0.0321	1.29	-196.043	0.002	1.05
Indicator Variable – Foreign GP Fund	39.883	0.032	1.366			
India minus USA GDP Growth Differential	10.713	0.005	1.233			
US GDP Growth				-19.937	0.026	1.857
	Model 1 Statistics			Model 2 Statistics		
Number of Observations	44			109		
Adjusted R^2	0.615			0.174		
F-Statistic	F-Statistics: 15.047 with 5 and 39 Degrees of Freedom. P-Value = 0.000			F-Statistics: 5.601 with 5 and 104 Degrees of Freedom. P-Value = 0.000		

Source: Author.

The results confirm that past reputation and performance have played an instrumental role in affecting the fund-raising potential of the individual fund managers (GPs). The quantum of funds raised and the number of deals funded over the past five years are indicative of the reputation of the GP players not only in terms of fund-raising but also for portfolio management. Both these skills are found to be significantly important in raising additional funds.

We have used the number of past exits as a proxy for past performance of the GPs. It should be noted that in our analysis, we have considered only the successful exits (namely IPOs and M&As) and have excluded bankruptcy as a form of exit. Thus, using these measure of exits as a proxy for good performance seems reasonable to us. All the three variables representing performance and reputation have a positive sign and are highly significant.

We have also deployed a few control variables to ensure the robustness of our results. This was done to control for the effect of factors other than performance and reputation on the fund-raising potential. The first one here is the GP type (domestic or foreign; private, corporate, or government). This variable attempts to control for the access to diverse sources of funds available to each type of GP. The indicator variable for government-backed GP has a negative sign, indicating that the government-owned GPs have raised much lower quantum of funds on an average compared to the private players. This is expected as there exist significant restrictions on the fund-raising by government-owned GPs. First, a majority of the government-owned entities are not permitted to raise funds abroad. Second, a significant section of potential fund providers in India such as pension funds and insurance companies are not allowed to make allocations to VC funds as part of their investment portfolios (Bain Consulting 2011; Planning Commission 2012).

The indicator variable for foreign GPs has a positive sign, indicating that foreign funds have a much higher fund-raising potential compared to domestic ones. Foreign VCs have access to much diverse sources of funds compared to their domestic counterparts and this seems to have enhanced their fund-raising potential.

The other control variable concerns the relative macroeconomic environment in which these VC and PE funds have been raised. Given the fact that more than 80 per cent of the Indian PE and VC funds are raised abroad (particularly in the US), the variables on *US GDP growth* in absolute terms and the one pertaining to the *relative GDP growth differential between India and US* play an important role in determining the fund-raising potential. Better and robust performance of the Indian economy vis-à-vis the US thus results in higher funds raised by GPs operating in India (more VC/PE funds pushed to India) from overseas.

Coming to the relative comparison of the VC and PE fund-raising models, we find that the quantum of historical funds raised and successful exits uniformly affect both kinds of fund-raising. However, the quantum of PE fund-raising is determined by the number of deals funded historically by the PE fund manager. The reason for the same could be as follows: PE investments are typically focused on areas that warrant a high interface with the government. Given the fact that investments in such sectors are often riddled by complex regulations/procedures and also the fact that India's record at the *relative ease of doing business* is not particularly noteworthy (Transparency International 2014; World Bank 2015), having a significant exposure to a larger number of deals is definitely a must-have attribute that the fund providers would potentially look for.

To summarize the results of the regression models pertaining to the fund-raising potential, we conclude that performance and reputation have played an important role in determining the quantum of funds raised by VC and PE fund managers. However, the role played by these factors cannot be looked at in isolation from the situation at the macroeconomic level. Thus, to conclude, during periods of macroeconomic boom, the better performing fund managers will tend to raise a higher quantum of funds than what they would have in relatively recessionary periods.

5

High-Tech Clusters in India

Introduction

The aim of this chapter is to present an in-depth analysis pertaining to the demand (Dd) side of the venture capital (VC) ecosystem. The demand side comprises start-ups into which the VC funds are directed. The focus here is to understand the nature of systematic influences that impact the emergence and growth of start-ups, especially start-up clusters. For ventures in high-technology domains, the start-up ecosystem, incubators/business accelerators, and most importantly VC funds play a vital role. Then there are other attributes pertaining to macroeconomic parameters, industrial structure, infrastructure, and government policies that are givens.

Literature also points out that start-ups rarely emerge on a stand-alone basis. Rather, they do so in the form of geographic clusters. Such clusters are often specialized in their respective domains (such as biotechnology or information technology), resulting in the accumulation of a critical mass of relevant skills (Reynolds 1993; Reynolds and Storey 1993). The positive externalities resulting from the same in the form of 'knowledge spillovers' are regarded as one of the most important determinants behind the emergence of such clusters (Jaffe, Trajtenberg, and Henderson 1992).

Conceptual Framework on Demand for VC Funds

The broad framework for analysing the demand for VC funds has been given in Figure 5.1, followed by the proposed hypotheses.

Proposed Hypotheses

Hypothesis 1: Robust macroeconomic conditions have a positive impact on the emergence of high-tech clusters.

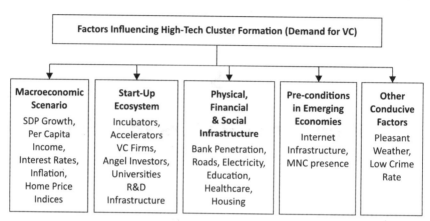

Figure 5.1   Conceptual framework
Source: Author.

Hypothesis 2: Robust start-up ecosystem parameters have a positive impact on the emergence of high-tech clusters.

Hypothesis 3: Presence of robust physical, financial and social infrastructure have a positive impact on the emergence of high-tech clusters.

Hypothesis 4: Factors such as Internet penetration and a distinct presence of multi-national corporations (MNCs) have a positive impact on the emergence of high-tech clusters.

Hypothesis 5: Conducive conditions, such as pleasant weather conditions and low crime rates, positively impact the emergence of high-tech clusters.

Each of these hypotheses has multiple hypotheses embedded within.

Sample, Data, and Methods of Analysis

This study based on secondary data covers the early-stage companies from six major Indian start-up hubs (Bangalore, Chennai, Hyderabad, Kolkata, Mumbai/ Pune, and the National Capital Region [NCR]) between 2005 and 2013. Due to the geographical proximity of Mumbai and Pune, they have been considered here as a single cluster. Similarly, owing to the geographical proximity of New Delhi, Gurgaon, and Noida, these have been considered together in the NCR cluster. We have chosen these cities since about 93 per cent of the early-stage start-ups during the period under study have emerged from these hubs (Venture Intelligence 2014). About 65 per cent of the start-ups in our sample belong to high-technology domains – information technology (IT) and IT enabled services (ITES), biotechnology and life sciences. Even when they belong to other sectors, IT is understood to be the major enabler.

Variables

The dataset for this study comprises a balanced panel of six start-up hubs in India such that cross-sectional or time series information (or both) on each of them is available for the period 2005 to 2013 (with annual frequency). These data have been compiled from the sources stated in Table 5.1.

As seen in Table 5.1, data on certain series were available at both time series and cross-sectional levels, while for others at either cross-sectional or time series levels. For the set of variables where the data were available at cross-sectional level alone (with no time series variation), we have imputed the same cross-sectional level values across all the time periods for each cross-sectional unit. For those where the data were available at time series level alone (with no variation in cross-sectional values), the same time-varying values have been imputed for each cross-sectional unit. Similarly, data on certain series were available at the state level and not city level. In such cases, the state level values have been imputed at the city level (based on the state that the city belongs to).

Dependent variable: Since the primary objective of this study is to explore the ecosystem related factors that contribute to the emergence of geographical start-up clusters, the dependent variable is the number of start-ups (varying across geography and year).

Independent variables: The independent variables can be classified into the following broad categories: those directly related to the start-up ecosystem, those associated with the available infrastructure in a particular geography, and those that are a proxy for the overall health of the macroeconomy in that geography.

Methods of Analysis

We have used two main statistical techniques for analysis here: exploratory factor analysis (EFA) and pooled OLS regression. The rationale for using these techniques has been provided in this section.

To start with, we perform EFA with the aim of grouping the independent variables into meaningful factors/constructs that capture the underlying dimensions in the data. We then use the factor scores for these constructs to build regression models in order to predict the potential drivers responsible for the emergence of the start-up clusters. We have used OLS regression technique in this regard. All analysis was performed using SPSS 21.0.0.0 and R 3.1.0 statistical software. For *EFA*, we report the scree plot, factor loading matrix, eigenvalues, and the variance

Table 5.1   Variable definitions and data sources

Variable Name	Level of Aggregation	Data Source
No. of Start-Ups	CS, TS	Venture Intelligence
No. of VC Funds	CS, TS	Venture Intelligence
No. of Incubators	CS	Venture Center, National Science and Technology Development Board (NSTEDB)
No. of Incubated Companies	CS	Venture Intelligence
No. of Angel Investments	CS	Venture Intelligence
State Domestic Product (at Constant Prices)	CS, TS	Central Statistical Organization
City-Level GDP	CS	Global Metro Monitor, Brookings Institution
Interest Rates (Annual average Call Money Rates)	TS	Reserve Bank of India – Handbook of Statistics on Indian Economy
Inflation Rate (Change in WPI – All commodities Base 2004–5 = 100)	TS	Reserve Bank of India – Handbook of Statistics on Indian Economy
Industry Sector /SDP Ratio and Service Sector SDP/ Aggregate SDP Ratio	CS, TS	Central Statistical Organization
Home Price Indices	CS	National Housing Bank
Electricity Installed Capacity (MWh)	CS	Central Electricity Authority
Highways (Km)	CS	National Highways Authority of India
Population (City and State)	CS	Census of India, 2011
No. of Telephone Connections (per 1,000 Population)	CS	Telecom Regulatory Authority of India
Internet Users (per 100,000 Population)	CS	India Market Research Bureau, 2013
No. of Universities	CS	Ministry of Human Resources and Development
Hospitals/Clinics (per 100,000 Population)	CS	National Health Mission, Ministry of Health, GoI
Housing Units (per 100,000 Population)	CS	Census of India, 2011
Bank Penetration, Credit and Deposit Penetration	CS	Reserve Bank of India
No. of MNCs	CS	Ministry of Corporate Affairs
IPC Crimes (per 100,000 Population)	CS	National Crime Records Bureau, Ministry of Home, GoI
R&D Units (Public Sector, Private Sector and Universities)	CS	Department of Science and Technology, Government of India
Weather (Temperature – Mean and Std. Deviation)	CS	World Weather Online

Source: Author.

explained. For *pooled OLS regressions*, we report the T-values, adjusted R^2, F-statistic and variance inflation factor (VIF) values.

Exploratory Factor Analysis (EFA)

We have about fourteen independent variables in our analysis. A preliminary analysis revealed that most of these are highly correlated with each other. Thus, using them together in the same regression model would have potentially led to severe multicollinearity problems. The presence of high multicollinearity, in turn, results in large standard errors and insignificant estimates (Gujarati 2012). Thus, we had to devise a method to bypass the multicollinearity problem without compromising on the available information. EFA as a technique enables us to overcome this problem.

The essential purpose of EFA is to describe the covariance relationships among many variables in terms of a few underlying but unobservable random quantities called factors (Johnson and Wichern 2008). Thus, EFA can be used for summarization of data on multiple correlated variables into a smaller number of underlying dimensions (Hair 2015). Each of these underlying dimensions are mutually orthogonal to each other. The initial solution thus obtained is then *rotated* to get more meaningful results.[1] The estimated values of these factors are known as factor scores, which can be used for further analysis. In our context, orthogonality implies that bi-variate correlations among the factor scores of these multiple dimensions are zero. Thus, using these constructs together in the same regression model is now possible as we have got over the multicollinearity problem.

Discussion of Results

This section comprises three subsections. To start with, we present the descriptive statistics (mean values) for each geographic cluster. This is followed by results from the EFA procedure, which classifies the independent variables into underlying dimensions. After this, we present the results from the OLS regression.

Preliminary Data Analysis

Table 5.2 presents the mean values (by geography) for the dependent and all independent variable categories.

---

[1] *Factor rotation* refers to an orthogonal transformation of factor loadings as well as the implied orthogonal transformation of factors. Since the original loadings may not be readily interpretable, it is the usual practice to *rotate* them until a 'simpler structure' is achieved (Johnson and Wichern 2008).

On an average, Bangalore has the highest number of start-ups, closely followed by Mumbai/Pune and NCR. Hyderabad (Andhra Pradesh/Telangana) ranks highest in terms of physical infrastructure, namely the length of highways, while Mumbai/Pune (Maharashtra) ranks highest in terms of the installed electricity capacity.

Table 5.2   Descriptive statistics by geography

Variables	Bangalore	Chennai	Hyderabad	Kolkata	Mumbai/Pune	NCR
Number of Start-Ups	**422**	98	103	16	394	292
Number of VC Firms	37	9	6	1	**89**	25
Number of Incubators	20	**32**	19	7	20	**32**
Number of Incubated Companies	**87**	40	24	8	92	**95**
Number of Angel Investments	**86**	29	16	0	**100**	54
SDP Growth Rate	7.26	9.15	**10.17**	6.85	9.14	9.99
City GDP (USD Bn)	110	78.3	75.2	150.1	**379**	294
IT and ITeS Exports (in USD Mn)	**19,896**	10,958	9,417	1,984	14,063	9,542
Number of MNCs	271	199	78	55	**781**	1,550
Electricity – Installed Capacity (in MWh)	13,941	20,717	17,285	8,709	**32,505**	7,501
Length of Highways (Km)	6,294	5,006	**7,068**	2,910	6,335	80
Internet Penetration	26%	41%	32%	**68%**	46%	13%
Bank Branches (per 100,000 Population)	**286**	216	179	338	181	98
Number of Technical Institutes	874	1,353	**1,904**	212	1,203	78
R&D Institutions (Public)	18	11	14	**23**	16	18
R&D Institutions (Private)	343	353	371	167	**916**	239
Number of Universities (with R&D Set-ups)	33	**45**	23	19	29	12
MNCs	271	199	78	55	781	**1,550**
Weather (Range of Temperature)	19	18	24	22	26	31
Number of Crimes (Registered under Indian Penal Code)	30,300	17,800	16,400	26,400	48,000	88,000

Source: Author.

Note: Cities with the highest mean values for each variable have been marked in **bold**. The mean values for the variables Interest Rates and Inflation are not given as they vary across time and not across geography

In terms of the educational infrastructure, Andhra Pradesh/Telangana ranks highest with regard to the number of educational institutes, and in terms of bank branch penetration, Bangalore ranks the highest, while NCR ranks the lowest. Further, Kolkata ranks the highest in terms of Internet penetration, while NCR is again the lowest.

As regards the high-tech start-up-specific infrastructure, Mumbai/Pune and Bangalore rank the highest in terms of presence of VC firms. Chennai and NCR both are at the top in terms of the number of business incubators, while NCR and Bangalore rank highest in terms of the number of incubated companies and angel investments. Mumbai/Pune and Bangalore rank the highest in terms of angel investments. Bangalore (Karnataka) ranks highest in terms of its value of IT and ITES exports, followed by Mumbai/Pune (Maharashtra). NCR has the highest presence of MNCs.

About the research and development (R&D) infrastructure, the number of public sector R&D institutions is the highest in Kolkata, while those in the private sector are highest in Mumbai/Pune. Similarly, the R&D institutions within university set-ups are highest in Chennai.

City-level real gross domestic product (GDP) is the highest for Mumbai/Pune, followed by NCR. Andhra Pradesh ranks highest in terms of state domestic product (SDP) growth, whereas NCR is way above other regions in terms of the number of registered crimes. About the range of average monthly temperatures, the lowest variation is in Bangalore and Chennai, with the difference between the minimum and maximum temperatures being in the range of 18° Centigrade, while it is the highest for NCR with the same range being 31.

Results from EFA

We performed the EFA procedure separately for each category of factors affecting the high-tech clusters. The number of factors to be extracted was based on the latent root (eigenvalue) criterion. The rationale for the latent root criterion is that any individual factor should account for the variance of at least a single variable if it is to be retained for interpretation. We decided on the total number of factors to be considered based on both technical metrics (scree plots and eigenvalues) and intuitive logic. *Varimax rotation* was applied to the principal components in order to extract the factors. Variables with high factor loadings (> 0.60) were chosen to represent factors.

Thus, we performed six EFA procedures in all. To identify the underlying dimensions for the construct related to macroeconomic scenario, we use the following variables: SDP growth, services sector output to SDP ratio, industry sector output to SDP ratio, interest rates, inflation rate, home price indices, city

GDP (in USD billion). Based on the EFA results, this construct was further divided into three sub-constructs, namely services sector dominance index, interest and inflation rates, and SDP growth.

For identifying the underlying dimensions of the construct on physical, financial, and social infrastructure, we use the following variables: length of highways (in kilometres), healthcare facilities (per 100,000 population), credit outstanding (per million population), bank deposits (per million population), and housing units (per 100,000 population). After performing the EFA procedure, this construct was subdivided into two sub-constructs: one, financial and social infrastructure and, two, physical infrastructure (Table 5.3).

The construct on educational infrastructure comprised two variables: number of technical institutes and number of universities. Both variables loaded on just one underlying sub-construct.

Table 5.3   Exploratory factor analysis procedure

Constructs	Sub-Constructs	Variables Loaded on	Eigenvalues
Construct 1: Macroeconomic Scenario	Services Sector Dominance Index	Services Sector Output to SDP Ratio, Industry Sector Output to SDP Ratio, Home Price Indices and City GDP (USD Bn)	2.971
	Interest Rates & Inflation	Interest Rates & Inflation Rates	1.693
	SDP Growth	SDP Growth Rate	1.017
Construct 2: Physical, Financial, and Social Infrastructure	Financial and Social Infrastructure	Healthcare Facilities per 100,000, Credit Outstanding (per Mn Population) and Deposits (per Mn Population)	3.12
	Physical Infrastructure	Housing Units (per 100,000 Population) & Electricity – Installed Capacity	1.786
Construct 3: Educational Infrastructure	Technical Institutions & Universities	Number of Technical Institutions & Number of Universities	1.844
Construct 4: Internet Infrastructure	Tele-density	Telephone Penetration & Internet Penetration	1.58
	Broadband Subscribers	Broadband Subscribers	1.01
Construct 5: R&D Infrastructure	Universities R&D	University Set-ups R&D Units	1.867
	Private R&D	Private Set-ups R&D Units	0.793

Contd

Contd

Constructs	Sub-Constructs	Variables Loaded on	Eigenvalues
Construct 6: Start-Up Ecosystem	VC Firms and Critical Mass	Number of Angel Investments, Number of VC Funds, Number of Incubated Companies, Number of MNCs, IT and ITeS_Exports (in USD Mn)	3.624
	Incubators	Number of Incubators	1.454

Source: Author.

The construct on Internet and telecommunications infrastructure comprised three parameters: Internet penetration, telephone penetration, and broadband subscribers. This was further subdivided into two sub-constructs: tele-density and broadband subscribers.

The R&D infrastructure related construct comprised three variables: public sector R&D units, private sector R&D units, and university R&D units. This was further subdivided into two sub-constructs: university R&D and private sector R&D. Public sector R&D did not load on either of these sub-constructs.

Finally, the construct pertaining to the start-up ecosystem comprised the following variables: number of angel investments, number of incubators, number of VC funds, number of incubated companies, number of MNCs, IT and ITES exports (in USD million). This got divided into two sub-constructs: one, VC firms and critical mass and, two, incubators. The quantum of angel investments, incubated companies, MNC presence, and IT and ITES exports emanating from the region are all indicative of the presence of a critical mass in terms of human, technological, and intellectual resources.

Discussion of Results

With the factor scores for each of the sub-constructs obtained from the EFA procedure, we built three OLS regression models. Three separate models had to be built owing to the multicollinearity issues among the sub-constructs. In addition to the factor scores, we have used certain other variables such as crime rates and weather conditions for each of the geographical clusters as explanatory variables in our models. In addition to the OLS models, we perform the relative importance analysis to understand the weightage of each of the model variables. This is based on the computation of standardized coefficients.

SPSS 21.0.0.0 was used for analysis. As model results, we present β coefficients, significance levels, variance inflation factors, adjusted R^2 values, and the model F-statistic (with P-values). Further, we also present the standardized coefficients and perform a relative importance analysis of model variables using the same.

Table 5.4 Ordinary least squares regression results

Model Variables	Model 1 β Coefficients	Model 1 Variance Inflation Factor	Model 2 β Coefficients	Model 2 Variance Inflation Factor	Model 3 β Coefficients	Model 3 Variance Inflation Factor
	Dependent Variable: Number of Start-Ups					
Constant	24.537***		29.528***		228.341***	
Services Sector Dominance Index	5.763*	1.767				
Interest Rates & Inflation	5.438**	1.029				
SDP Growth	-1.15	1.635				
Financial & Social Infrastructure	9.438***	1.602				
Universities R&D	2.839	1.841				
VC Firms and Critical Mass			19.190***	1.662		
Incubators			3.430*	1.173		
Private Sector R&D			-0.013	1.835		
Physical Infrastructure						
Internet Users (Mn)					2.179**	1.214
Crimes per Mn (Registered under Indian Penal Code)					-0.003**	1.219
Average Monthly Temperature					-7.810***	1.013
Model Diagnostics						
Adjusted R^2	0.264		0.691		0.493	
Model F-Statistic	F-value 4.803 with p-value of 0.004		F-value 40.54 with p-value of 0.000		F-value 18.188 with p-value of 0.000	

Source: Author.

Note: *** Significant at the 0.001 level (2-tailed). ** Significant at the 0.01 level (2-tailed). * Significant at the 0.05 level (2-tailed).

The construct on 'VC firms and critical mass' alone constitutes 30 per cent of the total weight in terms of the order of importance among the predictor variables.

Thus, VC funding emerges as one of the principal drivers contributing to the emergence of high-tech start-up clusters. This might lead us to conclude that a strong presence of VC funds in a particular geography naturally results in high prospects of it emerging as a start-up cluster. However, this result should not be misread as VC *causing* entrepreneurship. Rather, the causation is likely to be the other way around (Dossani and Kenney 2002), that is, the presence of start-ups with prospects for high return attracts more VC firms to a region. Thus, based on our results, all that we can say is that there exists a strong association between VC and start-ups. In case of India, just three clusters, namely Bangalore, Mumbai/Pune, and NCR are home to 78 per cent of the total VC fund managers operating here (Venture Intelligence 2019), thus revealing a strong geographical coincidence. Bangalore has the highest proportion of early- and growth-stage focused VC firms while Mumbai has the highest proportion of late-stage focused VC firms, particularly private equity firms. Bangalore is also home to the highest proportion of foreign VCs and those focused on high-tech sector investments. Mumbai has the highest proportion of VC firms focused on social sector investments.

The geographical proximity of the VC firms and start-ups has been well supported by literature. VC funding has been considered critical for incubating nascent businesses, particularly in high-technology domains. Intangibility of assets, coupled with novel revenue models that delay profits until the long run, is the mainstay of such ventures which, in turn, make them ineligible for funding from other conventional financial intermediaries (Barry 1994; Fried and Hisrich 1994). Further, given the high level of agency risks in the VC-funded projects, most VC fund managers generally prefer to fund projects that are not too geographically distant from where they are located (Cumming and Dai 2010). This seems to have been one of the foremost reasons for the joint emergence of start-ups and VC funds in the same geography. Moreover, VC funds not only influence the emergence of start-ups but affect their growth and survival as well. In fact, VC-funded companies provide a strong signal to the labour market, which consequently attracts better quality of human capital – the primary asset for high-tech companies (Gompers and Lerner 2004). All the factors just discussed are together responsible for the strong nexus between high-tech start-ups and VC funding.

Another critical element that seems to have a major influence is the presence of 'critical mass' – that is, pre-existence of a critical mass of relevant businesses and human capital. High quality human capital is the most vital resource for high-tech start-ups. Presence of a critical mass of high-tech businesses (including the pre-incubated companies and angel investments) indicates adequate availability of capital and skill sets. It is also well understood that localization of knowledge due to the presence of a critical mass results in significant positive externalities in the form of *knowledge spillovers* (Jaffe, Trajtenberg, and Henderson 1992).

These clusters facilitate networking among start-up employees and ease access to specialized suppliers, scientific knowledge, and technological expertise indigenous to the area (Ketels 2003). This critical mass is represented by the concentration of MNCs and angel investments in the region. Bangalore, ranking the highest in terms of IT and ITES exports, is reflective of the presence of critical mass therein.

Table 5.5 Relative importance analysis

Variable Names	Standardized Coefficients	Absolute Values of Standardized Coefficients	Order of Importance of Variables
Services Sector Dominance Index	0.275	0.275	9%
Interest Rates & Inflation	0.259	0.259	8%
SDP_Growth	-0.055	0.055	2%
Financial & Social Infrastructure	0.45	0.45	15%
Universities R&D	0.135	0.135	4%
VC Firms and Critical Mass	0.914	0.914	30%
Incubators	0.164	0.164	5%
Private Sector R&D	-0.146	0.146	5%
Physical Infrastructure	-0.19	0.19	6%
Internet Users (Mn)	0.298	0.298	10%
Crimes per Mn (Registered under Indian Penal Code)	-0.19	0.19	6%
Average Monthly Temperature	-0.546	0.546	18%

Source: Author.

Note: * Since variables SDP Growth and Average Temperature occur in two regression models, the average values of standardized coefficients were used

MNCs, particularly those in technology related arenas, have been the forerunners of high-tech clusters. As discussed, the most prominent example of this is Bangalore, which has been home to about 140 MNC development centres, and 750 large and small domestic IT firms as early as in 2001, contributing to more than 40 per cent of India's total exports (of USD 8.3 billion) with about 60,000 IT professionals being employed there (Patibandla and Peterson 2002). These factors collectively provided an impetus to the emergence of Bangalore among the top ten start-up hubs in the world. The role of MNCs in effecting technology transfer has been well recognized. In the context of start-ups, it is important to understand the role played by US-trained engineers from these MNCs in transferring the know-how and market information to the host countries, and help jump-start local entrepreneurship here (Saxenian 2006). In fact, the large pool of angel investors in India is essentially drawn from these MNCs – Google, Yahoo, Amazon, and others. These foreign-trained engineers from MNCs not only influence technology transfer and know-how when they return home to work or start businesses, but are also seen to significantly influence the process of policy formation and other aspects of the institutional environment for start-ups. A prominent example of the same in India is iSPIRT – Indian Software Products Industry Round Table (a think tank that is aimed at influencing policies for software product start-ups in India) – that has been started by returnee technology professionals from the US who first moved to India as a part of their multinational organizations and then took on the role of entrepreneurs and angel investors here. Such highly skilled returnees are now increasingly transforming the processes of brain drain into 'brain circulation' as they return home to establish entrepreneurial ventures while maintaining their social and professional links to the US. In doing so, they export first-hand knowledge of US capital markets and business models to the emerging markets (Saxenian 2006).

The presence of incubation facilities is another vital element in the high-tech start-up ecosystem. However, quite surprisingly, this variable explains only 5 per cent of the total weight in terms of the order of importance of the variables. Currently, there are about 104 active business incubators in India. About 47 per cent of them belong to three start-up hubs, namely Bangalore, Mumbai/Pune, and NCR. Interestingly, about 30 per cent of these incubators are located in Chennai (and Tamil Nadu) alone. Yet Chennai is not one of the topmost start-up hubs. The probable reason for this could be that the growth of an incubated company into a successful start-up warrants the presence of a vibrant start-up ecosystem, which perhaps Chennai lacks. In fact, just 5 per cent of the VC firms have a physical office in Chennai; similarly, just 10 per cent of all angel investments belong to Chennai. The low presence of VCs and angel investors could probably be the reason that despite the highest presence of incubators, the city is yet to emerge as a prominent start-up hub.

This observation can also be corroborated based on the evidence from the literature. It must be understood that not merely the number of incubators, but rather their 'functionality' is important from the viewpoint of cluster formation. While there are about 180 incubators operating in India today, very few of them are worthy in the true sense (Maital et al. 2008). In fact, most incubators within the academic set-ups focus on providing merely physical infrastructure (Maital et al. 2008). Without them facilitating access to other critical services such as mentoring, access to VC firms, angel investors, and other vital networks, they might not be very effective in augmenting the viable deal flow in the start-up ecosystem (Ministry of MSME 2013). Moreover, apart from 'idea incubators', there exists a strong need for the establishment of technology business incubators (TBIs) that provide access to the required machines and equipment to test and manufacture products on a pilot scale, which are almost missing from the Indian scene. Such TBIs have played a major role in the start-up ecosystem in Israel and the US (Ministry of MSME 2013).

Physical infrastructure does not seem to have any significant influence on the emergence of start-ups in the region. However, this is not to berate its importance, but rather look upon it as a minimum must-have condition for any region to emerge as a start-up cluster (Joshi 2018a). However, financial and social infrastructure (that is, robust banking as seen from high bank deposit and credit penetration, healthcare, and housing) is certainly an important factor. Moreover, Internet and telecommunications infrastructure can be regarded as the mainstay of such new-age high-tech businesses. In fact, low Internet penetration has been identified as a key impediment to innovation in emerging economies (Aubert and Reiffers 2004). Given that about 65 per cent of the high-tech start-ups in India belong to the information and communication technology (ICT) domains, it should not be surprising that high tele-density emerges as an essential precondition for high-tech cluster formation. Together, the financial, social, and Internet related infrastructure account for 25 per cent of the importance weight among all explanatory variables.

The sub-construct related to educational infrastructure emerged insignificant. Once again, this is not to berate the role of educational institutes. Rather, these facilities can be viewed as a minimum 'must-have' for high-tech cluster emergence. Moreover, since labour as a resource is highly mobile in India, the physical location of the educational institutes does not matter. Similarly, the R&D infrastructure related variables did not emerge significant as well. The presence of neither university R&D set-ups nor public and private R&D set-ups is related to the emergence of start-up clusters. This goes against the evidence presented by Bala Subrahmanya (2017a), which attributes the emergence of Bangalore and Hyderabad clusters to the strong public sector R&D set-ups therein. While the R&D set-ups may contribute indirectly by making available a pool of talented human capital, particularly scientists and innovators, they do not seem to directly impact the process of start-up formation in terms of commercializing the research from these R&D set-ups. There are many possible reasons for the same. To start with, the linkages between industry and academia are still not quite strong in India. Where they exist, they are restricted to the limited top-tier engineering and management institutes. This is quite in contrast to that seen in Silicon Valley, where many of the highly successful companies of today have been incubated as start-ups in the university set-ups of Stanford and Berkeley. A study by Basant and Chandra (2007) about India reveals that even among the top-tier institutes, only a miniscule proportion had successfully managed entrepreneurial spin-offs. The factors for the dismal performance in terms of encouraging entrepreneurship is attributed to a number of factors – lack of seed funding, inappropriateness of research for commercialization, and other institutional and regulatory barriers pertaining to intellectual property (Basant and Chandra 2007).

We used the variable on SDP growth as a proxy for the overall macroeconomic environment. Quite interestingly, this did not seem to influence the process of start-up creation. This finding contradicts the previous findings in literature, namely there exist more opportunities to start new firms in growing economies (Gompers and Lerner 2004; Jeng and Wells 2000; Cumming and Macintosh 2006; Cherif and Gazdar 2011). While we believe that the findings from the literature are definitely valid at the macro level, wherein more firms are likely to appear in growing economies, the specific geographic locations where these start-ups will emerge depend more on the specific micro aspects of the local ecosystem. Again, this is not to berate the role of macro factors, but rather goes on to justify the fact that a strong macro economy is a minimum must-have condition.

High interest rates seem to have positively contributed to the emergence of start-ups. The sub-construct on interest rates and inflation contributes to 8 per cent of the total weight in terms of variable importance. In general, high interest rates make bank borrowing relatively dearer and thus increase the demand for venture capital (Gompers and Lerner 2004). This, coupled with the fact that VC was available in abundance in India during the period under consideration owing to the economic downturn in other developed economies (Bain Consulting 2012), has been a very important factor contributing to the emergence of start-ups.

Apart from these, it was interesting to note that weather was an important attribute in impacting start-up cluster emergence. Bangalore has been known to have pleasant and salubrious weather throughout the year (Sudhira, Ramachandra, and Bala Subrahmanya 2007). Bangalore's favourable weather is found to foster a culture of optimism and openness, as stated by Jones (2017). This favourable weather has contributed significantly to attracting investments and technology workforce to the city on a continuous basis (Bala Subrahmanya 2017b). Among all start-up hubs, both the mean and standard deviation of temperature are the lowest for Bangalore.

Above all, social peace and harmony, as indicated by low crime rates, is an extremely important component for ensuring the vibrancy of start-up clusters. Lower the number of registered crimes, higher the likelihood of the emergence of a start-up cluster. This factor alone contributes to 8 per cent of the total variation in the dependent variable. A high rate of crime and conflicts has been looked at as a major impediment to both VC investment and entrepreneurship (Bonini and Alkan 2009).

6

Investment Strategies

Introduction

Having analysed the venture capital (VC) industry from a macro perspective, we now probe the micro decision-making aspects of VC firms (general partners or fund managers). In this chapter, we investigate the investment decisions of VC firms. Here, we assess the kind of *tacit/latent signals* and *tangible business attributes* used by the VC firms in their investment decision making, given the huge information asymmetry risks encountered by them. Based on the literature survey, industry reports, and our discussions with the VC professionals, we have classified the VC firms in our sample into three distinct types of segments.[1] The aim of this chapter is to probe the investment decisions for each of these VC firm segments. The objective of this chapter is manifold: First, to identify, categorize, and quantify the comprehensive set of signals used by VC firms in assessing venture level risks (simultaneously, we also identify and quantify the relevant tangible business attributes that are regarded important by the VC firms). Second, to distinctly identify how these sets of signals (and tangible factors) differ across the three dominant segments of VC firms in our sample. Third, to identify the sets of signals that are distinct in the Indian cultural milieu. Finally, to derive managerial implications based on our findings that would be valuable to the VC and the entrepreneurial communities.

The rest of this chapter is organized as follows: to start with, we present a conceptual model of VC investment decisions and arrive at testable hypotheses based on the same. We then proceed to the description of the research design for this study. This is followed by the discussion of results.

---

[1] Based on their stage of funding (early versus growth/late), ownership type (foreign versus domestic), and by the composition of their top management team, or TMT (prior founding experience versus prior financial investing experience).

Conceptual Model of VC Investment Decisions

VC firms base their investment decisions about the prospective deals on both tacit signals and tangible business attributes. Based on the available literature, the tacit signals may be broadly classified into entrepreneur and founding team related signals, deal and VC firm related signals, and the overall macroeconomic and policy related factors (Figure 6.1).

The tangible attributes relate to market characteristics, business model, nature of competition, and the financials. Based on the latent signals and the tangible

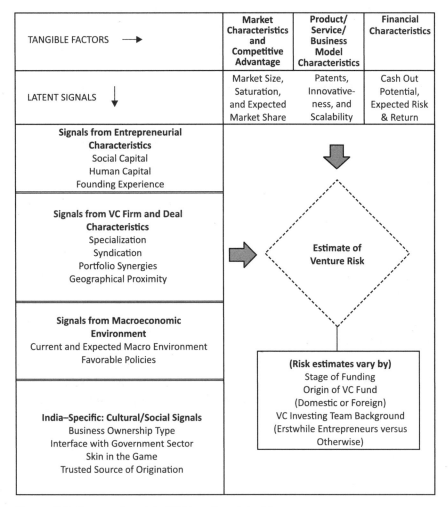

Figure 6.1 Proposed model of VC investment decisions

Source: Author.

attributes discussed earlier, we arrive at the following hypotheses regarding VC investment decisions:

Hypothesis 1: In the absence of tangible historical performance data on the venture, the VC firms extensively rely on *entrepreneurial signals*.

Hypothesis 2: *Specialization* and *syndication* are extensively used by the VC firms as viable strategies for overcoming information asymmetry risks.

Hypothesis 3: *Geographical proximity* is an important attribute in overcoming both adverse selection and agency risks emanating from information asymmetry.

Hypothesis 4: VC firms consciously assess *portfolio synergies* while making new investments, as it enables them to reduce risks.

Hypothesis 5: *Macroeconomic* and *policy related signals* are important for the VC firms while making their investment decisions.

Hypothsis 6: In the Indian context in general, the VC firms consciously stay away from funding *family-owned businesses* and prefer to fund only *first-generation entrepreneurs*.

Hypothesis 7: The VC firms in India do not prefer investing in domains having *high interface with the government*.

Hypothesis 8: The VC firms in India insist on *skin in the game* on part of the founders.

Hypothesis 9: In India, the VC firms consciously look for *formal sources of deal origination*.

Hypothesis 10: *Competition, barriers to entry, scalability, cost structure, gestation period*, and *financial robustness* are all important considerations for VC firms while making their investment decisions.

Data Analysis

This section describes the research design and the methods of analysis adopted for the purpose of this study. A description of the sample, the variables, and their definitions, modes of data collection, and the methodology used is presented in the following sections.

Sample and Data

Data Collection

This analysis is based on primary data collected from the investment professionals of seventy-two active VC firms operating in India during the period from June

2013 to May 2014. The data was collected by administering semi-structured questionnaires followed by in-depth face-to-face/telephonic interviews. We presume that the responses obtained by us appropriately represent the *true* views of the VC firm, since our interviewees (VC professionals) possessed significant decision-making authority in their respective capacities and were executing both VC investments and portfolio management responsibilities in the VC firms that they belonged to.

The questionnaire used for this analysis aimed at assessing the importance/favourability of each attribute (as mentioned in the item) from the viewpoint of funding the prospective deal. Each item was ranked on a scale of 1–5 (1 being least important/favourable and 5 being the most important/favourable). The questionnaire comprised fifty questions, which were divided into four broad categories, namely (*a*) entrepreneur and founding team related signals, (*b*) deal and VC firm related signals, (*c*) macroeconomic and policy related attributes, and (*d*) tangible business attributes. The items concerning the signals relevant in the Indian context were embedded in the other sections of the questionnaire (and not specified as a separate section in itself).

Variables

We use the following variables in our analysis:

Variables from Primary Data

Constructs and Sub-constructs relating to Latent Signals and Tangible Business Attributes: These comprise the quantified values (of the sub-constructs) pertaining to the latent signals and the tangible business attributes. For this, we use the factor scores obtained from subjecting the questionnaire data to the exploratory factor analysis (EFA) procedure.

Variables from Secondary Data

VC Segment related Variables: We have three separate categories of VC segment related variables, one each for the funding stage focus, ownership type, and the VC firm top management team (TMT) composition. Based on their funding stage focus, the VC firms have been divided in to two categories: early stage and growth/late stage. The growth- and late-stage-focused VC firms have been combined into a single category, namely 'later' stage focus. Based on their ownership type, the VC firms have been divided into two categories: domestic and foreign origin. Based on the composition of their TMT, they have been divided into two types: prior founding experience and prior financial investing experience.

Other VC Firm Profile related Variables: These include variables related to the age of the VC firm, number of historical deals funded, proportion of syndicated deals (or sole deals), and location of the VC firm in India.

Methods of Analysis

We have used two broad statistical techniques for analysis here: EFA and logistic regression models. The detailed explanation of each of these techniques, along with a rationale for using the same, has been provided in this section. To start with, we perform EFA on the questionnaire data with the aim of validating and quantifying the construct values. The factor scores obtained therein are then used in the logistic regression models (along with other control variables) as predictors of VC investment behaviour.

All analysis was performed using SPSS 21.0.0.0 and R 3.1.0 statistical software. For *EFA*, we report the scree plot, factor loading matrix, eigenvalues, variance explained, and the Cronbach's alpha values. For *logistic regressions*, we report the model Chi-Square statistic, -2 log likelihood values, pseudo-R-squared values (Cox and Snell R-Square and Nagelkerke R-Square), Hosmer-Lemeshow goodness-of-fit values, percentage of correctly classified pairs and Wald-Chi-Square values corresponding to each β coefficient.

Exploratory Factor Analysis

The primary aim of using this technique is two-fold. First, the EFA procedure enables us to validate the proposed constructs. Second, it simultaneously enables us to quantify the underlying latent attributes that could not have been directly measurable otherwise. The quantification of latent attributes is done by computing the factor scores. Factor scores are the composite measures for each factor computed for each subject. Conceptually, the factor score represents the degree to which each individual observation (in this case VC firm) scores high on the group of items with high loadings on a factor. Thus, higher values on the variables with high loadings on a factor will result in higher factor score (Hair et al. 2015). The factor scores thus computed can directly be used as input variables in the regression models.

In case of the EFA procedure, it is important to measure the *reliability* and the *content validity* in case of questionnaire data. Reliability has been measured based on Cronbach's alpha. Content validity is the correspondence of the variables to be included in a scale and its conceptual definition (Hair et al. 2015). This form of validity is also known as face validity, which subjectively assesses the correspondence between the individual items and the concept through ratings by expert judges. In order to guarantee content validity, we discussed our questionnaire with four–five senior VC professionals in Bangalore and made changes based on their feedback.

Logistic Regression Analysis

The dependent variable(s) in this analysis are dichotomous in nature, that is, they take the value of either 1 or 0. In such cases, the predicted value would measure the conditional probability that the event would occur given the values taken by X_i. Simplistically, this can be modelled as a linear probability model (LPM) based on the ordinary least squares (OLS) estimates.

$$P_i = \beta_1 + \beta_2 X_i + u_i \qquad \qquad \text{... (6.1)}$$

However, modelling the phenomenon in the manner described would violate some of the critical assumptions of OLS regression, namely normality of disturbances (which is required for the purposes of statistical inference) and heteroscedasticity (Gujarati 2012). Moreover, if in equation 6.1, P_i represents the probability then it is essential that it takes a value between 0 and 1. However, there is no guarantee that this restriction will be fulfilled (Gujarati 2012). Furthermore, the validity of R^2 as a measure of goodness of fit is further questionable (Gujarati 2012).

Hence, to get over these issues, cases where the dependent variable is dichotomous are often modelled using other alternate approaches such as logistic and probit regression. Since in their original form probabilities are not constrained to values between 0 and 1, we need to restate the probability in a way that the new variable would always fall between 0 and 1 (Hair et al. 2015). We will discuss in detail the basic formulation of the logistic regression this subsection. We express the probability of the occurrence of the event i the following manner:

$$P_i = 1/1 + e^{-(\beta_1 + \beta_2 Xi)} \qquad \qquad \text{... (6.2)}$$

For ease of exposition, we can write the equation as:

$$P_i = 1/(1 + e^{Zi}) = e^{Zi}/(1 + e^{Zi}) \qquad \qquad \text{... (6.3)}$$

where, $Zi = \beta_1 + \beta_2 Xi$

Equation 6.3 represents the logistic distribution function. As Z_i ranges from $-\infty$ to $+\infty$, P_i ranges from 0 to 1 and P_i is non-linearly related to $Z_i (X_i)$. However, equation 6.3 is highly non-linear, not only in terms of X_i but also βs. Hence, we linearize equation 6.4 and then estimate the coefficients. For doing so, we need to undertake the steps given next. If P_i refers to the probability of an event, then $(1 - P_i)$ refers to the probability of non-event.

$$1 - P_i = 1/1 + e^{Zi} \qquad \qquad \text{... (6.4)}$$

Therefore, we can write

$$(P_i/1 - P_i) = 1 + e^{Z_i}/1 + e^{-Z_i} = e^{Z_i} \qquad \text{... (6.5)}$$

$(Pi/1 - Pi)$ is known as the odds ratio of the event.

Now, if we take the natural log of equation 6.5, we obtain

$$L_i = ln(Pi/1 - Pi) = Z_i = \beta_1 + \beta_2 Xi \qquad \text{... (6.6)}$$

L_i is the log of odds ratio – it is not only linear in X but also in parameters. It can be observed that as P_i goes from 0 to 1, the logit L varies from -∞ to +∞. Thus, although the probabilities lie between 0 and 1, the logit is not so bounded. Also, although L is linear in X, the probabilities are not.

Thus, we have overcome all the major problems associated with the LPM approach. With the logit value, we now have a metric variable that can have both positive and negative values, but that can always be transformed back to a probability value between 0 and 1. This value is now the dependent variable in the logistic regression model.

Alternatively, we could have used probit regression instead of logistic regression to model for binary dependent variable. In that case, we use a normal cumulative distribution function instead of a cumulative logistic function. The results obtained from both these classes of models are similar in most cases. However, in practice, many researchers choose the logit model because of its comparative mathematical simplicity (Gujarati 2012).

Discussion of Results

This section comprises two subsections. To start with, we present the results from the EFA procedure. This is followed by the presentation of the results obtained from the three sets of logistic regression analyses – for funding stage focus (early versus later), for ownership type (foreign versus domestic), and for VC firm TMT composition (erstwhile founders versus erstwhile finance professionals).

Exploratory Factor Analysis

The EFA was performed using the principal components algorithm. The number of factors to be extracted was based on the latent root (eigenvalue) criterion. The rationale for the latent root criterion is that any individual factor should account for the variance of at least a single variable if it is to be retained for interpretation (Hair et al. 2015). We decided on the total number of factors to be considered based on both technical metrics (scree plots and eigenvalues) and intuitive logic.

The questionnaire used for this analysis comprised four broad sub-sections.[2] We performed the EFA procedure *separately* for each of these sub-sections to clearly identify the underlying dimensions (sub-constructs) in each of them. Thus, we have four sets of EFA results. Alternatively, we could have run the EFA procedure on items from all the sub-sections put together. However, the results would have been extremely difficult to interpret in that case (since there are expected to be significant cross-loadings across different sub-sections of the questionnaire). Hence, we took the view that each section should be subjected to a separate EFA procedure. The results from the same are presented sequentially in the appendix to this chapter (Appendix 6A). The results explain the details of the items included in each construct.

The sub-constructs obtained from the EFA procedure were as follows:

Entrepreneur and Founding Team related Signals: Educational pedigree, team composition, business ownership type and owner characteristics, past start-up experience, past managerial experience, family background, and networking ability.

Deal and VC Firm related Signals: Negative synergies: competing deals; positive synergies: complementary deals, specialization, syndication, and portfolio diversification fit.

Macroeconomic and Policy related Signals: Favourability of the current scenario and policies, favourability of the future scenario and policies.

Tangible Business Attributes: Heavy cost structure, scalability, market size and growth, entry barriers, and limited government interface.

The details of the specific items loaded on each of the constructs described are given in Appendix 6A at the end of this chapter. In addition to the variables mentioned earlier, three more variables, namely *trust* (trusted and formal channels of deal origination), *skin in the game* (entrepreneurial stake in the venture), and *geographical proximity* (geographical proximity between the VC firm and the investee venture), were used. These were not subjected to the EFA procedure and the raw values (ratings assigned to them in the questionnaire) were used directly.

Logistic Regression Models

The factor scores (for each sub-construct) obtained from the EFA procedure along with the other control variables (mainly pertaining to the profile of the VC firm)

---

[2] Three pertaining to latent signals (entrepreneur and founding team related attributes, deal and VC firm related attributes, and macroeconomic attributes), and one pertaining to the tangible business attributes (market, competition, business model, cost structure, and so on).

were used as independent variables in the logistic regression models. To reiterate, the objective of building these models is to assess the nature of latent signals and tangible factors that drive the investment decisions for each segment of VC firms. In this section, we present the results from three sets of logistic regression models, namely for stage of funding, for ownership type, and for investing team background. These models predict the likelihood of a particular VC firm being an early-stage investor, being of foreign origin, or having an investing team with erstwhile prior founding background respectively.

Logistic Regression: Stage of Funding

The results from the logistic regression model on stage of funding are presented in Table 6.1. In these sets of models, *event* refers to the VC firm having an early-stage focus. Please note that we have built two sets of regression models – first, to analyse the role of latent signals and, second, to assess the influence of tangible business attributes. In case of the models measuring the impact of latent signals, two main variables, namely *business ownership type and owner characteristics*, and *limited government interface*, are highly correlated with each other. Hence, in order to get over the potential multi-collinearity issues, we have built separate models.

From the P-value corresponding to the model Chi-Square statistic given in Table 6.1, all the models pertaining to the stage of funding are highly significant. The Nagelkerke R-Square values are 0.74 and 0.78 for the models with latent signals as independent variables, while the same is 0.243 for the model with tangible business attributes. The Hosmer-Lemeshow goodness-of-fit statistic is also high for all models, indicating the proximity of the actual and predicted values. The proportion of observations correctly classified ranges from 76 per cent to 90 per cent. All the given metrics point to the robustness of the models.

Coming to the discussion of model variables, let us first discuss the variables pertaining to latent signals. Among these, *specialization* emerged as one of the most significant variables. This finding appears to be in tandem with what is suggested by the resource-based view (Barney 1991; Barney, Wright, and Ketchen 2001). However, quite interestingly, the early-stage venture capitalists (VCs) in India seemed to specialize more by *funding size* rather than by *sector/domain*.

When we probed the underlying reasons for the same during the course of our interviews with VC professionals, they indicated that the market for VC deals in India lacked sufficient depth at the time to permit a very high level of specialization, as in the US market. Thus, in general, the VC firms in India tend to specialize only quite modestly and that too mostly by funding size or stage of funding, not so much by sector/domain. The lack of depth in the market for early-stage deals in India may be seen from the fact that as of 2014 the aggregate volume of early-

Table 6.1 Logistic regression results: stage of funding

	Dependent Variable: Early-Stage VC Firm = 1; Growth/Late-Stage VC Firm = 0 Number of Observations = 70								
	Latent Signals						Tangible Business Attributes		
	Model 1			Model 2					
	Beta - Coefficient	Chi-Square Statistic	Exp(β)	Beta - Coefficient	Chi-Square Statistic	Exp(β)	Beta - Coefficient	Chi-Square Statistic	Exp(β)
Constant	-5.438*	2.899	.004	-16.772*	10.288	0.000	-0.994**	9.084	0.370
Latent Signals									
Business Ownership Type and Owner Characteristics	1.702***	7.526	5.485	-	-	-	-	-	-
Specialization (by Funding Size)	1.644***	5.565	5.177	-	-	-	-	-	-
Proportion of Non-Syndicated Deals	2.399*	3.727	11.017	-	-	-	-	-	-
Trust	-0.758*	3.647	.468	-	-	-	-	-	-
Educational Pedigree	-0.982*	3.232	.374	-	-	-	-	-	-
Limited Government Interface				3.978***	9.993	53.372	-	-	-
Tangible Business Attributes									
Heavy Cost Structure	-	-					-0.618**	4.452	.539
Scalability	-	-					-0.500*	3.283	.606
VC Firm Profile Related Variables									
Historical Deals	0.13**	4.273	1.145	0.128**	5.392	1.137	-	-	-
Historical Exits	-1.066*	6.394	.344	-0.913***	6.779	.401	-	-	-
VC Investing Team with Prior Founding Experience							1.516	5.759**	4.555

Contd

Contd

	Model Statistics		
Nagelkerke R²	0.743	0.784	.243
Cox and Snell's R²	0.543	0.575	0.178
-2 Log Likelihood	37.342	32.512	78.604
Model Chi-Square Statistic	55.017 with 7 Degrees of Freedom. P-value 0.000	59.848 with 3 Degrees of Freedom. P-value 0.000	13.755 with 3 Degrees of Freedom. P-value 0.003
Hosmer-Lemeshow Goodness of Fit Statistic	0.997	0.941	0.618
% Correctly Classified	90.0%	87.1%	75.7%

Source: Author.

Note: * Indicates significance at 10% level. ** Indicates significance at 5% level. *** Indicates significance at 1% level stage investments in India is only about USD 240 million compared to that of USD 700 million in China and USD 6.3 billion in the United States (Planning Commission 2012).

Syndication too emerged as an important signal of investment for early-stage VCs. However, quite interestingly, *syndication* seemed to have an opposite sign (negative) than expected. As an indicator of syndication, we have used the variable *proportion of non-syndicated deals* in our model. Our analysis showed that early-stage VCs seemed to have a higher proportion of *non-syndicated* deals (consequently, a lower proportion of *syndicated* deals) compared to their growth- and late-stage counterparts. Although this finding seemed counter-intuitive initially, it has been well supported by recent literature in this domain (Hopp and Rider 2011; Nitani and Riding 2013; Joshi 2019). Moreover, in India, co-investment is primarily used as a mechanism to augment the deal size (that is, when the funding requirements are too large for an individual VC firm to fund on its own) and not so much to alleviate the information asymmetry risks. Furthermore, the average deal size for early-stage VC deals itself is much lower in India compared to the developed world such as the United States—the average size of an early-stage deal is about USD 0.8 million in India compared to USD 1.5 million for the United States (Ernst and Young 2014). Low deal size reduces the need for syndication. Above all, syndication as a tool for alleviating information asymmetry becomes more relevant when VCs tend to be highly specialized by sectors (Gompers and Lerner 2004; Barry 1994). In this context, syndicating with a VC firm that was specialized in another domain enabled a VC to get access to *idiosyncratic* knowledge relevant to the new sector. However, the Indian VC funds did not practise sector-specific specialization to start with (since the market for deals lacked the requisite depth). Thus, the lack of sector-specific specialization could probably explain why syndication might not have been very important to early-stage VCs in general. In fact, many Indian VC firms also believe in strong negative synergies associated with syndication if practised indiscriminately (Lerner 1994).

Among *entrepreneur and founding team* related signals, only *educational pedigree* turned out to be significant. However, this variable too had an opposite sign (negative). Although prima facie this may seem counter-intuitive, we can reason it out as follows. Most VC professionals in our sample did mention that a prodigious educational pedigree was by itself no guarantee of business success. While it was certainly important for high-technology businesses, in other consumer-driven businesses, meticulous execution ability was what mattered the most. Even in cases where the *educational pedigree* of the founders did matter, it merely acted as a signal for the prospective employees, thus enabling the investee firm to get better talent on board rather than being a direct guarantee of success.

Coming to the economic, political, social, and cultural signals relevant to India, we found *business ownership type and owner characteristics* to be an important signal for the early-stage VCs. This factor assesses how the VC firm views attributes such as the prospective venture (not) being a family-owned business and the entrepreneur being a first-generation entrepreneur. The early-stage VCs were very particular that they would refrain from funding family-owned businesses and fund only first-generation entrepreneurs. It was quite commonly felt that family-owned businesses usually had significant corporate governance issues associated with them. The founders were often not willing to get external talent on board, particularly at senior levels and in positions of financial control (Romano, Tanewski, and Smyrnios 2001; Upton and Petty 2000). Moreover, such firms were not open to third-party audits. Above all, an intense involvement from the VC firm was often looked upon as an unnecessary intrusion rather than value-add. It was also commonly believed that *first-generation entrepreneurs* were often more receptive to feedback compared to those with a family background in business. To sum up, *business ownership type and owner characteristics* were regarded by most early-stage VCs as an important signal about the extent of agency problems in the future.

Limited government interface was another important attribute of the businesses funded by early-stage VCs. Tackling corruption and other bureaucratic hurdles in terms of securing permits and licenses were considered to be major deterrents to investments in regulated sectors. Since the opportunity cost for VC resources is quite high, they did not favour domains involving too many procedural and policy bottlenecks. Even where the VCs invested in sectors that called for high government intervention, they carefully chose *niche ancillary* areas wherein the interface with government bodies would be minimal – for example, the VCs investing in the education sector will scrupulously stay away from investments in the K12 format and would rather prefer to invest in educational and school software or private training academies. This finding is well supported by literature as well. In fact, political risk (as defined by frequent changes in regulations relating to products/ pricing, FDI, and relative taxation) has been identified as one of the leading deterrents of VC investments worldwide (Henisz and Williamson 1999; Henisz and Delios 2001). Also, given the fact that India ranks 142 out of 158 on the *ease of doing business* index developed by the World Bank (2015) and 85 out of 175 on the *public sector corruption* index developed by Transparency International (2014), it should not be surprising that a majority of the early-stage VC firms in our sample preferred to consciously back out from funding businesses that warranted a high government interface.

Trust assesses the role of formal deal origination channels such as investment banks and academic incubators. While most VC firms in principle believed in originating their deals through *trusted* or *warm* origination channels, they mentioned that they typically did not consider the deal referrals from investment bankers too seriously as the same were believed to be deliberate *hard sells*. On similar lines, not all academic incubators were regarded as effective conduits of origination of high quality deals. Above all, deals from industry-backed accelerators were preferred over those coming from their academic counterparts. The reasons for the same are two-fold. First, most VCs found the process of intellectual property (IP) transfer (for ventures belonging to science and technology domains) from academic institutes in India to be quite tedious. Second, academic institutes were known to ask for a very high share of equity. Furthermore, most VC firms believed that their best deals were those that had been actively pursued by the VCs themselves through their own networks.

Coming to the *tangible business attributes* driving investment decisions, it was found that early-stage VC firms in general preferred to stay away from businesses with a *heavy cost structure*. This variable assesses factors such as whether the proposed business warrants a huge upfront investment in the form of sunk costs. This can be explained in the following manner. To start with, the early-stage VC firms typically have much smaller fund sizes compared to later-stage ones. The average fund size for early-stage VC firms is about USD 79 million compared to the later-stage ones where the same is around USD 230 million (Venture Intelligence 2019). Thus, naturally, they would tend to stay away from cost-heavy businesses that require them to burn up a large portion of their funds upfront.

Another attribute that turned out to be significant in this category pertains to *scalability*. This variable assesses the importance that the VC firms attach to the scalability *of the funded business over their expected investment horizon*. Model results reveal that scalability is not considered as an important attribute by the early-stage VC firms. Almost all the VC professionals in our sample believed that while scalability was no doubt important, given their fund constraints, it would not be possible for the early-stage VCs to scale up the business over their investment horizon. They would rather focus on developing the product/service as a proof of concept and getting customer validation before inviting participation from the other upstream growth-stage VC firms for the purpose of scaling up the business. Thus, scaling-up is more a prerogative of growth-stage VC firms and not necessarily earlier-stage ones. This explains the negative sign on this variable in our regression model.

Among the VC firm profile related variables, *number of historical deals* and *number of exits* turn out to be significant attributes. While the former has a positive coefficient, the latter has a negative one. Typically, the average deal size for the early-stage deals is much smaller thus permitting the VC firms to fund a large number of small deals. This explains the positive sign on the *number of historical deals*. However, it must be pointed out that the early-stage VCs have also witnessed a much smaller number of successful exits so far. There could be two possible explanations for the same: First, that most of the early-stage deals have been executed post 2008, and thus the complete investment–exit cycle is not yet complete. Second, in general, the early-stage businesses have a higher failure rate and thus the number of successful exits is expected to be lower. We also find a much higher proportion of *VC investing teams with prior founding experience* among early-stage VCs compared to later-stage ones. Having set up ventures of their own in the past confers *niche* skills on VC professionals that enable them to identify and tap opportunities at the early stages of the prospective venture. Each of these results are quite well supported by the literature (Cumming and Johan 2010; Patzelt, zu Knyphausen-Aufseß, and Fischer 2009).

Logistic Regression: Ownership Type (Foreign versus Domestic Origin)

We now move on to the discussion of regression results for the model on ownership type. The results from the logistic regression models by ownership type (foreign versus domestic) have been given in Table 6.2. In this regression, *event* refers to the VC firm being of foreign origin. From the P-value corresponding to the model Chi-Square statistic given in Table 6.8, all the models pertaining to the VC ownership type are highly significant. The Nagelkerke R-Square values are 0.605 and 0.395 for the models with latent signals as independent variables, while the same is 0.354 for the model with tangible business attributes. The Hosmer-Lemeshow goodness-of-fit statistic is also high for all models, indicating the proximity of the actual and predicted values. The proportion of observations correctly classified ranges from 71 per cent to 86 per cent. All of the given metrics point to the robustness of the models.

Coming to the discussion of model variables, we find that *syndication* is an important signal relied on by the foreign VCs while making their investments. The foreign VCs in our sample have a lower number of *non-syndicated deals* (consequently, a higher number of *syndicated deals*) compared to the domestic VCs. This finding is well supported by the academic literature. It has been found that the information asymmetries between the VC and its portfolio companies are often difficult to resolve when the portfolio company is located outside the VC's own home country (Schertler and Tykvova 2011). Although the foreign VCs have relatively rich experience in terms of experience, international network, and financial resources, they are often constrained by information friction due to geographic distance (Delloite 2012). Co-investing with the local VCs aids in alleviating the information asymmetry arising due to geographical and cultural differences (Dai, Jo, and Kassicieh 2012).

Table 6.2 Logistic regression results: ownership type (foreign versus domestic)

	Dependent Variable: Foreign VC Firm = 1; Domestic Stage VC Firm = 0 Number of Observations = 70								
	Latent Signals						Tangible Business Attributes		
	Model 1			Model 2					
	Beta-Coefficient	Chi-Square Statistic	Exp(β)	Beta-Coefficient	Chi-Square Statistic	Exp(β)	Beta-Coefficient	Chi-Square Statistic	Exp(β)
Constant	.985	.149	2.677	-.918	.297	.399	.798	1.169	2.221
Latent Signals									
Portfolio Diversification Fit	0.971**	4.544	2.641	-	-	-	-	-	-
Business Ownership Type and Owner Characteristics	1.034**	3.905	2.813	-	-	-	-	-	-
Proportion of Non-Syndicated Deals	-2.246*	3.699	.106	-	-	-	-	-	-
Past Start-Up Experience	2.276**	3.862	9.744	-	-	-	-	-	-
Geography	-0.923**	4.885	.398	-	-	-	-	-	-
Trust	1.076**	4.590	.032	-	-	-	-	-	-
Limited Government Interface	-	-	-	.715	2.351	2.044	-	-	-
Tangible Business Attributes									
Long Gestation period	-	-	-	-	-	-	-0.415*	2.845	0.660
Heavy Cost Structure	-	-	-	-	-	-	-0.578*	3.465	0.561
Ecosystem (Low Ecosystem Changes)	-	-	-	-	-	-	1.440**	4.181	4.221
VC Firm Profile-Related Variables									
Early-Stage Deals	-3.452***	8.294	.032	-2.802***	9.616	.061	-	-	-
SEBI Registered	-1.622*	3.295	.069	-1.918***	7.622	.147	-1.502	5.637	0.223
Located in Mumbai	-3.505***	8.372	.030	-1.534**	5.213	.216	-	-	-

Contd

Contd

	Model Statistics		
Nagelkerke R^2	0.605	0.395	0.354
Cox and Snell's R^2	0.448	0.292	0.262
-2 Log Likelihood	52.683	70.049	72.964
Model Chi-Square Statistic	41.539 with 9 Degrees of Freedom. P-Value 0.000	24.173 with 4 Degrees of Freedom. P-Value 0.000	21.258 with 4 Degrees of Freedom. P-Value 0.000
Hosmer-Lemeshow Goodness of Fit Statistic	0.832	0.877	0.498
% Correctly Classified	85.7%	71.4%	71.4%

Source: Author.

In fact, studies show that partnering with local VCs is a prominently used strategy by the foreign VC firms to invest in informationally *opaque* early-stage ventures. In general, foreign VC firms prefer investing in businesses whose potential has been well established, and shun investing in ventures belonging to emerging domains unless backed by significant local partnerships with other VCs (Zhang et al. 2007). Typically, domestic and foreign VCs possess different types of skill sets. While the domestic companies have well-developed regional networks with potential vendors, customers, and other significant stakeholders in general, foreign VCs possess the financial muscle and networks to scale up and grow internationally (Devigne et al. 2013). Thus, *syndication* of deals between the two parties enables each of them to leverage the benefits from both parties.

Specialization as a signal did not turn out to be significant in our models. This may possibly be attributed to two factors. On the one hand, the Indian market is not yet deep enough in terms of the number of prospective deals available for investment. The depth of the market can be established by the volume of VC investments in a region – the average annual VC investments between the years 2006 and 2013 were USD 31.2 billion in the United States compared to that of USD 1.23 billion for India (Ernst and Young 2014). On the other hand, the foreign VCs have relatively larger fund sizes (compared to their domestic counterparts), thus making *niche domain specialization* even more difficult in the face of an already existing low-depth market. The average fund size of foreign VCs is USD 95 million compared to USD 53 million for domestic ones (Venture Intelligence 2019).

It is also observed that foreign VCs consciously stay away from *early-stage deals*. It is well-understood that foreign VCs prefer investing in informationally transparent ventures (Dai, Jo, and Kassicieh 2012; Joshi and Bala Subrahmanya 2015, 2019). Early-stage ventures, particularly in the technology domains, have a huge level of information asymmetry associated with them, consequently adding an additional layer of risks. Handling these risks warrants a deep understanding of local conditions. Since such abilities of foreign VCs are likely to be quite limited, they stay away from such ventures. Also, early-stage companies require a much higher level of involvement on the part of the VC firm (Gupta and Sapienza 1992; Joshi, 2018b). The domestic VC firms are better positioned to assist the early-stage businesses by providing contacts to relevant external parties for soliciting feedback on critical processes and critically reassessing initial ideas based on this feedback (Devigne et al. 2013). Thus, in general, the local VCs are more likely to possess the skill sets required for investing in and managing the early-stage ventures; investments in such ventures is usually considered a prerogative of the domestic VCs.

Another signal that is considered important by the foreign VC firms is *past start-up experience* of the prospective founder. Since local networks of the foreign VC firms are expected to be quite limited, they seem to place a high value on prospective founders who have set up ventures of their own in the past. Such founders are likely to have well-developed networks of their own due to their prior involvement with community-based entrepreneurial clubs, events, and media – above all, their prior *social capital* compared to others (Hsu 2007). Our findings are well supported by the resource-based view of the firm which believes that tacit knowledge possessed by the firm comes from their erstwhile founding experience and hence would enable them to have an intimate understanding of the legal and institutional mechanisms. To sum up, such founders are seen to be well endowed with resources that translate to superior performance since such resources are valuable, rare, inimitable, and non-substitutable (Barney 1991; Dimov and Shepherd 2005). Links to existing networks and an intimate understanding of legal and institutional mechanisms may be viewed as one of such potential sources of tacit knowledge.

Geographical proximity is another important signal used by all categories of VC firms in general. Higher physical distance intensifies the magnitude of information asymmetry risks multifold (Cumming and Dai 2010). On the one hand, higher physical distance restricts the ability of the VCs to interact with entrepreneurs and consequently intensifies the moral hazard; on the other, it distances the VCs from the local *niche* networks, thus increasing the incidence of adverse selection as well (Cumming and Dai 2010). Thus, in general, VC firms are known to have a strong local bias in their investments (Dai, Jo, and Kassicieh 2012). However, in our regression model, the variable *geography* enters with a negative sign. This means that geographical proximity is not regarded important by the foreign VC firms. This can be explained in many possible ways. First, the market for deals in India lacks enough depth to permit intense geographical specialization. Thus, the VC firms are forced to invest in deals even if the ventures are geographically quite distant from the location of their offices. Second, many foreign VC firms have more than one regional office in India, spread across different geographical regions. Thus, in principle, they do ensure that the location of the investee firm is closer to at least one of their local offices. Third, they intensely syndicate with local VC firms when investing in geographically distant ventures. Syndication with the local VC firms ensures smooth information flow and monitoring (Bergemann and Hege 1998; Wright, Lockett, and Pruthi 2002; Manigart et al. 2006) which makes up for the physical distance. Another important point worth noting in this regard is that while investing locally has advantages in the form of mitigating information asymmetry, it also results in excessive competition among VCs, thus artificially enhancing the deal valuations and consequently decreasing returns (Gompers and Lerner 2000; Cumming and Macintosh 2006). Therefore, it might be possible that over-concentration of VCs in certain geographies could potentially result in the reduction of the local bias, as VCs explore other geographic regions for potential investments.

Portfolio diversification fit of the prospective deal is another important signal in the context of foreign VC firms. As discussed earlier, VC firms may either have *deal-specific* or a *portfolio-specific* view to investments. Our results reveal that compared to the domestic VCs, foreign VCs are more likely to assess how well a prospective deal fits their pre-existing portfolio from the viewpoint of risk diversification. We believe there are two reasons for the same. Since the relative deal sizes are much larger for foreign VCs, risk diversification becomes a necessity to consciously avoid overexposure to certain sectors or investment stages. The average size of an early-stage deal is about USD 4.8 million for foreign VCs compared to that of USD 2.4 million for domestic VCs (Venture Intelligence 2019). Moreover, since the relative fund size is also much higher for foreign VCs compared to their domestic counterparts, diversification is also feasible. The average fund size of foreign VCs is USD 95 million compared to USD 53 million for domestic ones (Venture Intelligence 2019). Although many domestic VCs would certainly like to practise diversification, their smaller fund sizes inhibit them from doing so.

Moving on to the set of signals that matter in the Indian social, cultural, political, and economic milieu, we find that foreign VCs tend to place a higher weight on *business ownership type and owner characteristics*. Thus, they consciously tend to stay away from any offshoots of family-owned businesses and insist on funding first-generation entrepreneurs alone. It is well understood that family-owned businesses are associated with a significant magnitude of potential corporate governance issues, thus compounding the intensity of impending moral hazard (Upton and Petty 2000; Romano, Tanewski, and Smyrnios 2001). It is also widely believed in the VC community that, in general, the first-generation entrepreneurs are more receptive to feedback and mentoring from the VCs. Since the foreign VCs already encounter a significant magnitude of other information asymmetry risks, it should not be surprising that they stay away from businesses that have an additional risk of impending moral hazard.

The next signal that is relevant, particularly more so in the Indian scenario, is *trust* – which refers to originating deals from a trusted source such as investment banks and academic incubators. This variable enters with a positive sign, indicating that foreign VCs heavily rely on such formal deal origination sources. This result is as per our expectations. Given the limited extent of their local networks, it is quite unlikely for foreign VCs to originate their deals by proactively sourcing the same through informal channels. Thus, reliance on formal channels is expected to be quite high.

Quite interestingly, we find that the variable *limited government interface* is insignificant. This implies that foreign VCs do not consciously stay away from domains that warrant a high government interface. During the course of our interactions, most VCs revealed to us that the lack of depth in the market for deals prevents them from imposing such additional constraints, although they do agree that dealing with government bodies can often be a frustrating task in India. Moreover, projects warranting a greater level of interaction with the government machinery are typically large projects and foreign VCs usually possess the requisite scale to fund them. Rather, the foreign VCs handle the risks emanating from such projects head-on by deploying the services of specialized consultants. The larger foreign VCs in India typically have specialized teams for each domain such as real estate, healthcare, energy, and so on, which would, in turn, solicit the services of highly specialized consultants (in these respective domains) who are well versed with understanding the systemic procedures.

Coming to the *tangible business attributes*, we find that foreign VCs consciously stay away from businesses with a *heavy cost structure* and *long gestation periods*. In general, there is a consensus that foreign VCs look for high growth and high potential businesses such that it will guarantee them quicker exits (Zhang et al. 2007). Thus, they consciously stay away from funding ventures that will potentially curtail this objective. Above all, they prefer funding the development of those types of products/services whose adoption might not warrant significant changes to the existing *ecosystem*. Greater ecosystem changes would warrant a longer period for scaling up the business and would go against the fundamental principle of quick exit.

Among the variables pertaining to the VC firm profile, we find that most foreign VC firms are not registered with the Securities and Exchange Board of India (SEBI). As discussed earlier, it is not mandatory for foreign VC firms to be registered with SEBI; rather, they can invest in India via the automatic approval route of the Reserve Bank of India (RBI) by adhering to the foreign direct investment (FDI) norms. Since SEBI registration imposes harsh constraints on the VC firms pertaining to the terms of investment, most of them prefer to bypass this route.

Logistic Regression: VC Investing Team Background (Erstwhile Founding Background versus Otherwise)

In this section, we present the results from the logistic regression models on VC investing team background. The detailed results have been given in Table 6.3. In this regression, *event* refers to the VC firm having an investing team with prior founding experience. Each of the constructs, namely *entrepreneurial signals, deal and VC firm related signals, macroeconomic and policy related signals*, and *tangible business attributes*, constitutes multiple sub-constructs.

As can be seen from Table 6.3, we have built four separate models to accommodate the effect of all the possible latent signals. Due to the presence of multi-collinearity, all these variables cannot be included in a single model. Additionally, we have built a separate model to capture the effect of tangible business attributes. From

Table 6.3 Logistic regression results: VC investing team background

	Dependent Variable: VC Investing Team with Past Founding Experience = 1; Otherwise = 0 Number of Observations = 70									
	Latent Signals								Tangible Business Attributes	
	Model 1		Model 2		Model 3		Model 4			
	Beta-Coeff	Chi-Square Statistic	Beta-Coeff	Chi-Square Statistic	Beta-Coeff	Chi-Square Statistic	Beta-Coeff	Chi-Square Statistic	Beta-Coeff	Chi-Square Statistic
Constant	-.573	.727	-1.349	.796	-1.358***	11.705	-1.530***	13.397	-0.972***	6.631
Latent Signals										
Business Ownership Type and Owner Characteristics	0.688*	3.435	-	-	-	-	-	-	-	-
Complementarities	-0.611*	3.189	-	-	-	-	-	-	-	-
Proportion of Non-Syndicated Deals (between 29 % and 43%)	2.160*	3.235	-	-	-	-	-	-	-	-
Past Start-Up Experience	1.252*	2.810	-	-	-	-	-	-	-	-
Limited Government Interface	-	-	.405	1.347	-	-	-	-	-	-
Tangible Business Attributes										
Entry Barriers	-	-	-	-	-	-	-	-	1.355**	4.232
VC Firm Profile Related Variables										
Hi-Technology Focus	-	-	-	-	1.115**	3.710	-	-	-	-
Early-Stage Focus	-	-	-	-	-	-	1.479***	6.280	-	-
VC Firm Age	-0.249**	4.465	-0.261**	6.235	-1.673	2.256	-1.663	2.197	-1.409	3.949
SEBI										
Delhi										

Contd

Contd

	Model Statistics				
Nagelkerke R^2	0.424	0.230	.122	0.175	0.188
Cox and Snell's R^2	0.288	0.157	0.083	0.119	0.128
-2 Log Likelihood	55.993	67.887	73.766	70.958	70.229
Model Chi-Square Statistic	23.813 with 5 Degrees of Freedom. P-value 0.000	11.920 with 2 Degrees of Freedom. P-value 0.000	6.041 with 2 Degrees of Freedom. P-value 0.049	8.848 with 2 Degrees of Freedom P-value 0.012	9.577 with 2 Degrees of Freedom. P-value 0.008
Hosmer-Lemeshow Goodness of Fit Statistic	0.901	0.231	.844	.838	0.261
% Correctly Classified	80.0%	72.9%	74.3%	74.3%	80.0%

Source: Author.

Note: * Indicates significance at 10% level. ** Indicates significance at 5% level. *** Indicates significance at 1% level the P-value corresponding to the model Chi-Square statistic, it can be seen that all the models pertaining to the VC investing team background are significant. The Nagelkerke R-Square values range from 0.12 to 0.424 for the models with latent signals, while the same is 0.188 for the model with tangible business attributes.

The Hosmer-Lemeshow goodness-of-fit statistic is also high for all models, indicating the proximity of the actual and predicted values. The proportion of observations correctly classified ranges from 73 per cent to 80 per cent. All of the given metrics point to the robustness of the models. Coming to the discussion pertaining to the model variables in particular, it can be seen that *specialization* emerges as an important signal for the VC firms with prior founding background. The VCs in this category are seen to specialize by both funding stage and domain. The variables *high-technology focus* and *early-stage focus* both have significant positive signs. This indicates that the VC investors with prior founding background are usually specialized early-stage investors in high-technology domains (Joshi 2018b, 2018c).

This finding has been well supported by literature. In this regard, it must be understood that most of the investors in this category are erstwhile serial entrepreneurs with the pedigree of having established successful technology companies in the past. Thus, they are expected to possess significant knowledge of emerging technologies. Also, their assessments of the technological risks of projects in the high-technology domains are likely to be more appropriate (Patzelt, zu Knyphausen-Aufseß, and Fischer 2009). This could be the possible reason for the *high-technology focus*. Investing in *early-stage* ventures is an attractive proposition since it is possible to buy large equities of these businesses at that stage at substantially lower rates and consequently make substantial profits on exit (Patzelt, zu Knyphausen-Aufseß, and Fischer 2009). Of course, the uncertainties associated with early-stage ventures are also quite high owing to the presence of agency problems and technology risks (Wright and Robbie 1998). However, the past founding experience of these VC firms better equips them to handle such risks compared to the other VC firms with no such commensurate experience (Zarutskie 2010).

The relationship with respect to *syndication* is quite interesting. The VC firms with prior founding experience engage in only moderate syndication, that is, neither too high nor too low. There exists an inverted U-shaped relationship between proportion of syndicated deals and the propensity of a VC firm to possess prior founding experience (about 29–43 per cent of their deals are non-syndicated). The reason for the same is two-fold. The fund size of most of such VC firms is likely to be quite small, as these are mainly early-stage investors, and also since a large section of such funds may be *non-pooled* in nature. Thus, there exists a need to co-invest with other VCs in order to augment the deal size. However, they consciously avoid over-syndication since that can potentially reduce their control over the investee companies. Since the *niche* investing and portfolio management skills of such founder-backed VCs are quite important to the overall success of the venture, they consciously avoid over-syndication for the purpose of maintaining their control over the investee firm.

Past start-up experience is a highly valued trait that such founder-backed VCs look for in potential entrepreneurs. Given their own founding background, they understand quite well the value of such experience and hence naturally seem to place a premium on it. This can also be supported based on the *similarity hypothesis* from the cognitive bias theory (Shepherd 1999; Zacharakis and Meyer 1998; Zacharakis and Shepherd 2001; Franke et al. 2006). This hypothesis states that 'the higher the similarity between the profile of a venture capitalist and the profile of a start-up team, the more favorable the evaluation by the venture capitalist will be'. Franke et al. (2006) have found that VCs with prior experience of working in either start-ups or large firms will tend to prefer teams with individuals coming from these backgrounds. Our model results lend further credence to their hypothesis.

Further, we find that the VCs with prior founding experience do not take a *portfolio-level view* to investments, but rather rely on a *deal-level view*. Consequently, they do not look for *positive synergies* in the form of *complementarities* of the prospective deal with those already existing on their portfolio. This result is as per our expectations mainly owing to two reasons: first, smaller fund size prohibits them from leveraging portfolio synergies and, second, they derive their *niche* from *specialization* and thus consciously stay away from *portfolio diversification* (by leveraging such synergies).

Coming to the signals that matter in the Indian milieu, *business ownership type and owner characteristics* emerges significant. Thus, the VCs with prior founding background consciously stay away from funding family-owned businesses and prefer funding only first-generation entrepreneurs. As explained earlier, the magnitude of agency risks is significantly high for such ventures owing to impending corporate governance issues and hence the VC firms would consciously prefer to stay away from them (Upton and Petty 2000; Romano et al. 2001).

Quite interestingly, the VC firms in this category do not stay away from businesses that have a high interface with government bodies. Thus, the variable *limited government interface* is highly insignificant. In fact, many companies funded by the VCs in this category are engaged in products pertaining to drug discovery, medical devices, or banking and finance related technologies and applications. All of such businesses would involve patents, licenses, and permissions and consequently warrant a high interaction with various government bodies. Since these VCs are highly specialized in their niche domains, it enables them to get into such *niche* businesses.

This brings us to explaining the aspects pertaining to the *tangible business attributes* that are important to the VCs in this category. Among these, we find that such VCs prefer to fund businesses with *high entry barriers*. Most of such entry barriers are, in fact, created by patents and other such *niche* and *tacit* aspects that are not easily imitable by other potential competitors (Tyebjee and Bruno 1984; Khan 1987; Kortum and Lerner 2000).

Among the VC profile related variables, VC age is significant and enters with a negative sign. This implies that the VC firms in this category are much younger in terms of their years of operation in India compared to their other counterparts. This again is an intuitive finding as it is a well-known fact that VC professionals with prior founding background are essentially the ones who have been successful entrepreneurs in the United States and have migrated back from there during the latter part of the last decade (Madhavan and Iriyama 2009).

Summary and Conclusions

Thus, to summarize, in this chapter we have identified the distinct set of latent signals and tangible business attributes used by Indian VC firms while making investment decisions. We investigated three diverse segments of VCs: early stage versus growth/late stage, foreign versus domestic VC firms, and VC firms with investment professionals having prior founding experience versus not.

We conclude that while some of these tacit signals and tangible attributes are common across all VC segments in general, others are distinctly different. Our findings from the results in this chapter have been summarized in Table 6.4. Based on the summarized results, it can be seen that early-stage VCs have a larger number of historical deals and fewer number of exits. They regard *syndication* and *specialization* to be important signals. They specialize by funding size. They do not invest in family-owned businesses and fund only first-generation entrepreneurs. They do not believe in originating their deals via the so-called trusted sources such as investment bankers and academic incubators. They prefer businesses that warrant only limited interface with government bodies. Among the tangible business aspects, they stay away from businesses with a heavy cost structure and do not regard short-term scalability as an important attribute.

The foreign VCs do not regard *specialization* to be an important signal but certainly consider *syndication* to be so. They take a *portfolio view* to their investments and consciously look for a *portfolio diversification fit* of a prospective deal. They value past start-up experience and originate deals through formal sources such as investment bankers and academic incubators. They do not consciously look for geographical proximity with respect to their investee companies. However, just as in the case of early-stage VCs, they too stay away from family-owned

Table 6.4 Summary of results

	Early Stage vs Growth/Late Stage VCs	Foreign vs Domestic VCs	VC with Prior Founding Experience vs Otherwise
Latent Signals			
Ownership Type and Owner Characteristics	+ (Significant)	+ (Significant)	+ (Significant)
Specialization	+ (Significant)	Insignificant	+ (Significant)
Syndication	- (Significant)	+ (Significant)	+ (Significant)
Trust	- (Significant)	+ (Significant)	Insignificant
Limited Government Interface	+ (Significant)	Insignificant	Insignificant
Portfolio Diversification/ Positive Synergies	Insignificant	+ (Significant)	- (Significant)
Past Start-Up Experience	Insignificant	+ (Significant)	+ (Significant)
Educational Pedigree	- (Significant)	Insignificant	Insignificant
Geographical Proximity	Insignificant	- (Significant)	Insignificant
Tangible Business Attributes			
Heavy Cost Structure	- (Significant)	- (Significant)	Insignificant
Scalability	- (Significant)	Insignificant	Insignificant
Long Gestation period	Insignificant	- (Significant)	Insignificant
Ecosystem	Insignificant	+ (Significant)	Insignificant
Entry Barriers	Insignificant	Insignificant	+ (Significant)
VC Firm Profile			
Historical Deals	+ (Significant)	Insignificant	Insignificant
Historical exits	- (Significant)	Insignificant	Insignificant
VC Firm Age	Insignificant	Insignificant	- (Significant)
SEBI Registration	Insignificant	- (Significant)	- (Significant)

Source: Author.

businesses and prefer funding only first-generation entrepreneurs. Among the more tangible business attributes, they do not invest in cost-heavy businesses and also those warranting a large gestation period. In addition, they are not too keen on investing in products/services whose adoption will warrant large changes to the existing ecosystem.

The VC firms with investing teams having prior founding experience are much younger in terms of their number of years of operation in India. Among signals, they significantly value *specialization*. They mostly invest in early-stage, high-technology businesses and practise only moderate level of *syndication*. They place a premium on the past start-up experience of prospective founders. Just like the early-stage and foreign VCs, they too stay away from funding family-owned businesses and show a bias towards first-generation entrepreneurs. Among the tangible aspects pertaining to business, they prefer investing in businesses whereby they can create strong entry barriers in the form of patents.

Thus, to summarize, in general, syndication, specialization, business ownership type and owner characteristics, past start-up experience, and trusted source of origination are found to be important across all VC firm categories. Among the tangible business attributes, VC firms usually prefer to stay away from ventures that warrant a heavy cost structure.

APPENDIX 6A   RESULTS FROM EXPLORATORY FACTOR ANALYSIS PROCEDURE

Exploratory Factor Analysis Results for Construct 1: Entrepreneur and Founding Team related Signals

This section comprised twenty items (questions) pertaining to the following aspects of the prospective founder(s): education, past work experience, past start-up experience, team size and composition, family background, and so on. The scree plot, factor loading matrix, variance explained, and the eigenvalues have been given in Figure 6A.1 and Table 6A.1.

Based on the scree plot, it can be seen that for the first seven factors, the eigenvalues are greater than 1. Thus, we have chosen the 7-factor solution for this analysis. As seen from the scree plot, the point corresponding to factor 7 is also the point where the curve elbows out.

The results from factor loading are given in Table 6A.1. However, prior to discussing the details of the factor loading matrix, we need to define each of the items here. To reiterate, the VC professionals were asked to rate the importance/favourability of each item from the viewpoint of funding the deal on a scale of 1 to 5 (1 being least important/favourable and 5 being most important/favourable).

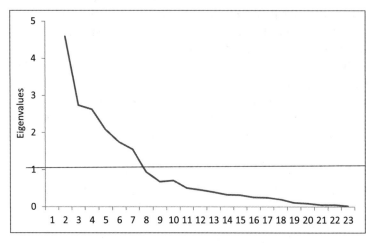

Figure 6A.1   Scree plot: entrepreneurial and founding team related signals
Source: Author.

The explanation of the items used for this EFA procedure is as follows: *Item 1*: The founding team consists of two–three core members. *Item 2*: The founders have known each other for a considerable period in the past. *Item 3*: The founders are college mates or ex-colleagues from previous job. *Item 4*: The founders complement each other's skill set in terms of technical and business expertise. *Item 5*: The founders have held leadership positions in their past jobs. *Item 6*: The founders have managed profit and loss responsibilities in their past jobs. *Item 7*: The founders have received significant global exposure in their previous jobs. *Item 8*: The founders have worked for mainly Indian companies in the past and have deep insight of the Indian market. *Item 9*: The founders have past experience of establishing other start-ups. *Item 10*: Founders have past experience of working for other start-ups. *Item 11*: The founders have a technical degree suitable for the proposed venture. *Item 12*: The founders have a business degree suitable for the proposed venture. *Item 13*: The founders are alumni of top tier educational institutions in India. *Item 14*: The founders hold a technical or business degree from one of the top schools abroad. *Item 15*: The founders are active members of alumni networks of their erstwhile educational institutions. *Item 16*: The founders are informally well networked with professionals from their erstwhile work organizations. *Item 17*: The founders belong to certain specific cultural business communities in India (for example, the Marwari business community). *Item 18*: The founders belong to a family that comprises highly educated and well-placed professionals. *Item 19*: The prospective entrepreneur is a first-generation entrepreneur. *Item 20*: The proposed business is *not* an offshoot of a family-owned business.

Table 6A.1 Factor loading matrix: entrepreneurial and founding team related signals

	Factors						
	1 Educational Pedigree	2 Team Composition	3 Business Ownership Type & Owner Characteristics	4 Past Start-up Experience	5 Past Managerial Experience	6 Family Background	7 Networking Ability
Item1	0.199	**0.749**	0.338	-0.158	0.059	0.102	0.019
Item2	-0.049	**0.836**	-0.119	0.094	-0.06	0.008	0.032
Item3	0.039	**0.806**	-0.228	0.112	-0.143	-0.045	0.083
Item4	0.058	**0.624**	0.465	-0.001	-0.123	-0.113	-0.096
Item5	-0.187	0.035	-0.258	0.135	**0.685**	-0.32	0.12
Item6	-0.103	-0.163	-0.225	-0.328	**0.682**	0.016	-0.069
Item7	-0.034	0.049	-0.082	0.512	**0.63**	-0.086	-0.001
Item8	0.059	-0.128	0.069	0.054	**0.695**	0.101	-0.032
Item9	0.146	0.122	0.021	**0.85**	-0.144	0.097	0.043
Item10	0.122	-0.033	0.049	**0.812**	0.073	-0.025	0.016
Item11	**0.943**	0.023	0.077	0.08	-0.03	0.055	0.058
Item12	**0.945**	0.04	0.025	-0.004	-0.02	0.072	0.098
Item13	**0.971**	0.068	0.052	0.062	-0.063	0.05	0.043
Item14	**0.957**	0.042	0.027	0.031	-0.062	0.086	0.053
Item15	0.173	-0.034	-0.051	-0.05	0.058	-0.085	**0.887**
Item16	0.039	0.104	0.192	0.061	-0.082	0.123	**0.866**
Item17	0.126	-0.032	-0.041	0	-0.066	**0.935**	-0.022
Item18	0.085	0.018	-0.109	-0.017	-0.005	**0.947**	0.059
Item19	0.089	0.128	**0.832**	0.041	-0.031	-0.124	0.045
Item20	0.077	0.001	**0.838**	0.128	-0.098	-0.153	0.004
Eigenvalues	4.595	2.74	2.633	2.075	1.739	1.55	1.338
Cumulative % of Variance	17.89%	28.94%	39.55%	49.59%	58.98%	68.37%	75.77%

Source: Author.

From the factor loading matrix presented in Table 6A.1, it may be seen that seven factors explain about 75.77 per cent of the total variability in the data pertaining to *entrepreneur and founding team related signals*. The intuitive interpretation of each of these factors is as follows.

Factor 1 has an eigenvalue of 4.595 and explains 17.89 per cent of the total variance. Items 11, 12, 13, and 14 are loaded on this factor. Since these items are indicators of the educational backgrounds of the founders, we have chosen to call this factor *educational pedigree*. Factor 2 has an eigenvalue of 2.740 and explains about 11.05 per cent of the total variance. Items 1, 2, 3, and 4 are loaded on this factor. Since these items mainly relate to the team size, composition, and the mix of skill sets, we have chosen to call this factor *team composition*. Factor 3 has an eigenvalue of 2.633 and explains about 10.60 per cent of the total variance. Items 19 and 20 are loaded on it. Since it measures the importance of attributes such as the business (not) being a family-owned one and the founder being a first generation entrepreneur, we call this factor *business ownership type and owner characteristics*. Factor 4 has an eigenvalue of 2.075 and explains about 10.041 per cent of the total variance. Items 9 and 10 are loaded on it. Since these measure attributes such as the founder having some kind of association with start-ups in the past (either as founder or employee), we choose to call this factor *past start-up experience*. Factor 5 has an eigenvalue of 1.739 and explains about 9.390 per cent of the total variance.

Items 5, 6, 7, and 8 are loaded on it. Since these are indicators of the managerial aspects and the qualitative aspects of the past work experience, we have chosen to call this variable *past managerial experience*. Factor 6 has an eigenvalue of 1.550 and explains about 9.388 per cent of the total variance. Items 17 and 18 are loaded on it. Since these measures the community and family backgrounds, we have chosen to call it *family background*. Factor 7 has an eigenvalue of 1.338 and explains about 7.409 per cent of the total variance. Items 15 and 16 are loaded on it. These items attempt to capture how well networked the prospective founder is within his academic and work peers. Hence, we have chosen to call this factor *networking ability*.

Thus, to summarize, the construct on entrepreneur and founding team related signals has seven underlying dimensions: *educational pedigree, team composition, business ownership type and owner characteristics, past start-up experience, past managerial experience, family background*, and *networking ability*.

Exploratory Factor Analysis Results for Construct 2: Deal and VC Firm related Signals

This section comprised nine items pertaining to deal and VC firm related attributes. The scree plot from the EFA procedure is given in Figure 6A.2. Based on the scree

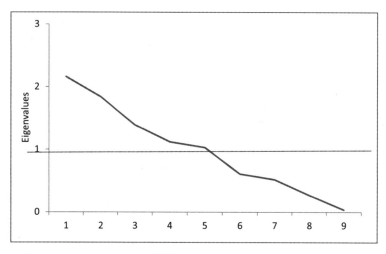

Figure 6A.2   Scree plot: deal and VC firm related signals
Source: Author.

plot, it can be seen that for the first five factors, the eigenvalues are greater than 1. Thus, we have chosen the 5-factor solution for this analysis. Also, we can see that the curve elbows out after the point corresponding to factor 5.

The results from factor loading are given in Table 6A.2. However, prior to discussing the details of the factor loading matrix, we need to define each of the items here. To reiterate, the VC professionals were asked to rate the importance/favourability of each item from the viewpoint of funding the deal on a scale of 1 to 5 (1 being least important/favourable and 5 being most important/favourable). The explanation of the items used for this EFA procedure is as follows: *Item 1*: The deal is consistent with the stage of investment that our VC firm specializes in. *Item 2*: The deal is consistent with the industry/sector that our VC firm specializes in. *Item 3*: The deal is consistent with the investment size that our VC firm specializes in. *Item 4*: There are other syndication partners in the proposed deal. *Item 5*: The deal seems appropriate from the angle of portfolio risk diversification. *Item 6*: We can leverage our current existing network of vendors, suppliers, bankers, lawyers, accountants, and customers for this deal as well. *Item 7*: We can bundle the offerings from this deal with those of others in our portfolio. *Item 8*: There is a potential risk of the offerings from this deal cannibalizing the market from other deals in our portfolio. *Item 9*: Financing of this deal may result in significant conflicts of interest with other existing deals in our portfolio.

The factor loading matrix along with the eigenvalues and the cumulative proportion of variance is given in Table 6A.2. As seen from the table, five factors explain about 84 per cent of the total variability in the data.

Table 6A.2   Factor loading matrix: deal and VC firm related signals

	Factors				
	1	2	3	4	5
	Negative Synergies – Competing Deals	Positive Synergies – Complementary Deals	Specialization	Syndication	Portfolio Diversification Fit
Item 1	-0.11	0.036	**0.876**	-0.096	-0.103
Item 2	0.041	-0.072	**0.503**	**0.679**	-0.038
Item 3	-0.057	-0.251	**0.592**	0.193	0.464
Item 4	-0.129	0.067	-0.175	**0.887**	0.002
Item 5	0.1	0.065	-0.046	-0.057	**0.93**
Item 6	0.113	**0.917**	0.091	-0.027	-0.048
Item 7	-0.135	**0.883**	-0.184	0.053	0.072
Item 8	**0.976**	-0.022	-0.08	-0.053	0.079
Item 9	**0.982**	0.011	-0.054	-0.059	0.025
Eigenvalues	2.161	1.849	1.392	1.128	1.032
Cumulative % of Variance	22.14%	41.02%	57.18%	71.71%	84.01%

Source: Author.

Factor 1 has an eigenvalue of 2.161 and explains about 22.14 per cent of variability in the data. Items 8 and 9 are loaded on it. Since these factors measure the negative synergies associated with funding mutually competing deals on the portfolio, we call this factor *negative synergies – competing deals*. Factor 2 has an eigenvalue of 1.849 and explains about 18.88 per cent of the total variability in the data. Items 6 and 7 are loaded on it. Since these measure the positive synergies associated with funding mutually complementary deals on the portfolio, we call this factor *positive synergies – complementary deals*. Factor 3 has an eigenvalue of 1.392 and explains about 16.16 per cent of the total variability in the data. Items 1, 2, and 3 are loaded on it. Since these items measure the fit of the prospective deal with respect to the specialization domain of the VC firm, we have chosen to call this factor *specialization*. Factor 4 has an eigenvalue of 1.128 and explains about 14.53 per cent of the total variability in the data. Items 2 and 4 are loaded on it. These factors pertain to sector specialization and the presence of other co-investors. However, since the item pertaining to co-investment has a much higher factor loading, we have chosen to call this factor *syndication*. Factor 5 has an eigenvalue of 1.032 and explains about 12.30 per cent of the total variability in the data. It has just one item, item 5, loaded on it, which measures the fit of the prospective deal from the point of view of portfolio risk diversification. Hence, we have chosen to call this factor *portfolio diversification fit*.

Thus, to summarize, the construct on deal and VC firm related signals has five underlying dimensions: *negative synergies – competing deals, positive synergies – complementary deals, specialization, syndication,* and *portfolio diversification fit.*

Exploratory Factor Analysis Results for Construct 3: Macroeconomic and Policy related Signals

This section comprised five items pertaining to macroeconomic and policy related attributes such as favourability of current and future macro scenarios to VC investments, robustness of the business model to economic cycles, and the overall favourability of the government policies towards VC investing in general. The scree plot from the EFA procedure is given in Figure 6A.3.

Based on the scree plot, it can be seen that for the first two factors, the eigenvalues are greater than 1. Thus, we have chosen the 2-factor solution for this analysis. As seen from the scree plot, the point corresponding to factor 2 is also the point where the curve elbows out. The results from factor loading are given in Table 6A.3.

However, prior to discussing the details of the factor loading matrix, we need to define each of the items here. To reiterate, the VC professionals were asked to rate the importance/favourability of the item from the viewpoint of funding the deal on a scale of 1 to 5 (1 being least important/favourable to 5 being most important/favourable). The explanation of the items used for this EFA procedure is as follows: *Item 1*: The market demand for the proposed product/service is resistant to economic cycles. *Item 2*: The existing macroeconomic scenario seems favourable for investing this deal. *Item 3*: The current government policies are favourable towards this sector. *Item 4*: I expect the government policies to

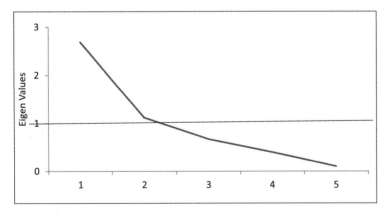

Figure 6A.3 Scree plot: macroeconomic and policy related signals
Source: Author.

continue to be favourable for exit. *Item* 5: I expect the macroeconomic outlook to be positive at the time of exit.

The factor loading matrix along with the eigenvalues and the cumulative proportion of variance is given in Table 6A.3. From the table, it can be seen that two factors explain about 76 per cent of the total variability in the data.

Factor 1 has an eigenvalue of 2.089 and explains 41.780 per cent of the total variability in the data. Items 1, 2, and 3 are loaded on it. It measures the favourability of the current macro scenario for investing in the deal. Hence, this factor is called *favourability of the current scenario and policies.* Factor 2 has an eigenvalue of 1.725 and explains 34.50 per cent of the total variability in the data. Items 4 and 5 are loaded on it. We call this factor *favourability of the future scenario and policies (for exit).*

Table 6A.3   Factor loading matrix: macroeconomic and policy related signals

	Factors	
	1	2
	Favorability of the current scenario and policies	Favorability of the future scenario and policies(for exit)
Item1	**0.843**	0.072
Item2	**0.886**	0.146
Item3	**0.731**	0.378
Item4	0.204	**0.907**
Item5	0.133	**0.856**
Eigenvalues	2.089	1.725
Cumulative % of Variance	41.78%	76.28%

Source: Author.

Thus, to sum up, the construct on macroeconomic and policy related attributes has two underlying dimensions, namely *favourability of the current scenario and policies* and *favourability of the future scenario and policies (for exit).*

Exploratory Factor Analysis Results for Construct 4: Tangible Business Attributes

This section comprised nine items pertaining to tangible aspects of a prospective deal. The scree plot from the EFA procedure is given in Figure 6A.4. Based on the scree plot, it can be seen that for the first five factors, the eigenvalues are greater than 1. Thus, we have chosen the 5-factor solution for this analysis. As seen from the scree plot, the point corresponding to factor 5 is also the point where the curve elbows out.

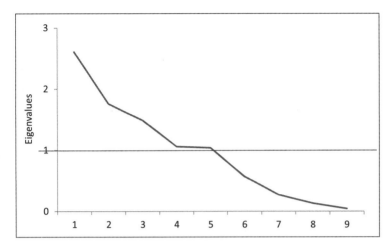

Figure 6A.4   Scree plot: tangible business attributes

Source: Author.

The results from factor loading are given in Table 6A.4. However, prior to discussing the details of the factor loading matrix, we need to define each of the items here. To reiterate, the VC professionals were asked to rate the importance/ favourability of each item from the viewpoint of funding the deal on a scale of 1 to 5 (1 being least important/favourable and 5 being most important/favourable). The explanation of the items used for this EFA procedure is as follows: *Item 1*: The proposed product/service is based on a patentable idea. *Item 2*: The existing market for the product is substantially large. *Item 3*: The market for the proposed product has a significant growth potential. *Item 4*: The barriers to entry for other competitors in this market are quite high; *Item 5*: The proposed business model is scalable. *Item 6*: The proposed business can be grown into a scalable one over our investment horizon. *Item 7*: The relative proportion of fixed costs in the overall cost structure is very high. *Item 8*: A significant proportion of the cost needs to be incurred upfront. *Item 9*: The extent of government interface in the proposed business is quite limited.

The factor loading matrix along with the eigenvalues and the cumulative proportion of variance has been given in Table 6A.4. From this table, it can be seen that five factors explain about 89 per cent of the total variability in the data.

Factor 1 has an eigenvalue of 2.615 and accounts for 29 per cent of the total variability in the data. Items 7 and 8 are loaded on it. Since these items measure the cost structure of the business, we have chosen to call this factor *heavy cost structure*. Factor 2 has an eigenvalue of 1.764 and accounts for 19.5 per cent of the total variability in the data. Items 5 and 6 are loaded on it. Since these measure aspects related to the scaling-up of the business model, we have chosen to call this factor *scalability*. Factor 3 has an eigenvalue of 1.490 and accounts for 16.56 per cent of the total variability in the data. Items 2 and 3 are loaded on it. We call this factor *market size and growth*. Factor 4 has an eigenvalue of 1.064 and accounts for 11.82 per cent of the total variability in the data. It has items 1 and 4 loaded on it. Since these attempt to capture the potential barriers to entry for a new entrant, particularly those arising from patents and intellectual property, we have chosen to call this factor *entry barriers*. Factor 5 has an eigenvalue of 1.040 and accounts for 11.55 per cent of the total variability in the data. Item 9 is loaded on this factor. Since it attempts to capture the extent of government regulation and intervention in the sector of the prospective deal, we have chosen to call this factor *limited government interface*.

Table 6A.4   Factor loading matrix: tangible business attributes

	Factors				
	1 Heavy Cost Structure	2 Scalability	3 Market Size and Growth	4 Entry Barriers	5 Limited Government Interface
Item 1	-0.016	-0.118	0.014	**0.902**	-0.175
Item 2	0.007	0.081	**0.952**	-0.014	-0.037
Item 3	-0.049	0.132	**0.943**	-0.024	-0.02
Item 4	0.131	0.366	-0.096	**0.643**	0.392
Item 5	-0.219	**0.877**	0.126	0.032	-0.055
Item 6	-0.087	**0.921**	0.11	-0.006	-0.066
Item 7	**0.976**	-0.136	-0.026	0.044	0.01
Item 8	**0.974**	-0.143	-0.016	0.013	0.036
Item 9	0.017	-0.122	-0.033	-0.047	**0.944**
Eigenvalues	2.615	1.764	1.49	1.064	1.04
Cumulative % of Variance	29.06%	48.65%	65.21%	77.04%	88.59%

Source: Author.

Thus, to summarize, the construct on tangible business attributes has five underlying dimensions, namely *heavy cost structure, scalability, market size and growth, entry barriers, and limited government interface*.

It must be pointed out that in this section of the questionnaire, we had other variables pertaining to financial details of the prospective deals such as the expected internal rate of return (IRR) and the expected earnings multiples. However, since most VC professionals refrained from answering these questions, we could not use this information in our analysis.

It is important to assess the reliability of the factors using Cronbach's alpha values. Cronbach's alpha values computed for each of the factors have been given in Table 6A.5.

Table 6A.5 Reliability statistics: Cronbach's alpha values

Entrepreneur and Founding Team Related signals	Cronbach's Alpha Values
Educational Pedigree	0.98
Team Composition	0.77
Business Ownership Type and Owner Characteristics	0.83
Past Start-Up Experience	0.8
Past Managerial Experience	0.66
Family Background	0.94
Networking Ability	0.74
Deal and VC Firm Related Signals	
Negative Synergies – Competing Deals	0.98
Positive Synergies – Complementary Deals	0.78
Specialization	0.53
Syndication	0.47
Portfolio Diversification Fit	Single Variable Construct; Cronbach's alpha values cannot be computed
Macro-economic and Policy Related Signals	
Favorability of the Current Scenario and Policies	0.79
Favorability of the Future Scenario and Policies.	0.78
Tangible Business Attributes	
Heavy Cost Structure	0.97
Scalability	0.85
Market Size and Growth	0.9
Entry Barriers	0.36
Limited Government Interface	Single Variable Construct; Cronbach's alpha values cannot be computed

Source: Author.

It must be noted here that for two factors, namely *portfolio diversification fit* and *limited government interface*, Cronbach's alpha values cannot be computed as these are single variable constructs. In general, in social science research, Cronbach's alpha values of 0.6 and above are acceptable (Bland and Altman 1997). From Table 6A.5, it can be seen that for most of the factors, we do have Cronbach's alpha values greater than 0.6. The factors for which Cronbach's alpha values were lower than the threshold were not used in further analysis. Rather, in such cases, we chose to use the individual raw values of one/more of the items therein.

7

Involvement and Value-Add in Investee Ventures

Introduction

The aim of this chapter is to investigate portfolio involvement strategies of the VC firms. In this context, portfolio *involvement* refers to the active participation by venture capital (VC) firms in various aspects of the investee venture. Specifically, we assess their involvement levels in six major areas – human resources (HR), business operations, marketing and business development, financial activities, business strategy, and crisis management. Further, we compute the *aggregate VC involvement index* and then cluster (and profile) the VC firms based on the same into three distinct categories: *most intensely involved* VC firms, *moderately involved* VC firms, and *least involved* VC firms.

To start with, it is important to reiterate that VC firms significantly differ from the other conventional financial intermediaries (namely banks and equity markets) in one principal aspect. Compared to the other financial mediators, VC firms are regarded as *active and personalized* sources of funding. Thus, the VC firms not only provide finance but are also known to actively intervene in other operational and strategic aspects of the investee ventures (such as administration, marketing and sales, recruitment, product development, and so on). This *activism* is necessitated by the need to tackle the risks emanating from agency problems associated with funding ventures in nascent and emerging domains (Elango et al. 1995; Sapienza, Manigart, and Vermeir 1996). While such agency risks exist in the developed VC markets as well, they pose difficulties in emerging markets with a weak institutional support (Wright, Lockett, and Pruthi 2002).

Accordingly, the objective of this chapter is manifold. First, to identify, categorize, and quantify the level of involvement of the VC firms in various aspects of the investee companies. Second, to divide the VC firms into distinct segments based on their aggregate intensity of involvement. Third, to identify the underlying attributes that drive this variation in involvement levels.

The rest of this chapter is organized as follows: To start with, we propose a conceptual framework based on literature and arrive at testable hypotheses based on the same. We then move on to the description of the research design for this study. This is then followed by the discussion of results. Finally, we summarize our findings and derive managerial implications.

Factors Governing the Level of Portfolio Involvement by the VC Firms

We understand that agency risks are the mainstay of VC-funded projects. Among the many possible mechanisms of tackling such risks, portfolio monitoring is one of the most commonly used (Sahlman 1990; Kaplan and Stromberg 2000).

Intensive monitoring is one of the ways to keep in check the opportunistic behaviour of entrepreneurs, that is, agency problems (Barry 1994). However, in addition to the *controlling* role, the VC firms play a significant *supporting* role as well. By this, we mean that the VC firms not only play the role of an overseer or a regulator but also that of a value-added service provider (Deakins, O'Neill, and Mileham 2000). Our conjecture is that the intensity of involvement in the funded ventures is not uniform; rather, it is driven by the magnitude of agency risks encountered by the investee firm. The broad framework for analysing the same has been presented in Figure 7.1 followed by the proposed hypotheses.

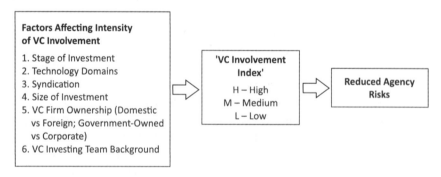

Figure 7.1   Proposed model of intensity of VC involvement
Source: Author.

Based on the conceptual framework just described, we propose the following hypotheses:

Hypothesis 1: *Early-stage* ventures and those in the *high-technology* domains warrant a higher level of involvement by the VC firms in all aspects. (*The magnitude of information asymmetry and consequently the agency risks are expected to be much higher in magnitude in such ventures – which merits greater monitoring.*)

Hypothesis 2: Corporate VC firms are likely to be intensely involved in the investee companies funded by them. (*Typically, corporate VC firms fund companies that have positive synergies with their core area of operations. Thus, these companies are looked upon as potential acquisition targets in the future.*)

Hypothesis 3: Presence of a *syndication* partner lowers the need for VC involvement. (*Since the monitoring responsibilities are shared among multiple partners, the intensity of involvement of each partner is expected to be much lower.*)

Hypothesis 4: Foreign VC firms are less involved in the investee ventures funded by them. (*Given their wide expanse of international experience but only a limited range of local networks, they are less likely to be actively involved in the day-to-day operations of the venture.*)

Hypothesis 5: VC firm top management teams (*TMTs*) with prior founding experience are likely to be intensely involved at operational levels. (*Given their own entrepreneurial experience, they possess the relevant skill sets to get involved at a hands-on level.*)

Research Design

This section describes the research design and the methods of analysis adopted for the purpose of this study. A description of the data, sample, variables, and their definitions, modes of data collection, and the methodology used is presented here.

Sample and Data

This study is based on primary data collected between June 2013 and April 2014 from a sample of active VC firms operating in India during this period. Semi-structured questionnaire followed by face-to-face/telephonic interviews were used as the primary tools for the data collection process. A separate questionnaire aimed at assessing the VC firms' *intensity of involvement* with the investee ventures was administered to the VC firm professionals for the purpose of data collection. Each item in this questionnaire evaluated the level of involvement by the concerned VC firm in the specific aspect (as mentioned in the question) on a scale of 1 to 5 (1 being least involved and 5 being most involved). This questionnaire comprised forty-five questions, which were further divided into six broad categories, namely HR, business operations, marketing and business development, financial activities, business strategy, and crisis management.

Variables

We use the following variables in our analysis:

Cluster Analysis Procedure (Segmentation and Profiling Variables): We compute *VC involvement indices* at both aggregate and domain specific levels (namely aggregate involvement, HR involvement, business operations involvement, marketing involvement, financial involvement, strategic involvement, and crisis situation involvement). These indices are then used as input variables to the clustering algorithm.

The clusters thus obtained are further analysed based on the VC firm profile related variables. These variables are – funding stage focus (early versus later), ownership type (domestic versus foreign), VC TMT composition (erstwhile founding experience versus erstwhile financial investing experience), Securities and Exchange Board of India (SEBI) registration, high-technology focus, corporate ownership, VC age (number of years of operation in India), the number of historical deals, successful exits, and degree of syndication (proportion of syndicated deals).

Methods of Analysis

We have used cluster analysis as the main statistical method for this analysis. To start with, we compute the *VC involvement indices* at aggregate and domain-specific levels and use the same in cluster analysis to segment the VC firms in our sample into three distinct categories (based on their overall intensity of involvement in the investee firm) – *most intensely involved VC firms*, *moderately involved VC firms*, and *least intensely involved VC firms*. Further, we profile each of these clusters based on the specific VC firm related attributes.

All the analyses were performed using SPSS 21.0.0.0 and R 3.1.0 statistical softwares. For cluster analysis, we report the cluster membership, cluster centroids, distance between final cluster centres, and the results from ANOVA analysis and the Chi-Square tests of independence (for the clustering variables).

Cluster Analysis Procedure

Cluster analysis is a group of multi-variate techniques whose primary purpose is to group objects based on the characteristics they possess (Hair et al. 2015). Thus, the aim of cluster analysis is to categorize n objects in k ($k > 1$) groups, called clusters, by using p ($p > 0$) variables. Cluster analysis classifies objects based on a set of user-selected characteristics. The resulting clusters should exhibit high internal (within-cluster) homogeneity and high external (between-cluster) heterogeneity. Cluster analysis works on the innate principles of pattern recognition and grouping.

However, grouping data into clusters is in most cases not an end in itself but rather a means to an end. Also, it is important that cluster analysis should have a strong conceptual basis. Thus, it is important to understand what variables logically explain why objects end up in groups that they do (Hair et al. 2015). In general, there exist two kinds of clustering algorithms – *hierarchical* and *non-hierarchical*. The *non-hierarchical* procedures assign objects into clusters once the number of clusters is specified (Johnson and Wichern 2008). The most commonly used non-hierarchical clustering algorithm is the *K-means* method. This algorithm works in the following manner: Partition the data into *K* initial clusters. Assign each item to a cluster whose centroid (mean) is the nearest. The notion of *nearness* is usually determined using Euclidian distance. The centroid for the cluster receiving the new item and for the one losing the old item is recalculated. This process is repeated unless no more new assignments take place (Johnson and Wichern 2008). The initial number of clusters is often determined based on prior research or data from another multi-variate analysis (Hair et al. 2015). The common element therein is that the researcher, while knowing the number of clusters to be formed, also has information about the basic character of these clusters (Hair et al. 2015). Since it has been pointed out that for social science research non-hierarchical clustering based on the *K-means* algorithm is most appropriate (Hennig and Liao 2013), we decided to use the same.

Since we have an *a priori* idea about the number of subgroups in our sample, we specify *three clusters* as the seed input to the *K-means* clustering algorithm. Further, our survey of literature revealed that a similar study had been taken up in the context of US VC firms by MacMillan, Kulow, and Khoylian (1989). In their study, they had divided the VC firms into three distinct categories based on their levels of involvement, namely *laissez faire* involvement (limited nature of involvement), moderate involvement, and *close tracker* involvement (high intensity of involvement). However, they could not explain the underlying reasons responsible for this variation in involvement levels. Thus, they concluded that VC firms exhibited different involvement levels solely because they elected to do so (MacMillan, Kulow, and Khoylian 1989). We believe that the above explanation is far from satisfactory and the presence of differences in the involvement levels warrants a more concrete explanation. Therefore, we have chosen to first divide the VC firms in our sample into three categories based on their levels of involvement (high, moderate, and low) and then explain in detail the potential drivers of this variation.

Any cluster analysis procedure warrants the usage of two sets of variables: first, the ones that are inputted into the clustering algorithm itself and, second, the ones that are later used to arrive at the cluster profiles. While the former are determined based on the primary objective behind the usage of the clustering procedure itself, the latter are determined based on the demographic (and other) characteristics across which the 'clustered' entities are expected to differ. In our context, we input the variables pertaining to the VC involvement levels (VC involvement scores and indices) as inputs to the clustering algorithm and those relating to the VC firm characteristics as profiling variables.

Discussion of Results

This section comprises four subsections. To start with, we discuss the results obtained from cluster analysis. To reiterate, the objective of cluster analysis in our context is to segment the VC firms into three distinct groups (namely *most involved* VC firms, *moderately involved* VC firms, and *least involved* VC firms) based on their intensity of participation in the funded ventures. Further, we profile each of these clusters based on their underlying attributes to arrive at the potential reasons explaining their differential intensities of involvement.

In this section, we present in detail the process of computation of the 'VC involvement indices', segmentation procedure, results from ANOVA and Chi-Square tests of independence, and finally the interpretation of results.

We have used the *K-means* algorithm for clustering the VC firms in our sample into appropriate subgroups. In the *K-means* algorithm, we need to specify the number of clusters *a priori*. Based on the reasons already discussed, we have chosen a three-cluster solution for our analysis. Since we are interested in segmenting the VC firms based particularly on their *levels of involvement* with the investee firm, we input variables corresponding to the same in our segmentation scheme. In this regard, we have created multiple indices pertaining to the *level of VC involvement*.

Indices of VC Involvement

The questionnaire data was used to arrive at VC involvement indices.[1]

Each item in the questionnaire attempted at measuring the intensity of participation by the VC firm in the specific micro-level activity of the investee venture (as specified in the question). Each item was rated by the VC firm executives on a scale of 1 to 5 (1 being least involved and 5 being most involved).

---

[1] The questionnaire administered by us to the VC firms was divided into six sections, each comprising multiple items: HR and organizational structure (eleven items), business operations (six items), marketing and business development (ten items), financial activities (seven items), business strategy (seven items), and crisis management (four items). The details of the items in each of these six sections have been given in Appendix 7A.

Based on the responses to the questionnaire, we compute six different *involvement scores* – one for each separate aspect of involvement. In addition, we also compute an overall index of VC involvement at the aggregate level. The procedure for doing so is as follows: There are eleven items in the HR and organizational structure category. We compute the HR involvement score as a simple sum of the ratings across all eleven items. Similarly, we compute the involvement scores for other arenas on involvement as well. The aggregate involvement index is computed as a simple sum of the values of the six different involvement scores. The detailed procedure for computing the same has been given in Table 7.1.

Table 7.1 Computation of VC involvement indices

No.	Type of Involvement	Number of Items in the Relevant Section of the Questionnaire	Index Computation
1	Human Resources Score	11	Sum across 11 items
2	Business Operations Score	6	Sum across 6 items
3	Marketing and BD Score	10	Sum across 10 items
4	Financial Activities Score	7	Sum across 7 items
5	Business Strategy	7	Sum across 7 items
6	Crisis Management Score	4	Sum across 4 items
7	Aggregate Involvement Index	Total Items = 45	Grand Sum across All 45 items

Source: Author.

Thus, we have seven variables in all – six separate involvement scores for each subcategory and the *aggregate involvement index* – which we feed in as inputs to the clustering algorithm. The three clusters of the VC firms are then obtained based on the distribution of the values of these indices across the VC firms in our sample.

Results: Cluster Analysis Procedure

The purpose of this section is to present the statistical results obtained from the *K-means* cluster analysis procedure. In this section, we present four sets of output: cluster membership, one-way ANOVA output for the input variables of the clustering procedure, final cluster centres, and distances between final cluster centres.

Table 7.2 shows the distribution of observations across the three clusters. To reiterate, we have specified a three-cluster solution as an input to the *K-means* clustering algorithm. Based on the results obtained, we found that first cluster comprises 41 per cent, second cluster 43 per cent, and third cluster 16 per cent of the total VC firms respectively.

Table 7.2 Cluster membership

Cluster Number	Number of Observations	Percentage of Observations
1	29	41%
2	30	43%
3	11	16%
Total	70	100%

Source: Author.

The one-way ANOVA table with respect to the variables inputted in the clustering scheme is presented in Table 7.3.

Table 7.3 One-way ANOVA results: cluster variables

	Cluster 1 (Most Intensely Involved)	Cluster 2 (Moderately Involved)	Cluster 3 (Least Intensely Involved)	F - Statistic	Significance (p-value)
	Average Values (for variables that are a part of the Clustering Scheme)				
Aggregate VC Involvement Index	201	173	136	153.086	0.000
Involvement Score – HR and Organizational structure	44	27	22	36.248	0.000
Involvement Score – *Business Operations*	25	20	12	23.629	0.000
Involvement Score – *Financial Activities*	34	32	30	5.283	0.007
Involvement Score - *Marketing and Business Development*	44	32	20	55.226	0.000
	Average Values (for variables that are not a part of the Clustering Scheme)				
Involvement Score – *Business Strategy*	34	32	32	1.875	0.121
Involvement Score – *Crisis Management*	19	18	18	1.423	0.248

Source: Author.

The results from the one-way ANOVA tests indicate the variables for which the mean values are significantly different across the three clusters. It also indicates the variables that contribute the most to our cluster solution. Typically, the variables having the highest F-statistic value contribute the highest towards the cluster solution.

Initially, we performed the cluster analysis with seven variables, namely *aggregate involvement index* and six separate involvement scores (for each sub-aspect of VC participation). However, we found that the involvement scores for business strategy and crisis management did not differ significantly across the three clusters. Hence, we excluded these two variables and executed the clustering algorithm once again with just the significant variables. The results thus obtained have been presented in Table 7.3. Our finding that the three clusters did not differ significantly for the levels of involvement in *business strategy* and *crisis management* is quite intuitive. These being the core aspects of VC participation, all VC firms are expected to be equally involved in this regard and thus no statistical differences across clusters could be found.

Table 7.3 also presents the average values for each of the clusters with respect to the involvement indices. This vector of average values for each cluster is also referred to as final cluster centres. We can observe that Cluster 1 ranks the highest in terms of both the aggregate involvement index and also with respect to the involvement in each of the micro aspects. Thus, the VC firms in this cluster are categorized as *most intensely involved*. Cluster 3 ranks the lowest in terms of each of the indices. Consequently, it is categorized as *least intensely involved*. Since Cluster 2 lies in between the Clusters 1 and 3 in terms of its involvement levels, we categorize the VC firms falling therein to be *moderately involved*.

Next, we present the output that gives the distance between final cluster centres. As indicated earlier, *cluster centres* refer to the vector of mean values of all the variables in each cluster. Thus, the column corresponding to the average values of each of the clustering variables for Cluster 1 (see Table 7.3) is known as the cluster centre vector for Cluster 1. Accordingly, we have the cluster centre vectors for Clusters 2 and 3. Table 7.4 presents the 3 x 3 symmetric matrix that gives the distance between the final cluster centres.

Table 7.4 Distance between final cluster centres

Clusters	1	2	3
1		31.931	74.15
2	31.931		42.52
3	74.15	42.52	

Source: Author.

Table 7.4 shows the Euclidean distances between the final cluster centres. Greater distances between clusters imply greater dissimilarities. Thus, the Euclidian distance between the cluster centres of Clusters 1 and 3 is 74.150, that between Clusters 2 and 3 is 42.520, and that between Clusters 1 and 2 is 31.931. From this, we can conclude that Clusters 1 and 3 are most different from each other in terms of their characteristics (with respect to those attributes that have been inputted into the clustering algorithm). This is expected as Cluster 1 comprises VC firms that are *most intensely involved*, while Cluster 3 comprises VC firms that are *least intensely involved*. Also, Clusters 1 and 2 are less different from each other, relative to Clusters 2 and 3.

Profiling of Clusters: Graphical Analysis

Having identified the clusters, the next task is to profile each of them based on their vital attributes. In this section, we present the profiling results that will enable us to further understand the underlying characteristics of each of the clusters. The clusters have been profiled with respect to the following attributes: funding stage focus (early versus later), ownership type (domestic versus foreign), VC TMT composition (erstwhile founding experience versus erstwhile financial investing experience), SEBI-registration, high-technology focus, corporate ownership, VC age (number of years of operation in India), the number of historical deals, successful exits, and degree of syndication (proportion of syndicated deals).

While profiling the clusters, we have compared the distribution of the specific attribute in the overall sample with its distribution in the three clusters.

Stage of Funding (Early versus Later)

Figure 7.2 presents the profiles of the three clusters with respect to their funding stage focus.

From the figure, it can be seen that the proportions of early-stage focused and later-stage focused VC firms are 37 per cent and 63 per cent respectively in the aggregate sample. However, the cluster comprising *most intensely involved* VC firms has about 55 per cent of early-stage focused VC firms but just 45 per cent of the later-stage focused VC firms. On the other hand, the cluster comprising *least intensely involved* VC firms has about 91 per cent later-stage focused VC firms but just 9 per cent early-stage focused VC firms. Similarly, the *moderately involved* VC firms too have an above average concentration of later-stage focused VC firms (70 per cent) and below average concentration of early-stage focused VC firms (30 per cent).

Thus, the clusters of *moderately* and *least involved* VC firms are more inclined towards funding later-stage ventures while the cluster on *most intensely involved*

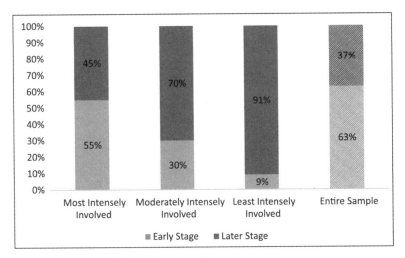

Figure 7.2 Cluster profile: funding stage focus

Source: Author.

VC firms seems partial to early-stage ones. This implies that the intensity of VC involvement proportionately varies with the stage of funding with the early-stage ventures warranting the highest involvement levels, while the late-stage ones warranting the least.

Ownership Type (Foreign versus Domestic)

Figure 7.3 presents the profiles of the three clusters with respect to their VC firm ownership type.

From the figure, it can be seen that at the aggregate level, 40 per cent of the VC firms in our sample are of foreign origin while 60 per cent are of domestic origin. However, the cluster comprising *least intensely involved* VC firms has the highest concentration of the foreign VC firms – with about 55 per cent of the VC firms in this segment being of foreign origin. On the other hand, the cluster of *moderately involved* VC firms has the least concentration of foreign VC firms – with 33 per cent of the VC firms being of foreign origin. It also has the highest concentration of domestic VC firms with about 67 per cent of the VC firms therein being of domestic origin. The *most intensely involved* VC cluster has a distribution of foreign and domestic VC firms that is more or less comparable to the overall sample distribution.

This implies that there exists a relationship between VC ownership type and its level of involvement; the foreign VC firms, in particular, are likely to be *least intensely involved*.

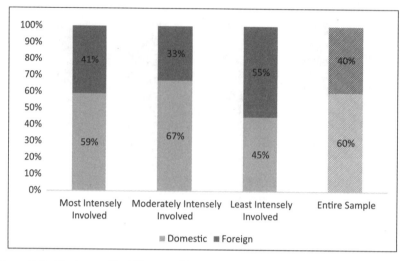

Figure 7.3 Cluster profile: VC ownership type
Source: Author.

VC Firm TMT Composition (Erstwhile Founding Experience versus Erstwhile Financial Investing Experience)

Figure 7.4 presents the profiles of the three clusters with respect to the composition of the VC firms' TMT.

From Figure 7.4, it may be seen that at an aggregate level, about 26 per cent of the VC firms in the sample have TMTs with *erstwhile* founding experience. However, in the *least intensely involved* cluster, only about 18 per cent of the VC firms possess similar experience. This reveals that there exists a correlation between the composition of the VC firm TMT and its level of involvement, wherein TMTs without prior founding experience are less likely to be involved with the investee VC firms.

High-Technology Focus

Figure 7.5 presents the profiles of the three clusters with respect to the high-technology focus of their investments. At the aggregate level, about 39 per cent of the VC firms exhibit a high-technology focus in their investments.

However, in the cluster of *most intensely involved* VC firms, as high as 52 per cent display a high-technology focus, while the same is only about 27 per cent and 30 per cent respectively for the VC firms belonging to the *least intensely involved* and *moderately involved* VC clusters. Thus, there seems to exist an obvious correlation

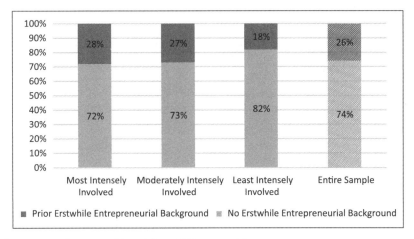

Figure 7.4   Cluster profile: VC firm TMT composition

Source: Author.

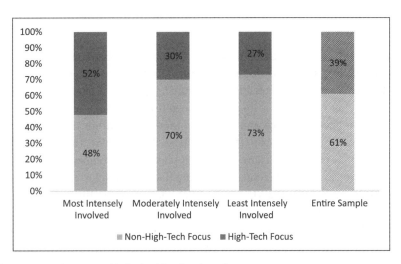

Figure 7.5   Cluster profile by high-technology focus

Source: Author.

here – with technology focused VC firms being more likely to be intensely involved in the ventures funded by them.

Corporate VC Firms

Figure 7.6 presents the profiles of the three clusters with respect to their nature of corporate ownership. Corporate VC firms are the VC arms of the larger corporate

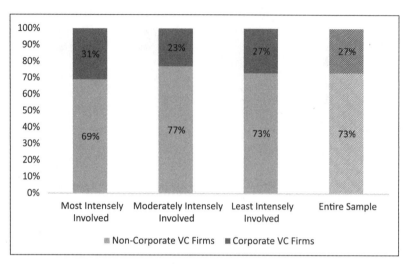

Figure 7.6 Cluster profiles: corporate VC firms
Source: Author.

entities – both multinational and domestic. These corporates are often known to fund fledgling start-ups (via their VC arms) that possess synergies with their core businesses, with the intention of acquiring them at a later point of time. The underlying rationale for this strategy could be explained as follows: as an organization becomes large and unwieldy, innovating within the organization often becomes quite unviable (Dougherty and Hardy 1996). However, lack of innovation may potentially cause a firm to lose out on its competitive advantage. This impediment can be overcome by funding fledgling businesses in the relevant domains of interest (via the VC arms) and at a later point in time merging them with the core business entities (Ivanov and Xie 2010).

˙ As seen from Figure 7.6, at an aggregate level, about 27 per cent of the VC firms are owned by larger corporate entities. However, among the *most intensely involved* VC segment, this proportion is marginally higher at 31 per cent. Thus, it can be said that in general, corporate ownership of VC firms results in a higher level of participation by the investing VC firms in the funded ventures, possibly owing to the existing synergies among their businesses and also because such ventures are viable acquisition targets in the future.

Age of Operation in India (in Years)

Figure 7.7 presents the profiles of the three clusters with respect to their age in terms of the number of years of operation in India. At an aggregate level, the average

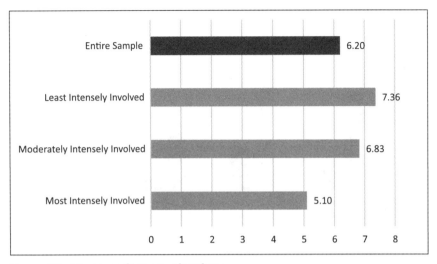

Figure 7.7 Cluster profiles: age of VC firms
Source: Author.

age of VC firms operating in India is about 6.2 years. However, the VC firms in the *least intensely involved* category are much older with an average age of 7.36 years, while those in the *most intensely involved* category are much younger with an average age of 5.1 years.

Thus, there seems to be a direct and linear relationship between the intensity of involvement and the age of the VC firm. We have noted earlier that the cluster on *most intensely involved* VC firms has the highest concentration of early-stage VC firms.

In general, early-stage investing is a recent phenomenon in India (Planning Commission 2012). This explains the fact that age of operation is the lowest for this cluster.

Historical Deals and Exits

Figure 7.8 presents the profiles of the three clusters with respect to their historically funded deals and successful exits.

At an aggregate level, the VC firms in our sample have, on an average, funded about eighteen deals and successfully exited about five deals so far (between the years 2006 and 2013). The highest number of deals have been funded by *moderately involved* VC firms (about twenty-three deals), while the lowest number of deals have been funded by *least intensely involved* VC firms (about ten deals). On similar lines, the *moderately involved* VC firms have witnessed the highest number of

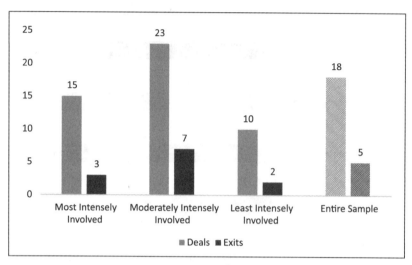

Figure 7.8 Cluster profiles: historical deals and successful exits
Source: Author.

successful exits (about seven exits) compared to the *least intensely involved* VC firms that have witnessed the lowest number of successful exits (about two exits).

It must be noted here that level of involvement and successful exits seem to be correlated, with *moderately involved* VC firms witnessing higher success rates in terms of exits.

Syndication (Co-Investment with Other VC Firms)

Figure 7.9 presents the profiles of the three clusters with respect to the proportion of syndicated deals in their portfolio.

At an aggregate level, about 45 per cent of the total funded deals are syndicated with other VC firms. However, the *most intensely involved* VC firms syndicate only about 38 per cent of their deals. On the contrary, the *moderately involved* and *least intensely involved* VC firms syndicate about 51 per cent and 48 per cent of their deals respectively. The low syndication among the *most intensely involved* VC firms could possibly explain their high level of involvement in the investee firms.

Discussion of Results

Based on the results just discussed, we present the summary profile of the three clusters in our sample.

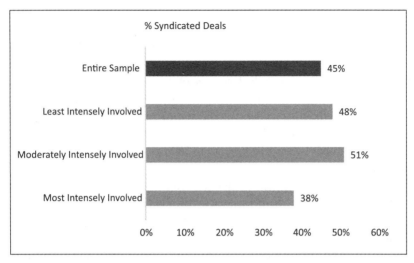

Figure 7.9 Cluster profiles: syndication

Source: Author.

Most Intensely Involved VC Firm Cluster

The *most intensely involved* cluster of VC firms has the highest concentration of early-stage VC firms and the lowest concentration of later-stage ones. They also exhibit the highest concentration of VC firms with erstwhile founding experience and also the ones focused on high-technology domains. They have a lower proportion of foreign VC firms compared to the overall sample. They are also the youngest in terms of their years of operation in India. They have the highest incidence of corporate VC firms. In general, they syndicate a much smaller proportion of their deals.

From this description, it appears that the profile of the VC firms in this category resonates quite well with their high intensity of participation in the investee ventures. It must be noted that the VC firms in this cluster are mostly early-stage firms focused on funding ventures in high-technology domains. Ventures in such domains are known to exhibit very high levels of agency risks, thus warranting the highest level of participation from the VC firm (Sapienza 1992; Sapienza, Manigart, and Vermeir 1996). Assistance from the VC firms is mandated not only to tackle the agency risks, but to provide assistance in all aspects of the business processes in general (Hellman and Puri 2002). In fact, it has been widely observed that VC firms are known to add the maximum value in the earlier stages of a venture (Sapienza 1992).

These VC firms are also much younger compared to those in other clusters, thus indicating that early-stage investing is still a relatively nascent phenomenon in India

(Planning Commission 2012). Moreover, there exists an overwhelming presence of corporate VC firms in this cluster. It must be understood that the corporate VC firms tend to fund ventures engaged in developing those technologies/services/products that they find difficult to innovate and develop in-house owing to the inflexibilities associated with the large size of their parent entity (Dougherty and Hardy 1996). Consequently, they fund such businesses via their VC arms and merge them with their parent entity at the appropriate time. Thus, if the investee venture has essentially been looked upon as a potential acquisition target in the future, it should not be surprising that the VC firm is intensely involved in the funded entity.

Further, the VC firms in this cluster syndicate with other VC firms to the least possible extent. Earlier, we have seen that syndication is primarily used as a strategy to tackle the adverse selection risks while venturing into newer domains. Thus, the VC firms specialized in a particular domain/sector actively co-invest with their counterparts (who are specialized in other arenas) while investing in domains in which they lack the *tacit* knowledge. However, we also found that the VC firms in India are not much *domain specialized* to start with, owing to low market depth. Thus, they do not need to syndicate much. In fact, this low level of syndication itself explains why the VC firms in this category tend to be most intensely involved in their investee companies. Since they do not have many co-investors to share their portfolio management responsibilities, it is not surprising that these VC firms are most actively involved in their portfolio companies.

Least Intensely Involved VC Firm Cluster

The *least intensely involved* cluster of VC firms has the lowest concentration of early-stage VC firms and the highest concentration of later-stage ones. It also has the highest proportion of foreign VC firms and the lowest incidence of VC firm TMTs with erstwhile founding experience. Most of these invest in *non-high-technology* domains, that is, the more conventional sectors. They are the oldest in terms of their years of operation in India. They have funded the least number of deals and witnessed the least number of successful exits.

From this description, it can be inferred that the characteristics of the VC firms in this category match quite well with their very low intensity of participation in the investee ventures. To start with, most of these firms are growth- and later-stage firms, focused on investing in more conventional domains. Naturally, the magnitude of agency risks is much lower for the ventures funded by the VC firms in this category. For later-stage businesses, significant historical performance data are available to the VC firms while making investment decisions. Unlike the early-stage investments, here the business model is in place, revenue model tested, customer validation acquired, and cash has started flowing inwards (Ruhnka and Young 1987). Consequently, the information asymmetry is much lower. Moreover, since these businesses are in the more conventional domains, the risks arising owing to the *liability of newness* are also expected to be quite limited (Baum 1989; Certo 2003). All these factors warrant lower levels of intervention by the VC firm. Moreover, the nature of the intervention warranted is more strategic in nature rather than at a hands-on level. Consequently, the VC firms in this cluster are least intensely involved.

It may be seen that this cluster has the highest concentration of foreign VC firms. Owing to the geographic distance and cultural differences, the foreign VC firms are less likely to be connected with the local *niche* networks (Dai, Jo, and Kassicieh 2012). A link with such networks is essential if the VC firm needs to get intensely involved in day-to-day business processes. The lack of such networks thereof is one of the principal reasons for the low level of involvement by the VC firms with the investee ventures.

It is further interesting to note that although the VC firms in this category are the oldest in terms of their years of operation in India, yet they have funded and successfully exited the least number of deals. It must be noted here that a large proportion of the older domestic VC firms fall in this category. Moreover, their primary focus is on later-stage investments. We must understand that the average deal size for a later-stage deal is significantly larger compared to an early-stage one (according to Venture Intelligence [2014], the average deal size of an early-stage deal is about USD 3.46 million compared to that of USD 7.17 million for a later-stage one). Thus, given the fund size, it should not be surprising that they can accommodate fewer deals compared to the VC firms focused on early-stage ones.

Moderately Involved VC Firm Cluster

The *moderately involved* VC firm cluster has the highest concentration of domestic VC firms and the lowest concentration of foreign VC firms. It has an above average proportion of later-stage VC firms. It also has the least concentration of corporate VC firms. Also, most of the VC firms in this segment do not have a high-technology focus in their investments. They have funded the greatest number of deals historically and also witnessed the highest number of successful exits. They are also known to intensely co-invest with other VC firms.

Thus, in general, the profiles of the *moderately involved* and *least intensely involved* VC firms are more or less comparable. Both have an above average concentration of later-stage VC firms. However, among these, the *least involved* cluster has a higher concentration of foreign VC firms while the *moderately involved* cluster has a higher concentration of domestic VC firms.

Primarily being of domestic origin and also much older than the average (in terms of their number of years of operation in India), the VC firms in this category are likely to have quite well-entrenched local networks (Wright, Lockett, and Pruthi 2002). This enables them to get involved intensely in the investee ventures. However, since the majority of these ventures belong to later stages of investment, they do not warrant the same level of intervention as the ones at earlier stages (Ruhnka and Young 1987). Thus, we observe that the VC firms in this category tend to be involved in their investee companies only to a moderate extent.

Another intriguing feature of the VC firms in this cluster is that they have funded the highest number of deals historically. One of the possible reasons for this is that these VC firms have been in business for a much longer period than the average (as seen from the above average years of operations in India). However, in that case it can be argued that the *least involved* VC firms have been in business for an even longer period (compared to the *moderately involved* VC firms); however, they have funded a relatively lower number of deals. Hence, a more appropriate explanation in this regard can be provided on the basis of their intensity of syndication. It can be seen that among the three clusters, the VC firms in this category are known to syndicate most intensely. This probably enables them to support a much larger number of deals, since deal funding is now shared with other co-investing partners (Lerner 1994; Cumming 2006). Co-investment not only helps in pooling together funds but also substantially reduces the intensity of monitoring on the part of any individual VC firm (Lerner 1994). Thus, the presence of a high proportion of syndicated deals in the portfolios of the VC firms in this cluster is probably an explanation for their moderate intensity of involvement.

It is further interesting to note that the VC firms from this cluster have witnessed the highest number of successful exits. Literature reveals that there exists a strong correlation between the degree of intervention by the VC firm in the funded venture and its performance (Macmillan, Kulow, and Khoylian 1989; Arthurs and Busenitz 2006). In general, high degree of intervention by the VC firms is known to result in better performing ventures. This correlation can be explained by the *value-add* role played by the VC firms (Sapienza, Manigart, and Vermeir 1996). However, it must be noted that the relationship between the degree of VC intervention and performance of the investee firm is not linear. In general, too much intervention by the VC firm is known to result in VC–entrepreneur conflicts. Thus, an intervention in *moderation* and that too only in certain aspects of the venture are known to constitute a significant value-add (Macmillan, Kulow, and Khoylian 1989; Busenitz, Fiet, and Moesel 2004; Arthurs and Busenitz 2006). With respect to our sample, although prima facie it is difficult to isolate the underlying causes behind this nature of relationship between the moderate intensity of VC involvement and the high number of successful exits, the results seem to be well supported by the literature.

APPENDIX 7A   QUESTIONNAIRE II – LEVEL OF INVOLVEMENT

Section A: Please rate your level of involvement with a funded venture on a scale of 1 to 5. (**1 indicates least intensely involved while 5 indicates most intensely involved**).

The aim of this questionnaire is assess the intensity of involvement in the investee company

The major areas of involvement have been classified into 5 categories – HR, Operations, Financial, Strategic and Crisis Management

Measurement Scale: 5 – Most Involved to 1 – Least Involved					
Level of Involvement in HR practices	5	4	3	2	1
1. Identifying personnel for the most important positions from your own network					
2. Actual interviewing and recruitment of key personnel					
3. Negotiating terms of employment and compensation					
4. Designing incentive structures for entrepreneurs					
5. Keeping the core team focused and motivated					
6. Arresting attrition of key personnel					
7. Insisting the top management to sign 'no-compete' agreements with respect to competitors					
8. Putting in place professional performance management systems					
9. Provide feedback to key personnel in performance appraisals					
10. Setting up Employee Stock Option Plans and determining vesting schedules					
11. Putting in place an organizational structure					

Measurement Scale: 5 – Most Involved to 1 – Least Involved					
Level of Involvement in Business Operations	5	4	3	2	1
12. Recommending and facilitating access to key vendors and distributors					
13. Actual development of the product/service/ business offering					
14. Monitoring the quality of product/service through formal and informal channels					
15. Setting up internal quality management systems					
16. Setting up standard operating procedures for performing the relevant tasks					
17. Pushing the investee firm to apply for external professional quality certifications					

Comments If Any (Other HR, Organizational Structure, and Business Operations related tasks not captured in the above questions):

_____

_____

_____

_____

_____

_____

Measurement Scale: 5 – Most Involved to 1 – Least Involved					
Level of Involvement in Marketing	5	4	3	2	1
18. Set up the marketing plan					
19. Clearly lay down the key marketing targets					
20. Directly assist in the *4 P*'s of market strategy – Price, Product, Positioning, and Promotion					
21. Actively participate in Business Development					
22. Evaluating other potential markets and facilitating access to the same					
23. Monitoring market share					
24. Track marketing strategies perceived by competitors					
25. Direct participation in facilitating customer validation of the proposed concept					
26. Bring in best practices from other similar funded ventures on their portfolio					
27. Market Research and Demand Forecasting					

Comments If Any (Other Marketing related tasks not captured in the above questions):

_____

_____

_____

_____

_____

_____

Measurement Scale: 5 – Most Involved to 1 Least Involved					
Level of Involvement in Financial Activities	5	4	3	2	1
28. Putting in place key financial metrics for evaluating the venture					
29. Identifying major heads of cost					
30. Establishing *lean* procedures to keep costs under control					
31. Prioritizing and allocating resources based on the identified key drivers					
32. Assessing cash-flow projections, management accounts and audited financial statements					
33. Appointing CFO from your own network of contacts/ Insisting on audit by a *top 4* auditing firm					
34. Analysing the variance between projected and actual estimates					

Comments If Any (Other Financial Involvement related tasks not captured in the above questions):

_____

_____

_____

_____

_____

Measurement Scale: 5 – Most Involved to 1 Least Involved					
Level of Involvement in Strategy	5	4	3	2	1
35. Identifying the potential follow-on sources of funding					
36. Facilitating and negotiating strategic alliances between investee firm and other co-investors					
37. Take an official position on the governing board of the investee firm					
38. Providing mentorship support and advice to the entrepreneurs in strategic areas					
39. Laying down guidelines on the approximate timing of exit					
40. Lay down clear conditions governing the Appropriate channel of exit					
41. Lay down corporate governance guidelines					

Measurement Scale: 5 – Most Involved to 1 Least Involved					
Level of Involvement in Crisis Situations	5	4	3	2	1
1. Replace the CEO if the venture is not performing well					
2. Assist when the venture gets involved in corporate governance mess ups					
3. Step in when there are issues in adherence to regulatory guidelines					
4. Intervene in the event of disputes among co-founders.					

Comments If Any (on Strategic and Crisis Period Intervention):

_____

_____

_____

_____

_____

_____

8

Venture Capital Exits
What Drives Success?

Introduction

This chapter probes in detail the final phase in the venture capital (VC) firms' lifecycle, namely exit from the funded investee companies. The term *exit* refers to the divestment of the company from the VC firms' portfolio (Schwienbacher 2009). As there are no other avenues for disposing of the VC firms' stake in the investee ventures and since the VC-backed companies do not pay out any dividends, exit is the only way for a VC firm to redeem its return on investment (Schwienbacher 2009). Therefore, the exits are as important as the entry decisions themselves. Moreover, exit is also a signal of the quality of the concerned VC firm, which is crucial for follow-up fund-raising. Thus, any study pertaining to VC investments cannot be deemed to be complete unless we have analysed the last crucial stage in the lifecycle, that is, exit from funded ventures.

Although, there are several interesting issues that can be analysed in the context of VC exits, our focus is on understanding the determinants of *successful* exits in the face of huge agency risks encountered by the investing VC firms. In this study on VC exits, the primary unit of analysis is the individual VC firm. Thus, the incidence of successful exits has also been analysed at the VC firm level.

It is a well-documented fact that VC firms exit the investee companies using one of the following five exit routes: initial public offering, or IPO (stock market listing of the funded company), strategic sale (merger and acquisition [M&A] of the funded company with a strategic partner based on mutual synergies of the participating businesses), re-financing (selling off its own stake to another upstream VC firm), re-purchase (purchase of the VC firms' stake by the firm founders), and write-offs (company files for bankruptcy). IPO is regarded as the most profitable exit route, with an internal rate of return (IRR) of 80 per cent, followed by M&A (Cochrane 2005). The rates of return are comparatively much lower for two other exit types, namely re-finance and re-purchase. Write-offs yield negative returns. In our analysis, we do not intend to look into the individual rates of return from these different exit routes. Moreover, we only have the information pertaining to the IPOs and strategic sales (namely M&A exits) for the VC firms in our sample. Since these two are the topmost profitable exit channels, we deem the exits via these routes as *successful*. We then model for the 'success rate' of the VC firms (based on the definition of being 'successful' just discussed) and probe the underlying drivers explaining the same.

Factors Governing Successful Exits

We have seen earlier that information asymmetry is the mainstay of VC-funded projects in general. This is quite pertinent even during the final stage of the VC lifecycle, that is, exit from investee companies. At this stage, there exists significant asymmetry between the sellers of the given firm's equity and its potential buyers (Cumming and MacIntosh 2003a, 2003b). In general, the sellers have greater access to information about the entrepreneurial firm in terms of its *true* quality. Moreover, they have an enhanced ability to evaluate that information owing to their lengthy involvement with the firm and also have a superior understanding about the *space* in which the investee venture operates (namely its industrial environment, number of competitors and their niche skills, and so on). Some buyers are relatively less well positioned to resolve these information asymmetries compared to others, consequently reducing the price at which the VC firm's interest is sold (Cumming and MacIntosh 2001). In general, greater information risks result in a heavier discounting of the investee firm's future cash flows. Consequently, the buyers who are less able to resolve these information asymmetries will pay less for the VC firm's interest in the entrepreneurial firm compared to the ones who are better positioned to do so. On the contrary, the VC firm as a seller would prefer to select the buyer who is best able to resolve the underlying information asymmetries since that enhances the prospective valuation of the venture (Cumming and MacIntosh 2003a, 2003b).

In this regard, the potential buyers in an IPO and M&A are known to best resolve information asymmetries (Cumming and MacIntosh 2001, 2003a, 2003b). This can be seen from the fact that the IRR on IPOs and M&As are typically the highest compared to other exit routes (Cumming and Johan 2008). This finding has been noted in the context of empirical studies pertaining to VC exits for several countries including the United States, Canada, the United Kingdom, and Continental Europe (Cumming and MacIntosh 2003a, 2003b; Cochrane 2005; Nikoskelainen and Wright 2007). Thus, in general, there exists a pecking order in terms of the profitability of exits. It has been shown empirically that the VC exits display the following rank order (in decreasing order of their profitability): IPOs, M&As, re-financing, re-purchase, and write-offs (Cumming and MacIntosh 2003a, 2003b).

There are various aspects that govern the profitability of VC exits: the profile of the market that the start-up operates in, the profile of the VC firm, and finally the profile of the start-up itself. Scale of the firm, sector/domain of operations, current and future expected size of the focus market, specific market segment (B2B or B2C), degree of innovation in the product offering (especially in the context of it being disruptive of the prevailing status quo), geography in which the start-up is located, and the purchasing capability of potential buyers are just a few of these factors. However, for the purpose of this study, we have focused only on those factors that are indicative of the level of agency risks. These include: syndication (co-investment with other peer VC firms), stage of investment and sector focus of the VC firm, social capital of VC firm (proxied by its age and experience), its ownership type (foreign or domestic), and its geographical location in India (proxy for synergies with the other elements in the entrepreneurial ecosystem).

The conceptual framework in Figure 8.1 is aimed at identifying determinants of *successful* exits based on the factors that determine the resolution of agency risks.

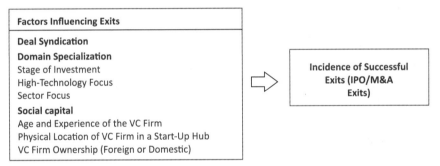

Figure 8.1 Proposed model of agency risks and VC exits
Source: Author.

Our basic premise is that *successful* exits (as indicated by IPO and M&A exits) are related to the overall magnitude of agency risks, such that VCs who are more adept at resolving agency risks are likely to experience a higher incidence of profitable exits.

Propositions

In this section, we develop propositions based on the conceptual framework just outlined here.

Syndication: Agency Risks and Incidence of Profitable Exits

VCs are often pressurized to make the quickest return in possibly the shortest time frame, which can be attributed to the intense pressure on the fund managers to raise successive VC funds. This drives a VC firm to time exit events so as to accelerate positive returns and to delay negative returns. Owing to syndication, a VC who invests in a start-up company faces a discernible risk that it may disagree at some point with the company's other VC investors concerning what constitutes a proper exit event (Bartlett 2006). Thus, syndicating with other VCs often results in enhanced agency risks. On the contrary, syndication also reduces agency risks for VC investors in a variety of ways. By co-investing with other investors, a VC investor reduces its exposure to the firm-specific agency risk it would otherwise bear if it made the entire investment on its own (Bartlett 2006). At the same time, syndication helps VC investors diversify their investment portfolios. Additionally, syndication by facilitating better selection and monitoring of deals plays a critical role in reducing the information asymmetries inherent in VC investment. Thus, there are indications that syndication can either deter or enhance the chances of a profitable exit (IPO/M&A).

Based on this, we advance proposition 1:

Hypothesis 1: Co-investing with other VC firms enhances the prospects of an IPO/M&A exit. (*Syndication with other VC firms is known to better mitigate the adverse selection and agency risks associated with the investee ventures. Their collective network is also critical from the viewpoint of enhancing the pool of prospective buyers.*)

Domain Specialization: Agency Risks and Incidence of Profitable Exits

Conventional finance theory propounds the existence of positive relationship between the risk of an investment and the return required by the investor. However, owing to diversification, the overall risk of a diversified VC portfolio will be much lower compared to the average of its individual investments (Manigart, Joos, and de Vos 1994). Thus, the commensurate return from a well-diversified portfolio is also expected to be much lower. On the contrary, the return required for a less-diversified portfolio of investments will be significantly higher (Norton and Tenenbaum 1993). Hence, according to the conventional finance theory, the greater the specialization of the VC firm portfolio (by stage, sector, technology, or focus market), the more the outcomes of the investments are likely to be correlated with each other. The resulting risk will thus be higher and will accordingly require a higher return to compensate for the same compared to a non-specialized VC firm.

Resource-based theories predict exactly the opposite. The resource-based view characterizes the firm as a collection of tangible and intangible resources (Barney 1991). The VC firms that specialize in a certain domain allow VC managers to gain a better understanding of the specifics. This deeper knowledge allows them to make better investment decisions compared to a non-specialized VC firm. Their superior understanding facilitates both assessment of inherent risks and monitoring of investee companies, consequently reducing business risks (Manigart, Joos, and de Vos 1994). This implies that a specialized VC firm will require a lower return for an investment in their area of specialization. Based on this discussion, domain specialization (by funding stage, sector, and high-technology focus) can possibly lead to a greater or a lower incidence of profitable exits, namely IPOs and M&As.

Based on this, we advance propositions 2, 3, and 4:

Hypothesis 2: VC firms focused on funding early-stage companies are less likely to witness IPO/M&A exits. (*The magnitude of information asymmetry associated with early-stage deals is usually quite high and often difficult to resolve owing to the nascency of such ventures.*)

Hypothesis 3: VC firms focused on funding ventures in high-technology domains are less likely to have IPO/M&A exits. (*Ventures in high-tech domains have huge information asymmetry due to the intangibility of assets that are often difficult to value and liquidate.*)

Hypothesis 4: VC firms focused on funding social sectors are likely to experience a lower proportion of IPO/M&A exits. (*Social-sector-focused ventures are often located in distant second-tier towns. Among other factors, geographical distance makes it difficult to resolve agency risks.*)

Social Capital: Agency Risks and Incidence of Profitable Exits

Social capital is a form of non-economic knowledge and is distinct from human capital. Social capital refers to the relational and structural resources attained by leveraging the network of social relationships (Mosey and Wright 2007). Thus, a critical source of social capital is an individual's social network. Networks provide a conduit for the exchange of information and resources that allows VC firms to gain access to opportunities and resources, save time, and tap into advice and moral support that may otherwise be unavailable. In the VC industry, where information on deals is rarely public, social capital in the form of inter-firm relationships is likely to play a crucial role in granting access to better quality deals (Sorenson and Stuart 2001).

The age of the VC firm and its investment experience in a certain geography are important proxies for its level of social capital (Lu, Tan, and Huang 2013). Prior experience in the VC industry is likely to significantly enhance contacts with the VC–entrepreneurial ecosystem, thus augmenting the level of social capital and making VCs adept at selecting and supporting their investees (Zarutskie 2010).

Additionally, the presence of a vibrant ecosystem in terms of the presence of incubators, accelerators, business angels, and incubated companies (Joshi and Satyanarayana 2014) is an important factor considered by the VC firms in determining their geographical location. Co-location with other elements of the ecosystem enhances their social capital or compensates for lack of the same. The social capital endowment thus has a vital role to play in effecting the incidence of profitable exits. Thus, VC firms with a higher level of social capital are likely to experience greater IPOs/M&As.

In general, foreign VC firms are known to possess limited social capital in the form of networks while investing in locations that are distinctly different from their place of origin (Devigne et al. 2013). This can possibly have a negative influence on their incidence of profitable exits. However, foreign VCs in India are also known to have deep pockets that enable them to wait long before they find an appropriate avenue for a profitable exit (Joshi 2015).

Based on this, we advance propositions 5, 6, and 7:

Hypothesis 5: More experienced VC firms have better prospects of IPO/M&A exits. (*VC firms that have greater investment and portfolio management experience can better resolve information asymmetry risks.*)

Hypothesis 6: VCs that are physically located in vibrant start-up entrepreneurial–VC ecosystem hubs have a higher likelihood of IPO/M&A exits. (*The formal and informal networks among VCs and entrepreneurs enable the former to better mitigate information asymmetries.*)

Hypothesis 7: Foreign VC firms have better prospects of IPO/M&A exits compared to their domestic counterparts. (*Given the fact that they invest in later-stage companies, the resultant information asymmetries are much lower in magnitude.*)

Research Design

This section describes the research design and the methods of analysis adopted for the purpose of this study. A description of the data, the sample, description of variables and their definitions, modes of data collection, and the methodology used is presented as follows.

Sample and Data

As discussed earlier, the purpose of this chapter is to understand the underlying characteristics of VC firms that result in *successful* exits. To reiterate, in our analysis, we have defined the IPO and M&A exits as 'successful' exits.

This study is based on secondary data obtained from the Venture Intelligence database (2019). These secondary data are available from the year 2005 onwards. Additional secondary data were obtained from the respective VC firm websites after validating the same with the VC firm professionals. Further details on each of these variables have been given in the next section. All analyses were performed using SPSS 21.0.0.0 and R 3.1.0 statistical softwares. In our analysis, we used the logistic regression procedure to model for the likelihood of successful exits. For the same, we report the model Chi-Square statistic, -2 log likelihood values, pseudo-R-squared values (Cox and Snell R-Square and Nagelkerke R-Square), Hosmer-Lemeshow goodness-of-fit values, percentage of correctly classified pairs, and Wald-Chi-Square values corresponding to each β coefficient.

Variables

We use the following variables in our analysis:

Logistic Regression (Dependent Variables): Our objective of modeling for successful VC exits can be attained in the following manner: To start with, we compute the proportion of successful exits (as defined by the IPO or M&A exits) for each VC firm in our sample. For this, we compute the ratio of total IPO and M&A exits to the aggregate number of deals funded (at the VC firm level). After doing so, we find that about 50 per cent of the VC firms in our sample have had no successful exits so far. Based on this, we create the variable *successful exits indicator* as a discrete variable which takes the value 1 if the VC firm has had at least one successful exit so far (that is, at least one IPO or M&A exit) and 0 otherwise (that is, if the VC firm under consideration has witnessed neither IPO nor M&A exits). This variable is used as the dependent variable in logistic regression models.

Logistic Regression (Independent Variables): The predictor variables in the regression models have been derived from both primary and secondary sources. From secondary sources, we obtain information pertaining to mainly VC firm profile related variables, namely stage focus (early versus later), high-tech focus (high-tech domains versus otherwise), ownership type (foreign versus domestic), VC firm top management team (TMT) composition (*erstwhile* founding experience versus *erstwhile* financial investing experience), corporate VC firms, VC firm age (number of years of operation in India), and so on.

Discussion of Results

It is important to take a quick look at the profile of *successful* exits of VC firms.

The distribution of successful exits has been presented in Figure 8.2. From Figure 8.2, it can be seen that about 49 per cent of the VC firms in our sample have not experienced any *successful* exits so far. About 21 per cent of them have experienced at least one IPO exit while about 51 per cent of them have witnessed at least one M&A exit. Thus, in general, the incidence of successful exits via the IPO route is much lower compared to that via the M&A route.

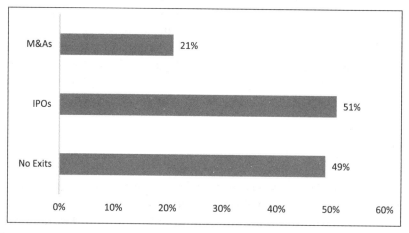

Figure 8.2   Distribution of successful exits
Source: Author.

The apparent dominance of the M&A exits over those via the IPO route could be possibly attributed to the stringent listing requirements of the major stock exchanges in India. Typically, the listing requirements of Indian stock exchanges have not been quite amenable to the listing of contemporary start-up firms. They often impose stringent listing requirements in terms of the paid-up capital invested by the promoters and are also known to have arbitrary rules, such as the proceeds from a public listing to be used to build tangible assets or invested in only plant and machinery (Planning Commission 2012). Since most technology businesses cannot necessarily meet such requirements, IPO exits have been quite rare for them.

We build the logistic regression models to analyse the incidence of IPO or M&A exits. For this analysis, we do not model for the IPO and M&A exits separately. Rather, these have been clubbed together and modelled as profitable exits. The dependent variable for the logistic regression takes the value of 1, if a VC firm has witnessed at least one IPO or M&A exit. It takes the value 0 if none of these two types of exits is encountered. Thus, active deals, write-offs, re-finance exits, and re-purchase exits have all been clubbed together in the '0' category. We admit that this is a limitation of our approach and can potentially hinder us from obtaining sharper results. However, given the fact that we did not have information pertaining to the other exits (write-offs, re-finance, and re-purchase) in our dataset, it was not possible to separate them out from the other active deals.

The results from the logistic models have been presented in Table 8.1. From the model diagnostics presented in the table, it may be stated that the model results are fairly robust. For the logistic regression model, F-statistics is significant, p-values corresponding to the Hosmer-Lemeshow goodness-of-fit statistic are high and percentage of pairs correctly classified above 65 per cent.

Among the model variables, *syndication* emerges significant. The indicator variable *absence of syndication* (zero syndicated deals) exhibits a negative relationship with the incidence of an IPO/M&A exit. This implies that syndicating with other VC firms enhances the likelihood of profitable exits. The underlying reasons for the same could be explained as follows: Syndication is known to enhance the level of due diligence associated with the initial investment in the investee firm (Cumming and Johan 2010; Joshi 2016; Joshi and Chandrasekhar 2018). By checking each other's willingness to invest in potentially promising deals, VC firms can pool correlated signals and thereby select better investments in situations of extreme uncertainty about the viability and the return potential of investment proposals (Sah and Stiglitz 1984; Hochberg, Ljungqvist, and Lu 2007). Moreover, individual VC firms tend to have investment experience that is both sector and location specific. Thus, syndication helps diffuse information across sector boundaries and expands the spatial radius of exchange, thus allowing VC firms to diversify their portfolios (Sorenson and Stuart 2001). In addition, syndication networks may help VC firms add value to the investee companies (Hochberg, Ljungqvist, and Lu 2007). Moreover, syndicates are known to make exit easier for successful start-ups as they increase the pool of contacts required to make M&A possible.

Having well-established VC firms in the syndicate is known to facilitate the IPO process as well through enhanced certification (Giot and Schwienbacher 2007). All of these indicate that syndication is one of the most potent methods to reduce the magnitude of agency risks. Thus, in general, VC syndication has been shown to be associated with higher returns (Brander, Antweiler, and Amit 2002; Nahata 2008).

Next, we find that VC firms focused on funding *early-stage deals* are less likely to have IPO/M&A exits. Typically, the degree of information asymmetry varies inversely with the firm's stage of development. Accordingly, the early-stage firms have the highest level of information asymmetry and therefore agency risks associated with them (Cumming and Johan 2010). The quality of management and the soundness of the firm's product/technology is often untested at the seed stage. Despite the VC firms' expertise in resolving information asymmetries, it seems inevitable that the valuation errors will be much greater for early-stage investments

Table 8.1 Logistic regression model output

VC Firm Profile Related Variables	Dependent Variable: Successful Exit = 1; No Successful Exit = 0 (Successful Exit = IPO or M&A) Number of Observations = 70									
	Model 1		Model 2		Model 3		Model 4		Model 5	
	B	Exp(B)	B	Exp(B)	B	Exp(B)	B	Exp(B)	B	Exp(B)
Early Stage of Funding	-1.667 (5.495**)	0.189			-0.946 (3.163*)	0.388	-0.985 (3.088*)	0.373	-1.18	0.307
High-Technology Focus	1.309 (3.379*)	3.704							-4.888	
Foreign VC Firm					0.99 (3.527*)	2.691				
Age of VC Firm			0.796 (20.152***)	2.217						
Social VC			-2.33 (3.681*)	0.097						
Zero Syndication							-2.868 (6.975***)	0.057		
Location – Bangalore									0.949 (2.934*)	2.583
Constant	-0.115 -0.085	0.891	-4.066 (16.798***)	0.017	0.019 -2	1.019	0.812 (5.467**)	2.253	0.187 -0.292	1.206

Model Statistics

Nagelkerke R Square	0.214	0.675	0.15	0.288	0.141
-2 Log Likelihood	84.711	47.626	88.62	79.929	89.172
Model Chi-Square Statistic	12.273 with 3 Degrees of Freedom. P-value = .007	49.357 with 2 Degrees of Freedom. P-value = .000	8.364 with 2 Degrees of Freedom. P-value = .015	17.054 with 2 Degrees of Freedom. P-value = .000	7.812 with 2 Degrees of Freedom. P-value = .020
Hosmer-Lemeshow Goodness of Fit Statistic	3.792 (P-value = .580)	9.957 (P-value = .191)	3.238 (P-value = .198)	0.538 (P-value = 0.764)	0.452 (P-value = 0.798)
% Correctly Classified	68.6	82.9	58.6	68.6	62.9

Source: Author.

(Nahata 2008; Cumming and Johan 2010). This kind of riskiness associated with early-stage investments adversely impacts their performance (Nahata 2008). Accordingly, the early-stage focused VC firms are found to experience a lower incidence of IPO/M&A exits.

In the Indian context, early-stage firms cannot easily take the IPO route as there are minimum listing requirements based on the scale of the business and historical record of profitability (Joshi 2015). The above regulations rule out the listing of early-stage firms on India's major bourses, namely the Bombay Stock Exchange (BSE) and the National Stock Exchange (NSE). However, the Securities and Exchange Board of India (SEBI) has also since started the small and medium enterprises (SME) trading platforms for listing stat-ups. But these are yet to gain traction and thus no start-up worth its name has listed on these new trading platforms. Hence, the lower incidence of IPO exits for early-stage start-ups in India is mainly owing to the reason stated here more than anything else. However, in the context of M&A exits for early-stage firms, the agency risks argument still holds. Naturally, their incidence of exits via the latter route is lower.

Further, we find that the VC firms having a high-tech focus have a greater likelihood of IPO/M&A exits. This finding is quite contrary to what has been observed in the case of other related empirical studies. It has been found that, in general, the incidence of success is much lower for firms in the high-tech domains. The underlying reasons for the same are manifold. As such, the high-tech firms are characterized by a greater level of information asymmetry compared to the ones in the more conventional domains, thus resulting in greater agency risks. Usually, the more sophisticated or innovative the technology, fewer will be the potential buyers who understand it well and hence value it appropriately. Accordingly, the risks associated with incorrect assessment are likely to be higher. Moreover, the technology firms are also associated with high asset-specificity. Should technology fail, such firms are likely to have very low asset salvage value (Cumming and MacIntosh 2001). Consequently, high-tech firms are known to be associated with a high failure rate.

However, other studies also point out that, historically, IPO investors have exhibited a greater appetite for technology firms (Cumming and Johan 2010) compared to the ones in non-technology domains. Besides, firms in high-tech industries have higher market-to-book ratios and greater growth options, and are therefore more likely to go public (Gompers and Lerner 2004). Alternatively, the high-tech firms are known to possess significant transaction synergies with respect to bigger firms making M&A exits more viable (Cumming and Johan 2010). In the case of India as well, the deals in the information technology (IT) and information technology enabled service (ITES) sectors have witnessed good liquidity and high returns so far (Bain Consulting 2014). Since these sectors come under the purview of high-tech domains, it can be said with a fair degree of confidence that in India as well firms focused on high-tech domains have been found to witness more profitable exits. Nevertheless, it must be pointed that in the Indian context, owing to impediments to listing technology companies on the stock markets, M&As and not IPOs have constituted a major portion of such successful exits (Bain Consulting 2014).

We also found that the *more experienced* VC firms (as explained by their age, that is, years of operation in India) have a higher likelihood of IPO/M&A exits. Greater VC firm experience has been found to be positively associated with a high likelihood of an IPO (Giot and Schwienbacher 2007). More experienced the VC firm, better is the initial deal screening process and also higher are the network effects (Black and Gilson 1998; Hege, Palomino, and Schwienbacher 2003). Such firms are also likely to add more value. For IPO exits in particular, experienced firms have better chances of building a strong IPO syndicate. Giot and Schwienbacher (2007) and Kaplan and Schoar (2005) have shown that greater the experience of the VC firm, more persistent are the returns across a sequence of funds managed by the same VC firm. Accordingly, VC reputation as measured by its age and experience in investing is naturally translated into more successful exits (Hochberg, Ljungqvist, and Lu 2007; Nahata 2008).

Lastly, we find that VCs focused on social-sector investments have a lower likelihood of successful exits. In India, typically the companies funded by such VCs are likely to be located in second-tier towns. The language and cultural barriers for city-based VCs increase with the geographical and cultural distance from the funded investee firms. Geographical proximity between the VC and the investee firm is another potential indicator of riskiness. It is a proxy for the extent of monitoring that is possible. Since monitoring is critical for reducing agency risks, shorter geographical distance is typically associated with lower risk (Sapienza 1992; Lerner 1995; Sapienza, Manigart, and Vermeir 1996; Manigart et al. 2000; Sapienza, de Clercq, and Sandberg 2005; Cumming and Dai 2010). Geographical distance impacts not only the agency risks but also those emanating from adverse selection. In the VC industry, the information on investment opportunities is not public. Rather, it is only discretely available through organizational networks. A high geographic distance reduces the effectiveness of these channels and thus affects the ability of the VC firms to access high quality investment opportunities (Cumming and Dai 2010). The risks resulting from geographical distance between the social-sector-focused VCs and the ventures funded by them are certainly likely to negatively impact the incidence of successful exits.

The variables on foreign VC firms and physical location of the firm in a vibrant entrepreneurial ecosystem did not emerge significant. To conclude, we establish propositions 1 to 5, but not propositions 6 and 7.

Chapter Summary

In this chapter, we focus on the agency risks encountered by VC firms and their impact on the incidence of profitable exits (IPO/M&As). We consider various parameters that proxy the underlying magnitude of agency risks and assess their impact on exits. The factors considered by us are syndication, specialization (namely investment-stage focus, high-tech focus), and social capital of the VC firm (age and experience of the VC firm, ownership type [foreign versus domestic]), and the geographical location of the VC firm in a prominent IT and start-up cluster.

This analysis which was performed using logistic regression technique throws up several interesting findings. To start with, we find that owing to high information asymmetry, the VC firms focused on early-stage funding witness a relatively lower proportion of successful exits. On the contrary, corporate VC firms, VC firms of foreign origin, and those focused on funding high-tech businesses witness higher success rates. Co-investing with other VC firms enhances the likelihood of success. Further, VC firms having greater experience of prior investing in India witness more successful exits.

Among other attributes, businesses with scalable business models and those warranting a limited interface with the government authorities exhibit a greater proportion of successful exits. Moreover, the investee firms in which the VC firms take on board positions have a higher incidence of successful exits.

9

Conclusion

Background

The aim of this study was two-fold. To start with, we were interested in analysing the principal components of the Indian VC ecosystem. For this, we identified the key stakeholders, gained an insight into their operations, and analysed how these elements interacted with one another to advance the interests of the Indian VC industry. The other purpose of this study was to probe in detail the decision-making processes of the individual VC firms at each critical stage of their investment lifecycle – investment in fledgling start-ups, involvement with the funded entity, and exits from the same.

At the outset, we surveyed the theoretical and empirical literature in this domain in order to familiarize ourselves with the findings from the previous studies. The literature survey covered both VC ecosystem related aspects and the aspects pertinent to the micro-strategic VC decision-making processes. The VC ecosystem comprised three core entities: limited partners (LPs, or fund providers), general partners (GPs, or fund managers), and entrepreneurs (fledgling start-ups). The LPs and GPs made up the supply side of the VC ecosystem while the entrepreneurs constituted the demand side.

To gain an insight into aspects of the strategic decision-making processes of the individual VC firms (GPs) at a micro level, we reviewed literature pertaining to the entire VC lifecycle – investment decisions, portfolio involvement intensity, and exit related strategies. We probed how the VC firms address the risks arising from information asymmetry, namely adverse selection and agency risks, at each subsequent phase during their lifecycle.

Summary of Findings and Inferences

The findings and inferences from this research study have been discussed under two broad heads: one, those pertaining to the VC ecosystem related macro aspects and, two, those related to the micro-strategic decisions during the VC lifecycle. These have been discussed in detail in the next two subsections.

VC Ecosystem in India: Findings and Inferences

To start with, we modelled for the supply side of the VC ecosystem using ordinary least squares (OLS) regression models. Two sets of models were built here: a macro-level model to identify the nature of *systematic* influences on aggregate fund-raising (that is, the funds raised in aggregate by all VC firms [that is, general partners] operating in India) and a micro-level model to understand the nature of *non-systematic* influences that determined the fund-raising potential of the individual VC firms.

Among the factors impacting the fund-raising, our findings indicated that strong macro fundamentals of the Indian economy relative to developed nations (as measured by the relative differences in the GDP growth), combined with the gradual evolution of the start-up ecosystem in India, played a critical role in attracting VC funds to India. Quite interestingly, not merely the aggregate GDP but the growth of the industrial sector (as measured by the index of industrial production, or IIP) in particular was significant in determining the aggregate quantum of fund-raising. We also found that the Indian stock markets had failed to play any significant role in influencing the flow of VC funds to India. Further, foreign funds had been the engine of growth of the VC industry. Moreover, the evolution of the Indian start-up ecosystem (as measured by the increase in the number of start-ups) had also played a key role in attracting these funds. To sum up, we could identify both 'pull' and 'push' factors for the emergence of the Indian VC industry. While *pull* factors related to the emergence of India as an attractive investment destination, the *push* factors were the ones that diverted these funds to India due to the waning of other profitable avenues for investment in the developed economies.

Among the *non-systematic* influences determining the fund-raising potential of the individual VC firms, their past performance and reputation were found to be important. Here, the number of historically funded deals, erstwhile successful exits, and the quantum of funds raised in the past were the vital factors that determined their fund-raising potential. Moreover, the government-owned VC funds in India had exhibited a substantially lower fund-raising potential. On the contrary, the foreign VC firms had displayed the highest fund-raising abilities.

After analysing the supply side of the VC ecosystem, we probed the demand side aspects (mainly comprising fledgling start-ups). The objective of this analysis was to gain an understanding about the attributes that had contributed to the emergence of start-ups. It must be understood here that VC may be regarded as *only one* of the critical enablers for the emergence of a vibrant start-up ecosystem. In fact, VC is never the pre-condition for the emergence of an entrepreneurship; rather, the explanation is the other way around (Dossani and Kenney 2002). Hence, it was important to identify the other elements of the ecosystem that had played a vital role in this regard.

At the outset, we found that the Indian start-ups were not really geographically widespread; rather, they had emerged in the form of clusters. While a similar pattern had been noticed the world over, we found it intriguing to identify the principal influences that had led to the origination of such clusters in India. Using the technique of panel data regression analysis, we studied six geographic clusters in India – Bangalore, Mumbai/Pune region, NCR, Hyderabad, Chennai, and Kolkata – from the period of 2006 to 2013. To start with, we found that the establishment of the VC firms and the emergence of start-ups had gone hand-in-hand. The other vital factor in this regard was the presence of a *critical mass* of relevant businesses and human capital specializing in high-technology domains. Our results revealed that, given the availability of the local pool of knowledge and talent, newer start-ups would naturally gravitate towards locations where such kind of *critical mass* was already present. Further, we found that not just *conventional infrastructure* (physical and educational infrastructure) but *relevant infrastructure* for high-tech businesses (tele-density and incubators) was important for the emergence of these clusters. This is not to belittle the role of physical infrastructure as such, but rather consider it as a minimum given parameter. Moreover, merely the presence of a high number of technical educational institutes did not seem to matter as much as the ones with well-established incubator set-ups. Among the *relevant infrastructure* parameters, the tele-density and broadband internet penetration were found to be the principal determinants of evolution of such high-tech start-up clusters. This was quite understandable since most of the new-economy businesses were heavily technology based wherein Internet was the prime enabler. Quite strikingly, core parameters about the economy such as the state domestic product (SDP) growth did not seem to affect the start-up growth at all. In fact, in our sample, the geographies with relatively higher SDP growth rates did not seem to possess the most vibrant start-up ecosystems at all. Again, this is not to decry the role of macro factors, but rather goes on to justify the fact that a strong macroeconomy is a minimum must-have. Interestingly, other factors such as a salubrious climate and rule of law played a critical role in the emergence of start-up clusters.

We believe that these findings obtained from analysing the supply and demand sides of the Indian VC ecosystem are quite insightful in guiding the future course of policy action. To start with, it must be understood that the growth of the VC industry based on *push* forces alone is not going to be sustainable in the long run. For ensuring a steady momentum, the *pull* forces need to be augmented significantly. Currently, the process of VC investing in India may be considered far from smooth.

Moreover, India performs poorly on global entrepreneurship rankings, ranked 74 among 79 countries (INSEAD 2012), and also on the *ease of doing business* index, ranked 146 out of 189 countries (World Bank 2015). For attracting global VC funds on a sustainable basis, this clearly needs to change. Our policymakers seem to have realized this, and recently many recommendations have been made in this regard, particularly with respect to setting up single-window clearances and industrial clusters (Planning Commission 2012). Yet it is well understood that the ground realities are drastically different from these recommended measures.

Our results also emphasize the significance of the industrial sector in the Indian economy. In our opinion, this finding is extremely important as it underlines the vitality of the industrial sector in India. As such, the industrial sector is known to have strong linkages to both agriculture and services sectors. It has been widely believed that regulatory bottlenecks to investments in areas related to the industrial sector (such as infrastructure, energy, and telecom) can prove to be a major deterrent to the emergence of India among the topmost destinations for VC investments in the future (Bain Consulting 2011, 2012, 2013). Moreover, of late, India's gross domestic product (GDP) growth has been primarily led by the service sector with IIP showing a negative or only a marginally positive growth. This is a cause for concern as it is likely to have severe consequences not only for VC fund-raising but for the overall economy in general (Bala Subrahmanya 2014).

Further, over-reliance of the Indian VC industry on foreign sources of funds is of major concern. While the importance of foreign funds is certainly well recognized, it is also vital that the VC resources need to be supplemented from the domestic sources as well. Currently, Indian pension funds are completely prohibited from investing in VC, while mutual funds are allowed to invest only 5 per cent of their corpus in the same (Dossani and Kenney 2002; Bain Consulting 2012). Incidentally, pension funds and mutual funds are the largest investors in the VC industry worldwide. Consequently, the fund-raising potential of the domestic funds is much lower compared to their counterparts overseas. The policy certainly needs to be amended in this regard.

Further, we found that the stock markets in India have so far not played a significant role in attracting VC funds. However, the world over, initial public offering (IPO) has been the most profitable exit route (Cochrane 2005). Hence, a lot needs to be done in the context of facilitating exits via the stock market route. In particular, over-the-counter exchanges need to be established in India. Small and medium enterprises (SME) exchanges were set up in 2012 (Bala Subrahmanya 2014). However, these are yet to gain traction. Moreover, Indian companies are not allowed to list on the overseas markets prior to domestic listing (Planning Commission 2012). Since domestic listing is already a matter of concern, it is proving to be a major bottleneck for the VC-funded companies. Of late, the

Securities and Exchange Board of India (SEBI) is planning to moot a series of measures in this regard. The most notable among these is the proposition to set up the Alternate Capital Raising Platform with the sole aim of providing an opportunity for the technology start-ups, new-age businesses, and e-commerce companies to raise capital (SEBI 2015).

Deal flow, particularly of viable early-stage deals, is another critical factor influencing both the supply and demand sides of the VC ecosystem. Currently, the flow of viable early-stage deals is not keeping pace with the inflow of VC funds (Bain Consulting 2012, 2013, 2014). This leads to over-valuation of the existing deals on the one hand and redirection of existing funds into growth-stage investments on the other. The setting up of more incubators and accelerators within the existing university and corporate set-ups for start-ups is an important step in this regard. While these trends are certainly quite encouraging, it must be said that merely setting up more incubators will not address the problem of lower volume of early-stage deals. To achieve the same, these incubators need to be 'functional'. While there are several incubators operating in India today, very few of them are really worthwhile in the true sense (Maital et al. 2008). In fact, most incubators within the academic set-ups focus on providing merely physical infrastructure (Maital et al. 2008). Unless they can provide other critical services such as mentoring, access to financial institutions, investors and other vital networks or key stakeholders, they will not be very effective in augmenting the flow of viable deals in the start-up ecosystem (Ministry of MSME 2013). Another point worth noting in this regard is that, so far, India has focused on the incubation of ideas alone. Technology business incubators (TBIs), which provide a technical entrepreneur access to the required machines and equipment to test and manufacture products on a pilot scale, are almost missing from the Indian scene. Such TBIs have played a major role in the start-up ecosystem in Israel and the US (Ministry of MSMEs 2013). Recognizing the importance of the same in the amendments to the Companies Act of 2013, investments in technology incubators (of academic institutions approved by the central government) were recognized under the corporate social responsibility (CSR) initiatives.

The most striking takeaway from the demand side analysis is that ensuring a high economic growth or building physical infrastructure alone is not going to be sufficient for the evolution of the VC–entrepreneurial ecosystem. For this, a futuristic vision and conscious efforts are warranted on the part of the policymakers. Moreover, owing to the network effects, the geographic locations of new start-ups are expected to naturally gravitate towards cities with a pre-established critical mass of high-technology businesses. Disrupting this chain with the intention of creating completely new start-up hubs is going to be clearly difficult. Thus, it appears that, rather than directing resources on creating completely new start-up clusters, it might be more realistic (at least during the short-term) for policymakers to focus on specific factors pertaining to the start-up ecosystem that are directly under their control. In case new hubs need to be created at all, then the vision could be to create science parks on the lines of Zhongguancun Science Park in China, which houses multiple stakeholders of this ecosystem – universities, research labs, multinationals, start-ups, VC firms, incubators, and accelerators (Anjum 2014). Creating a new start-up hub with just a one or two stakeholders is likely to meet with little success.

Another cause of concern regarding private sector VC firms is that they have migrated 'upstream' and now focus on funding the scale-up stages of new businesses rather than providing seed capital to the nascent ones (Grail Research 2012). Thus, in the true sense, they do not address the financial needs of these early-stage ventures. This void needs to be met by the public financial institutions by providing initial seed capital or establishing a fund-of-funds on the lines of the Yozma scheme in Israel (Ministry of MSME 2013).

While understanding the macro dimensions of the VC industry are certainly important, it is also vital to study the micro decision-making aspects therein. These will enable us to better understand the specific challenges that the individual VC firms encounter during their distinct lifecycle phases, given the magnitude of the information asymmetry risks in the Indian milieu. An insight into the same is necessary to facilitate appropriate mechanisms to reduce their intensity. The following section discusses our findings in the context of strategic decisions of the VC firms in further detail.

Strategic Decisions of VC Firms: Findings and Inferences

We systematically evaluated each phase of the VC lifecycle (investment decisions, portfolio involvement, and exits) with the aim of probing their strategic decision-making processes. Our primary conjecture here was that these practices were not likely to be uniform across all VC firms; rather, these were expected to vary substantially based on their intrinsic attributes. Accordingly, we studied three distinct VC firm segments: (*a*) based on their stage of funding (early versus growth/late stage), (*b*) their ownership type (domestic versus foreign), and (*c*) their top management team (TMT) background (erstwhile entrepreneurs versus prior finance professionals). These specific segments were chosen since these match well with the underlying themes of the contemporary VC literature.

VC Investment Decisions

To start with, we evaluated the investment decisions of the VC firms. The primary aim here was to understand the nature of signals used by the VC firms in the absence of concrete performance data on the investee venture.

The first VC segment to be analysed was based on the funding stage focus: early-stage versus growth/late-stage VC firms. To start with, we found that (contrary to what had been suggested in the signalling literature), the early-stage VC firms in India did not specialize much by sector or domain; rather they did so only by funding size. The lack of depth in the market for VC deals was pointed out as one of the principal reasons for their limited specialization. This feature further contributed to a low intensity of syndication. Unlike their western counterparts, the early-stage VC firms in India shied away from co-investments. In fact, in India, co-investing was primarily used as a tool for the augmentation of the deal size rather than for gaining investing insights into diverse domains.

The findings in the context of the signals pertinent to the Indian milieu were even more thought-provoking. Although the family-owned businesses had a potential to constitute a viable source of deal flow, the VC firms consciously stayed away from funding the same. The primary reason for this was that such projects entailed significant agency risks and severe corporate governance issues. Moreover, the VC firms preferred to do business with first-generation entrepreneurs, who were often found to be more receptive to feedback from the VC professionals. Furthermore, the VC firms preferred to invest in businesses with limited government interface. Given their past experiences with tackling corruption and other bureaucratic hurdles in terms of securing permits and licenses, it was not particularly surprising that VC firms preferred to stay away from such businesses. Among the potential sources of deal origination, the VC firms placed a higher weightage on deals coming from industry accelerators, but a lower value on those initiated by investment bankers and academic incubators. In fact, it was widely believed that the best deals were those that had been sourced by them proactively.

The next category of VC segment to be analysed was based on their ownership type: domestic versus foreign VC firms. For an overwhelming proportion of foreign VC firms, the lack of market depth (in terms of deals eligible for VC funding) was a major area of concern. Consequently, it had a profound impact on determining the nature of signals used by them to overcome the adverse selection risks at the time of investment. Thus, the foreign VC firms did not specialize much either by domain or funding size. They also did not insist on geographical proximity of the investee firms (to their own locations) that would have potentially facilitated better monitoring (consequently gaining better control over the ensuing agency risks). Similarly, although they did acknowledge the difficulty in dealing with the government sector in India, they did not stay away from businesses with a high government interface. In their opinion, imposing these extra constraints would further add to the lack of market depth. Rather, they had devised innovative means to circumvent these issues. Accordingly, to make up for the lack of specialization, they had established sector-specialized investment desks; to overcome the lack of geographical proximity, they had set up multiple offices across prominent VC hubs; and to overcome the friction associated in their dealings with government bodies, they had hired the services of specialized consultants. However, it needs to be pointed out here that such strategies were feasible for the foreign VC firms owing to their higher scale of operations resulting from their relatively larger fund sizes. While domestic firms would have liked to deploy similar mechanisms, their smaller set-ups prevented them from doing so.

The next prominent feature in the context of foreign VC firms was that they lacked deep local networks in India. It was widely agreed that although other formal conduits of local networks existed (for example, community based entrepreneurial clubs, such as TiE; other events, such as VC and entrepreneurial meet-ups; and media, such as Yourstory.com, to name a few), the ones that really mattered from the point of view of getting access to superior quality *niche* deals were in reality based on informal channels. Foreign VC firms in India were clearly not plugged into such networks. Consequently, they needed to take cognizance of this fact while making their investment decisions. Accordingly, foreign VC firms preferred to invest in informationally more transparent ventures, in which historical information on the company performance was directly available, consequently reducing their reliance on tacit signals. Thus, they minimized their exposure to early-stage ventures since these were thought to be informationally more opaque and at the same time would warrant a greater involvement in day-to-day operations (in the form of access to vendors, consultants, accountants, and so on) which clearly the foreign VC firms could not provide. Further, they syndicated extensively with other VC firms who were likely to be better engaged in the local ecosystem. Additionally, towards achieving this end, they placed a lot of credibility on the past start-up experience of a prospective founder. Such a founder, with prior entrepreneurial experience in India, would compensate for their limited networks. To this effect, the foreign VC firms were also known to place a greater value on the flow of deals coming in from formal origination channels such as investment bankers. Once again, their limited local networks greatly reduced their ability to source deals either proactively or via informal routes.

The last category of the VC segment was based on the VC firms' TMT composition: erstwhile entrepreneurs versus prior finance professionals. The VC firm TMTs with prior founding experience were generally found to be investing in businesses belonging to *niche* technology domains at the very early phases of their lifecycle. Having worked in similar domains, the VC professionals with prior founding experience were believed to be more adept at identifying such opportunities. They practised syndication only to a moderate extent, enough to augment the funding size but not high enough to result in a loss of control over the company. Given their own backgrounds, they greatly valued past start-up experience in the prospective founders. Moreover, just like the VC firms with an early-stage focus, the VC firms in this segment stayed away from family-owned businesses and businesses warranting a high government interface owing to the ensuing magnitude of agency risks.

These findings have important managerial implications as well as ramifications for determining the future course of policy. To start with, most VC firms find the low depth of the market for viable deals in India a major concern. The world over, professionals in the VC industry (and accordingly the VC firms) are known to be highly specialized in their niche domains of expertise. This attribute enables them to quickly identify nascent opportunities and take these companies to the next level by funding them at appropriate phases. The lack of depth in the Indian VC market potentially prohibits the establishment of similar highly specialized VC firms. For foreign firms in particular, this situation is even more difficult. For them, the lack of market depth, coupled with their large fund sizes, could potentially result in the classic situation of too much money chasing too few deals. Consequently, it leads to a significant over-valuation of the available deals. It has been widely believed in the VC community that currently e-commerce is a highly over-valued sector in India owing to the same reason (VC Circle 2014). Over-valuation results in high entry-level prices and consequently translates into a lower rate of return.

In the long run, it is extremely important that the market for deals becomes broad based. One such channel of viable deals is likely to be the university spin-offs (that is, commercialized version of academic research). Yet the number of such spin-offs in India is relatively fewer in number. In fact, the VC firms are not quite keen to fund such ventures since the academic set-ups demand too much equity in the venture. Moreover, there is always a disagreement regarding which party would own the intellectual property (IP) (Planning Commission 2012). These factors naturally reduce VC interest in investing in such ventures. The only way out of this situation is by enlightening the scientists and engineers about the commercial aspects of their IP. Currently, while the academic faculty and researchers are relatively well versed with the technical aspects of their innovations, their knowledge about the specific business aspects is fairly limited (Planning Commission 2012). This needs to change if the universities want to create more start-ups. Business courses, particularly the ones focusing on entrepreneurship, should be given their due importance in the technology universities. Currently, not many Indian universities have the resources to provide such courses (Planning Commission 2012).

Moreover, we found that although foreign capital is available in abundance in the VC industry, only a limited portion of it is getting allocated to the early investment stages. This finding further emphasizes the urgent need for introducing more channels of early-stage deals in the system – in the form of academic incubators, industry accelerators, and angel investing networks. Such formal channels are also important for the foreign VC firms, since they have only limited access to informal channels of deal-sourcing.

Our finding regarding the VC firms shunning businesses with a high government interface is particularly revealing. A lot needs to change here, particularly in the context of facilitating the procedures. Specific problem areas need to be identified and processes for improving customer experience established. Currently, starting a company takes on an average just three to six days in Singapore and the UK but more than twenty-five days in India (World Bank 2015). Although many measures have been proposed in this regard, such as single-window clearance, the ground reality is quite different.

Family-owned businesses have historically been quite important in India. Even today they contribute about two-thirds of the GDP and more than half of the private sector employment (PwC 2012–13). Yet a large proportion of VC firms stayed away from funding these businesses. Although on the negative side these might be potentially associated with significant agency risks, on the positive side it needs to be accepted that these businesses understand the local market conditions quite well. Besides, such entrepreneurs are likely to be better networked informally. They are also likely to be more adept at the informal procedures of navigating the domestic markets. This can be a valuable experience, particularly for foreign VC firms that do not have deep networks in India. Instead of building their networks from the scratch, they can simply piggyback on such networks. Keeping this in mind, instead of shunning the family-owned businesses right away, it might be worthwhile to assess if the agency risks could be resolved by putting in place appropriate contracting frameworks. In fact, of late, a few VC-funded businesses have started to resolve these issues by taking on the role of market aggregators, that is, firms that bring many small businesses on board (a marketplace model in e-commerce). A large section of these businesses is likely to be family owned. In such a business model, the VC firm need not deal with each business separately; rather, it needs to deal with just the corporate entity that serves as a *marketplace* for many such businesses.

Another noteworthy finding is that a large proportion of foreign VC funds in India still fall outside the purview of SEBI. This is of particular concern, as in reality SEBI registration confers several advantages on the registered VC funds compared to the other channels. In particular, registration with SEBI grants them tax pass-through status; it frees them the pricing guidelines of the Reserve Bank of India (RBI) (that is, guidelines stipulating the minimum price a foreigner must pay when purchasing the shares of an Indian company from a resident and the maximum price a person can receive when he sells to a non-resident) and grants exemption from lock-in period for IPO exits (on pre-issue capital). Yet many foreign VC funds bypass the SEBI route of investment in India. The reasons for doing so need to be probed thoroughly since a major section of funds falling outside the ambit of the central regulatory authority is not exactly a desirable outcome. Based on our literature survey, we could identify one such possible cause – the limited partners need to pay a capital gains tax on their investments in fledgling start-ups if they invest via the SEBI route but not if they enter via the Mauritius registry route. This results in a lack of parity which needs to be removed (Agarwal 2011).

We found that the VC firm TMTs with prior founding experience invest in truly niche businesses that have the potential to become disruptive innovations. Such innovations are associated with significant spill-over effects, which makes these qualify as public goods. As in the case of other public goods, since the costs are private but the benefits are public, private VC firms if left to themselves are less likely to fund such innovations. Consequently, such ventures will invariably be deprived of sufficient funds. Thus, there is a great role for public institutions to step in here and augment the sources of funds for VC firms focused on funding ventures in such niche domains.

VC Involvement with Portfolio Companies

After analysing the investment decisions of VC firms, we probed their strategies of involvement in their portfolio companies. We understand that the VC firms not only address the financial requirements of the investee firms, but get involved in other operational and strategic aspects as well. Our primary conjecture in this regard was that the overall intensity (and the specific aspects) of involvement was directly proportional to the magnitude of agency risks. Higher information asymmetry invariably warranted a higher level of participation. To start with, we computed the indices of VC involvement both at an aggregate level and at activity-specific levels (namely HR, business operations, marketing, strategy, finance, and crisis management). These indices were then used to cluster the VC firms (using the *K-means* algorithm) into three distinct groups based on their intensity of involvement: *most intensely involved*, *moderately involved*, and *least intensely involved* VC firms.

The analysis of the VC firm clusters, based on their involvement intensity, revealed several interesting findings. In general, the VC firms with an early-stage and high-technology focus and the ones with TMTs possessing erstwhile founding experience were found to be most intensely involved in their portfolio companies. The high intensity of involvement therein was clearly warranted by the relatively higher levels of information asymmetry that the investee ventures entailed. In addition, the corporate VC firms were also found to be most intensely involved in their investee ventures. Here, it was the strategic significance of such start-ups to the parent organization which probably resulted in a higher level of involvement from the investors.

On the contrary, VC firms with a late-stage focus in their investments and the ones focused on investing in conventional domains were found to be least involved in their funded companies – again owing to the relatively low levels of agency risks. Further, the foreign VC firms were found to be *least involved* as well, possibly owing to their limited local networks. The *moderately involved* VC firms were found to possess the highest concentration of domestic VC firms. Quite interestingly, the VC firms belonging to the *moderately involved* cluster ranked the highest in terms of the success rate of the funded ventures (that is, they had witnessed the highest number of successful exits historically). We found this result particularly remarkable, since it revealed how the magnitude of VC participation and the resultant value-add ultimately translated to venture success. Moreover, this finding revealed that the relationship between the intensity of VC intervention and the performance of the investee firm was not linear. Over intervention by the VC firm could potentially result in VC–entrepreneur conflicts, while too little intervention could lead to negligible value-add. Thus, an intervention in moderation, and that too only in specific chosen aspects of the venture, was found to constitute a significant value-addition from the point of view of the investee firm translating into successful exits.

These findings have important managerial implications for both entrepreneurs and VC firms. In the surveys of VC and private equity (PE) professionals conducted by Bain Consulting (2012, 2013, 2014), one common observation has emerged year over year. The entrepreneurs in India are not very receptive to intervention from the VC firms. They still view the VC firms as just fund providers and not necessarily as value-adding partners. This perception needs to change significantly. The entrepreneurs must recognize that, in general, VC funding possesses several added advantages over the conventional sources of finance. Moreover, the domestic and the foreign VC firms have their own areas of expertise that could be used to the advantage of these investee partners. While the domestic VC firms have deep local networks, the foreign VC firms possess the financial muscle and international exposure required for scaling up the businesses and granting them access to overseas markets (Devigne et al. 2013). Both these aspects are important to the entrepreneurs over distinct stages in their start-up lifecycle. Given the fact that a majority of the new-economy entrepreneurs are first-generation founders, they are likely to have limited *relevant* social networks. Hence, rather than creating such networks from the scratch, piggybacking on the pre-existing social capital of their funding partners could certainly provide a viable alternative.

Similarly, for the VC firms, it is important to ensure that they do not over-step their brief. There exists a thin dividing line between *intervention* and *interference*.

While the former results in value-add, the latter can be a nuisance. Entrepreneurs despise over-interference from their investors. In this regard, our results reveal that VC firms who intervene only to a *moderate* extent are likely to witness greater venture successes. Thus, it is important that the VC firms respect the entrepreneurial sentiments and do not over-step into the entrepreneur's territory resulting in conflicts that might ultimately impact venture success. Since successful exits are critical for both the parties, it is important that a healthy distance is maintained between the two.

Exits from Investee Companies

Finally, after analysing the investment and portfolio involvement strategies of the VC firms, we investigated their exits from the funded investee companies. Among the various (theoretical and empirical) issues related to VC exits, we chose to analyse the determinants of *successful* exits. To start with, we categorized the exits via the IPO and M&A routes as *successful*. We then built a set of models to gain insight into factors that drive *successful* exits. Our primary conjecture in this regard was that ventures in which buyers were better able to resolve the underlying information asymmetries resulted in higher valuations and consequently more *successful* exits.

This analysis threw up several interesting findings. To start with, we found that syndication (co-investment) significantly enhanced the chances of successful exits. In our opinion, the pooling of the financial and non-financial resources (during co-investment) and its resultant synergies contributed to reducing the magnitude of both adverse selection and agency risks. Further, it was found that the early-stage investments were associated with lower successes – primarily attributed to the information asymmetries therein that could not be resolved appropriately. On the contrary, although the investments in high-technology domains entailed higher information asymmetry, they still witnessed a higher success rate. This is more or less in tandem with what has been observed the world over wherein the IPO investors and larger corporates (resulting in M&A deals) have shown a greater appetite for technology firms. Further, we found that the ventures funded by corporate VC firms exhibited a higher success rate. This finding is intuitive, since, to start with, the corporate VC firms had funded ventures in arenas that were of strategic interest to them. They actively participated in these ventures by adding substantial value at each life stage, and later acquired these companies at an appropriate time. We also found that, in general, VC firms with a greater investing experience were likely to witness higher successes. Finally, we found that the local VC–entrepreneurial ecosystem had a significant role to play in enhancing the chances of successful exits. Accordingly, VC firms based in Bangalore (with one of the strongest ecosystems) had experienced substantially higher proportion of successful exits.

Our findings have important managerial implications and policy conclusions. For VC managers in particular, it is important to note that co-investing with other VC firms enhanced their prospects of successful exits. Moreover, our results had also revealed that early-stage firms had witnessed lower success rates for the ventures funded by them. However, in our earlier findings (in the context of VC investment decisions) we had also found that the early-stage-focused VC firms in India syndicated only to a limited extent. From this, it is important for us to join the dots and draw appropriate inferences. While these findings do not imply that co-investment alone would result in successful exits, the strong positive relationship between co-investment and venture success needs to be certainly acknowledged.

From the point of view of policy in particular, we have two important propositions. To start with, it must be acknowledged that the VC–entrepreneurial ecosystem has played an important role in ensuring successful exits. Thus, in order to ensure the long-run viability of the VC industry, it is important to focus on enhancing the quality and depth of the existing ecosystem. Further, our finding about the low success rate of the early-stage-focused firms partially explains why a majority of the VC firms in India are hesitant about investing in the early-stage companies. As observed by the Planning Commission (2012), India substantially lags behind the West in the provision of early-stage funding compared to its global peers. If private VC firms are not willing to come forward to meet this demand–supply gap in early-stage funding, the public sector needs to step in here. In fact, this has been the underlying pattern the world over, wherein the government has played a key role in the provision of early-stage risk capital.

Policy Implications

Based on the discussion so far, it is quite apparent that the Indian VC industry has come a long way. While the ongoing progress is certainly commendable, a substantial magnitude of regulatory and other ecosystem-enabling measures are warranted in order to take it to the next level. For this, the principal impediments to its sustainable growth need to be identified and addressed at the earliest. The findings from our study provide vital pointers to the same. Based on these, we would like to propose certain policy recommendations.

In general, the policy measures concerning the Indian VC industry may be divided into two distinct categories: first, those pertaining to the regulatory aspects of VC and, second, those related to the VC ecosystem and a conducive investing environment in general. These have been discussed at length in the following section.

Policy Measures relating to the Regulatory Aspects of the VC Industry

1. Till date, the Indian VC industry has been heavily reliant on the overseas funding sources. It has been estimated that more than 80 per cent of the VC funds invested in India have been raised abroad (Ernst and Young 2013). We believe that in the interest of the sustainability of the Indian VC industry, it is important to augment the sources of domestic funds as well. Currently, Indian pension funds, insurance companies, and provident funds are not allowed to invest in the VC sector at all (Planning Commission 2012). On the contrary, the same have been the major contributors to the VC investing pool the world over (Dossani and Kenney 2002). Thus, it is imperative that the Indian government takes cognizance of the same and liberalizes the domestic funding sources to some extent.

2. Moreover, a majority of these foreign sources of funds do not come under the purview of SEBI, the central regulatory authority of the VC industry in India. In fact, most of the foreign VC funds bypass the SEBI registration route and invest in India via the foreign direct investment route (with approvals from Foreign Investment Promotion Board and RBI) and the Mauritius registry route (by registering their business entity in Mauritius and routing their funds via that country to take advantage of the Double Taxation Avoidance Treaty). Although SEBI registration confers several advantages (in the form of tax pass-through, share pricing, and lock-in period of IPO), the foreign funds still see distinct advantages in circumventing this route (Agarwal 2011). It is important to probe the underlying reasons for this, since, given the growing influence of foreign funds, it is not desirable that a majority of them fall outside the ambit of the regulatory authority.

3. Although VC is available in India in abundance, a relatively smaller proportion of it is being currently directed into early-stage ventures. In this regard, our findings indicated that foreign VC firms in particular hedge their risks by investing only a minimal proportion of their funds in early-stage ventures and rather are eager to participate in the scale-up phases of the businesses where the underlying risks are expected to be much lower. Particularly, if these ventures belong to *niche* technology domains working on the creation of disruptive innovations, the availability of early-stage capital is even lower owing to the *public goods* characteristics possessed by the concerned product/service. We envisage a major role for government VC funds in this regard. There are two possible ways in which the public funding sources can support the VC industry. Either the government VC funds can invest in the early-stage ventures directly or it can create a fund-of-funds in which

the government agencies provide seed capital to multiple funds which can then enhance their fund size by finding appropriate investing partners either domestically or overseas. This can lead to a significant multiplier effect as noted from the Yozma scheme in Israel (Dossani and Kenney 2002).

4. As of 2014, long-term equity investments in listed companies are exempt from capital gains tax. However, this provision does not apply to unlisted companies. Since the early-stage VC investments are primarily in unlisted companies, this is a major cause for concern (Planning Commission 2012). It needs to change and unlisted companies need to be brought on par with the listed ones for taxation purposes. In fact, one of the reasons for the foreign VC firms investing in India via the Mauritius registry route is that it exempts them from paying such capital gains taxes (the SEBI-registered VC firms need to pay the same).

5. The most significant policy change is warranted in the arena of facilitating exits of VC-funded companies via the IPO route. Based on the current SEBI regulations, it is extremely difficult for technology-focused companies to get listed on the Indian stock exchanges (Bombay Stock Exchange and National Stock Exchange). Often these businesses are *top-line* based and not *bottom-line* based and hence do not have a historical track record of profitability – which is one of the pre-conditions for listing (SEBI 2015). Neither are these ventures allowed to list directly in overseas markets (Planning Commission 2012) prior to listing on Indian bourses. This needs to change and India needs to create an over-the-counter exchange on the lines of NASDAQ that facilitates the listing of these new-economy companies. In this regard, the government has established SME exchanges in 2012 (Bala Subrahmanya 2014), yet these exchanges suffer from a lack of liquidity owing to low business volumes. Only recently has SEBI proposed the setting-up of alternative capital raising platforms in this regard.

6. Above all, the government needs to expedite the process of closing down businesses. This is still a tedious and a time-consuming process in India (Planning Commission 2012). Businesses belonging to emerging domains, in general, witness a high failure rate. High procedural delays in closing down failed businesses may reduce the incentive to start newer ones.

Policy Measures relating to the Ecosystem Aspects of the VC Industry

1. The primary concern expressed by our sample VC firms related to the lack of depth of the market for viable deals in India. Moreover, this apprehension was not regarding the overall number of deals per se, but rather the availability

of specific types of deals amenable to VC funding. Thus, we feel that there strongly exists a need to augment the deal flow. Academic incubators and industry accelerators can play an important role in enhancing the same. However, among these sources as well, the VC firms preferred deals coming from industry accelerators. The deal flow coming out of the majority of the academic incubators was not really considered 'viable'. The primary reason for this is probably that very few of the 180 or so academic incubators in India can be considered operational in the true sense (Maital et al. 2008). The objective of establishing more incubators is not merely to provide physical infrastructure alone, but to grant these incubated companies access to social networks, that is, angel investors, VC firms, vendors, and initial customers. Given the current disconnect between the academic establishments and the industry, they often find it difficult to provide such access (Planning Commission 2012). Thus, it is important to identify ways to fill this gap. One of the ways to ensure this is to hire outside industry talent to head these incubators rather than having in-house academicians at the helm of affairs. These professionals could be erstwhile entrepreneurs, finance professionals, or even professionals with prior VC investing experience.

2. University spin-offs may constitute another potential source of deal flow. In this regard, the VC firms in our sample revealed that they find collaborating with Indian universities particularly difficult. Usually, the university staff handling the IP commercialization are not quite well versed with its commercial aspects. Consequently, they demand a high equity share which the VC firms are often reluctant to part with. For overcoming this impediment, it is important that an office of technology licensing be set up in all major universities – at least the ones in which there exists a scope of commercializing the existing research. Moreover, it might also be useful if entrepreneurship related courses are introduced in the regular curriculum to coach the technical personnel on the commercial aspects of their research. However, it is important that such courses are vocational in nature and emphasize on the practical aspects of establishing businesses and not merely the theoretical aspects therein.

3. In addition to the incubator/accelerator set-ups discussed here, it is important that TBIs are created. The current incubator/accelerators provide mechanisms for incubation of ideas alone. However, it is also important to have machines and equipment to create the working prototypes. Such TBIs have played an important role in the growth of start-ups in Israel (Ministry of MSME 2013).

4. Our study also revealed that development of start-ups progresses in the form of geographic clusters. Here, the presence of a *critical mass* (of existing companies and human capital) was an important attribute in influencing

the growth of more start-ups. Given that new start-ups will primarily develop in places where a *critical mass* already exists, at least in the short run it is important for the policymakers to focus on enhancing the depth of the ecosystem in the already existing geographies rather than focusing on developing completely new clusters. The long-run strategy would, however, be to artificially create an ecosystem on the lines of science parks in China, where multiple stakeholders are housed at a single location.

5. Moreover, it is necessary to significantly enhance the relative ease of doing business in India. The VC firms in our sample unanimously expressed their concern about the frictions involved in dealing with government authorities in India. The specific areas of their concern need to be understood and speedy steps implemented thereupon. The existing process of setting up a business involves an interaction with multiple authorities (Planning Commission 2012). This can lead to multiple opportunities for friction and delay. With this in mind, the government has established a 'single-window clearance' system. However, our interactions with the VC firms revealed that even this process is far from satisfactory.

6. India's growth story so far has mainly been service-sector driven. However, our findings revealed that the growth of the industrial sector has played an important role in attracting VC funds to India. This implies that the industrial sector cannot be ignored for too long. Thus, any impediments related to VC investments in areas coming under the purview of the industrial sector need to be rapidly removed.

Limitations and Scope for Future Work

This research study has some limitations.

1. The unit of analysis for this study is the individual VC firm. However, using funded deals as the analysis unit is likely to add further granularity to this investigation. Interesting dynamics about each deal can be unravelled if we sequentially study the multiple funding stages for each deal. In particular, it might enable us to answer questions pertaining to the manner in which the latent signals relied on or the involvement strategies deployed by the same VC firm differed across sectors or domains (for example, biotechnology versus cloud computing). The VC firms in our sample clearly indicated that the nature of signals used by them would vary based on the geographical location of the prospective entrepreneurs – in particular, the signals used in evaluating the deals coming from north India are likely to be distinctly different from the ones used while evaluating the same from south India. These differences may not be attributed to the differences in their respective

domains/sectors alone but rather to the prevalent institutional frameworks in these diverse geographies. Questions like these could have been probed into in further detail if we had access to deal-level data. In terms of strategies pertaining to VC exits in particular, there exist several other interesting issues. The most interesting among these are the timing and type of exit, degree of exit (complete/partial), and the pecking order of exits. Again, these could not be probed into in the current study owing to the lack of deal-level data.

2. Although we have studied the decision-making processes of the VC firms (pertaining to their investments, portfolio involvement, and exits), we have been unable to link the same to their financial performance at large. In fact, the proportion of successful exits has been used as a suitable proxy for financial performance. This was mainly because of the formidable challenge involved in getting the financial performance data.

3. In this study, we have probed three principal segments of VC firms: early versus growth/late-stage focus, foreign versus domestic VC firms, and VC firm TMTs with prior founding versus financial investing experience. However, there is great scope to expand the coverage to include more segments such as corporate VC firms or those focused on investing in social sectors in particular. Given the thrust provided by SEBI to impact investing, under its Alternative Investment Guidelines in 2013, it can be an important area for future study.

References

Acs, Z. J. and C. Armington. 2006. 'New Firm Survival and Human Capital.' In *Entrepreneurship and Dynamics in the Knowledge Economy*, edited by Charlie Karlsson, Börje Johansson, and Roger R. Stough, 141–64. New York: Routledge.

Agarwal, A. 2011. 'Investing in an Indian Startup: FDI or VC: Which Is the Better Route?' 17 January. Available at http://headstart.in/2011/01/17/investing-in-an-indian-startup-fdi-or-vc-which-is-the-better-route/ (accessed on 1 July 2015).

Amit, R., L. Glosten, and E. Muller. 1990. 'Entrepreneurial Ability, Venture Investments, and Risk Sharing.' *Management Science* 36(10): 1233–46.

———. 1993. 'Challenges to Theory Development in Entrepreneurship Research.' *Journal of Management Studies* 30(5): 815–34.

Amit, R., J. Brander, and C. Zott. 1998. 'Why Do Venture Capital Firms Exist? Theory and Canadian Evidence.' *Journal of Business Venturing* 13(6): 441–66.

Anjum, Z. 2014. *Startup Capitals: Discovering the Global Hotspots of Innovation*. Gurgaon: Random House India.

Annamalai, T. R. 2010. 'Value Creation from Venture Capital and Private Equity Investments: The Indian Context.' *Journal of Private Equity* 13(2): 67–75.

Arthurs, J. D. and L. W. Busenitz. 2006. 'Dynamic Capabilities and Venture Performance: The Effects of Venture Capitalists.' *Journal of Business Venturing* 21(2): 195–215.

Aubert, J. E. and J. L. Reiffers, eds. 2004. *Knowledge Economies in the Middle East and North Africa: Toward new Development Strategies*. Washington, D.C.: The World Bank.

Bain Consulting. 2011. 'India Private Equity Report.' Available at http://www.bain.com/publications/articles/bain-india-private-equity-report-2011.aspx (accessed on 1 July 2015).

———. 2012. 'India Private Equity Report.' Available at http://www.bain.com/publications/articles/india-private-equity-report-2012.aspx (accessed on 1 July 2015).

———. 2013. 'India Private Equity Report.' Available at http://www.bain.com/publications/articles/india-private-equity-report-2013.aspx (accessed on 1 July 2015).

———. 2014. 'India Private Equity Report.' Available at http://www.bain.com/Images/BAIN_REPORT_India_Private_Equity_Report_2014.pdf (accessed on 1 July 2015).

Bahrami, H. and S. Evans. 1995. 'Flexible Re-cycling and High-Technology Entrepreneurship.' *California Management Review* 37(3): 62–89.

Bala Subrahmanya, M. H. 2014. 'Why Does India's Economic Growth Process Falter?' *Economic and Political Weekly* 49(8): 18–20.

———. 2015. 'New Generation Start-ups in India: What Lessons Can We Learn from the Past.' *Economic and Political Weekly* 50(12): 56–63.

———. 2017a. 'How Did Bangalore Emerge as a Global Hub of Tech Start-ups in India? Entrepreneurial Ecosystem – Evolution, Structure and Role.' *Journal of Developmental Entrepreneurship* 22(01). https://doi.org/10.1142/S1084946717500017.

———. 2017b. 'Comparing the Entrepreneurial Ecosystems for Technology Startups in Bangalore and Hyderabad, India.' *Technology Innovation Management Review* 7(7).

Barney, J. 1991. 'Firm Resources and Sustained Competitive Advantage.' *Journal of Management* 17(1): 99–120.

Barney, J., M. Wright, and D. J. Ketchen. 2001. 'The Resource-based View of the Firm: Ten Years after 1991.' *Journal of Management* 27(6): 625–41.

Baron, J. N., M. T. Hannan, and M. D. Burton. 2001. 'Labor Pains: Change in Organizational Models and Employee Turnover in Young, High-tech Firms.' *American Journal of Sociology* 106(4): 960–1012.

Barry, C. B. 1994. 'New Directions in Research on Venture Capital Finance.' *Financial Management* 23(3): 3–15.

Barry, C. B., C. J. Muscarella, J. W. Peavy, and M. R. Vetsuypens. 1990. 'The Role of Venture Capital in the Creation of Public Companies: Evidence from the Going-public Process.' *Journal of Financial Economics* 27(2): 447–71.

Bartlett, R. P. III. 2006. 'Venture Capital, Agency Costs, and the False Dichotomy of the Corporation.' *UCLA Law Review* 54: 37–115.

Basant, R. and P. Chandra. 2007. 'Role of Educational and R&D Institutions in City Clusters: An Exploratory Study of Bangalore and Pune Regions in India.' *World Development* 35(6): 1037–55.

Baum, J. A. 1989. 'Liabilities of Newness, Adolescence, and Obsolescence: Exploring Age Dependence in the Dissolution of Organizational Relationships and Organizations.' *Proceedings of the Administrative Science Association of Canada* 10(5): 1–10.

Beaudry, C. and P. Swann. 2001. 'Growth in Industrial Clusters: A Bird's Eye View of the United Kingdom.' Stanford Institute for Economic Policy Research Discussion Paper, 1–38.

Bergemann, D. and U. Hege. 1998. 'Venture Capital Financing, Moral Hazard, and Learning.' *Journal of Banking and Finance* 22(6): 703–35.

Black, B. S. and R. J. Gilson. 1998. 'Venture Capital and the Structure of Capital Markets: Banks versus Stock Markets.' *Journal of Financial Economics* 47(3): 243–77.

——— (1999). 'Does Venture Capital Require an Active Stock Market?' *Journal of Applied Corporate Finance* 11(4): 36–48.

Bonini, S. and S. Alkan, 2006. 'The Macro and Political Determinants of Venture Capital Investments around the World'. Università Commerciale 'Luigi Bocconi', Milan, Italy.

Brander, J., W. Antweiler, and R. Amit. 2002. 'Venture Capital Syndication: Improved Venture Selection vs. Value Added Hypothesis.' *Journal of Economics and Management Strategy* 11(3): 423–52.

Brenner, R. 2003. *Merchants and Revolution: Commercial Change, Political Conflict, and London's Overseas Traders, 1550–1653.* London: Verso.

Busenitz, L. W., J. O. Fiet, and D. D. Moesel. 2004. 'Reconsidering the Venture Capitalists' "Value Added" Proposition: An Interorganizational Learning Perspective.' *Journal of Business Venturing* 19(6): 787–807.

Busse, M. and C. Hefeker. 2007. 'Political Risk, Institutions and Foreign Direct Investment. *European Journal of Political Economy* 23(2): 397–415.

Bygrave, W. D. and J. A. Timmons. 1992. *Venture Capital at the Crossroads.* Boston, MA: Harvard Business Press.

Campbell, T. S. 1979. 'Optimal Investment Financing Decisions and the Value of Confidentiality'. *Journal of Financial and Quantitative Analysis* 14(05): 913–24.

Casper, S. 2007. *Creating Silicon Valley in Europe: Public Policy towards New Technology Industries.* Oxford, New York: Oxford University Press.

Castilla, E. J., H. Hwang, E. Granovetter, and M. Granovetter. 2000. 'Social Networks in Silicon Valley'. In *The Silicon Valley Edge: A Habitat for Innovation and Entrepreneurship,* edited by C. M. Lee, W. F. Miller, M. G. Hancock and H. S. Rowen, 218–47. Stanford, CA: Stanford University Press.

Certo, S. T. 2003. 'Influencing Initial Public Offering Investors with Prestige: Signaling with Board Structures.' *Academy of Management Review* 28(3): 432–46.

Chacko, E. 2007. 'From Brain Drain to Brain Gain: Reverse Migration to Bangalore and Hyderabad, India's Globalizing High Tech Cities.' *GeoJournal* 68(2–3): 131–40.

Chan, Y. S. 1983. 'On the Positive Role of Financial Intermediation in Allocation of Venture Capital in a Market with Imperfect Information'. *The Journal of Finance* 38(5): 1543–68.

Cherif, M. and K. Gazdar. 2011. 'What Drives Venture Capital Investments in Europe? New Results from a Panel Data Analysis.' *Journal of Applied Business and Economics* 12(3): 122–39.

Chesbrough, H. W. 2002. 'Making Sense of Corporate Venture Capital'. *Harvard Business Review.* 80(3): 90–9.

Cochrane, J. H. 2005. 'The Risk and Return of Venture Capital.' *Journal of Financial Economics* 75(1): 3–52.

Cumming, D. J. 2006. 'The Determinants of Venture Capital Portfolio Size: Empirical Evidence.' *Journal of Business* 79(3): 1083–126.

———— 2010. 'Venture Capital Exits'. *Venture Capital,* 389.

Cumming, D., G. Fleming, and A. Schwienbache. 2005. 'Liquidity Risk and Venture Capital Finance'. *Financial Management* 34(4): 77–105.

Cumming, D. J. and J. G. MacIntosh. 2001. 'Venture Capital Investment Duration in Canada and the United States.' *Journal of Multinational Financial Management* 11(4): 445–63.

————. 2003a. 'A Cross-Country Comparison of Full and Partial Venture Capital Exits.' *Journal of Banking and Finance* 27(3): 511–48.

————. 2003b. 'Venture-Capital Exits in Canada and the United States.' *University of Toronto Law Journal* 53(2): 101–99.

Cumming, D. and N. Dai. 2010. 'Local Bias in Venture Capital Investments.' *Journal of Empirical Finance* 17(3): 362–80.

Cumming, D. and S. Johan. 2010. 'Venture Capital Investment Duration.' *Journal of Small Business Management* 48(2): 228–57.

Dai, N., H. Jo, and S. Kassicieh. 2012. 'Cross-border Venture Capital Investments in Asia: Selection and Exit Performance.' *Journal of Business Venturing* 27(6): 666–84.

Dahl, M. S., C. Ø. R. Pedersen, and B. Dalujm. 2005. 'Entrepreneurial Founder Effects in the Growth of Regional Clusters: How Early Success Is a Key Determinant.' DRUID, Working paper no. 05-18.

Dahl, M. S. and O. Sorenson. 2009. 'The Embedded Entrepreneur.' *European Management Review* 6(3): 172–81.

Dauterive, J. and W. Fok. 2004. 'Venture Capital for China: Opportunities and Challenges.' *Managerial Finance* 30(2): 3–15.

Davidsson, P. and B. Honig. 2003. 'The Role of Social and Human Capital among Nascent Entrepreneurs.' *Journal of Business Venturing* 18(3): 301–31.

Deakins, D., E. O'Neill, and P. Mileham. 2000. 'The Role and Influence of External Directors in Small, Entrepreneurial Companies: Some Evidence on VC and Non-VC Appointed External Directors.' *Venture Capital: An International Journal of Entrepreneurial Finance* 2(2): 111–27.

Delloitte. 2012. *Global Trends in Venture Capital: Outlook for the Future.* Available at http://www.bvca.co.uk/Portals/0/library/Files/News/2010/2010_0051_gtvc_slidepack.pdf (accessed on 1 July 2015).

Desai, N. 2002. 'Venture Capital at Crossroads.' Report by Private Equity Practice Group. Available at www.nishithdesai.com (accessed on 1 July 2015).

——— 2012. Special Report. *Indian Law Journal* 4(2).

Devigne, D., T. Vanacker, S. Manigart, and I. Paeleman. 2013. 'The Role of Domestic and Cross-border Venture Capital Investors in the Growth of Portfolio Companies.' *Small Business Economics* 40(3): 553–73.

Dimov, D. P. and D. A. Shepherd. 2005. 'Human Capital Theory and Venture Capital Firms: Exploring "Home Runs" and "Strike Outs".' *Journal of Business Venturing* 20(1): 1–21.

Dixon, R. 1991. 'Venture Capitalists and the Appraisal of Investments.' *Omega* 19(5): 333–44.

Dossani, R. and M. Kenney. 2002. 'Creating an Environment for Venture Capital in India.' *World Development* 30(2): 227–53.

Dougherty, D. and C. Hardy. 1996. 'Sustained Product Innovation in Large, Mature Organizations: Overcoming Innovation-to-Organization Problems.' *Academy of Management Journal* 39(5): 1120–153.

Drucker, P. 2014. *Innovation and entrepreneurship.* New York: Routledge.

Dumais, G., G. Ellison, and E. L. Glaeser. 2002. 'Geographic Concentration as a Dynamic Process'. *Review of economics and Statistics* 84(2): 193–204.

Elango, B., V. H. Fried, R. D. Hisrich, and A. Polonchek. 1995. 'How Venture Capital Firms Differ.' *Journal of Business Venturing* 10(2): 157–79.

Ernst and Young. 2014. 'Adapting and Evolving: Global VC Insights'. Available at http://www.ey.com (accessed on 1 July 2015).

Evans, P. B. 1992. 'Indian Informatics in the 1980s: The Changing Character of State Involvement.' *World Development* 20(1): 1–18.

Fama, E. F. and M. C. Jensen. 1983a. 'Separation of Ownership and Control.' *Journal of Law and Economics* 26(2): 301–25.

———. 1983b. 'Agency Problems and Residual Claims.' *Journal of Law and Economics* 26(2): 327–49.

Fiedler, M. O. and T. Hellmann. 2001. 'Against All Odds: The Late but Rapid Development of the German Venture Capital Industry.' *The Journal of Private Equity* 4(4): 31–45.

Fried, V. H. and R. D. Hisrich. 1994. 'Toward a Model of Venture Capital Investment Decision Making.' *Financial Management* 28–37.

Franke, N., M. Gruber, D. Harhoff, and J. Henkel. 2006. 'What You Are Is What You Like: Similarity Biases in Venture Capitalists' Evaluations of Start-up Teams.' *Journal of Business Venturing* 21(6): 802–26.

———. 2008. 'Venture Capitalists' Evaluations of Start-up Teams: Trade-offs, Knock-out Criteria, and the Impact of VC Experience.' *Entrepreneurship Theory and Practice* 32(3): 459–83.

Gereffi, G. 2005. 'The Global Economy: Organization, Governance, and Development.' *The Handbook of Economic Sociology* 2: 160–82.

Giot, P. and A. Schwienbacher. 2007. 'IPOs, Trade Sales and Liquidations: Modelling Venture Capital Exits Using Survival Analysis.' *Journal of Banking and Finance* 31(3): 679–702.

Gompers, P. A. 1995. 'Optimal Investment, Monitoring, and the Staging of Venture Capital.' *The Journal of Finance* 50(5): 1461–89.

———. 1996. 'Grandstanding in the Venture Capital Industry.' *Journal of Financial Economics* 42(1): 133–56.

———. 2000. 'The Determinants of Corporate Venture Capital Success: Organizational Structure, Incentives, and Complementarities.' In *Concentrated Corporate Ownership*, edited by Randall K. Morck, 17–54. Chicago: University of Chicago Press.

———. 2004. *The Venture Capital Cycle.* Cambridge, MA: MIT Press.

Gompers, P. A. and J. Lerner. 1999. 'What Drives Venture Capital Fundraising?' No. w6906, National Bureau of Economic Research.

Gorman, M. and W. A. Sahlman. 1989. 'What Do Venture Capitalists Do?' *Journal of Business Venturing* 4(4): 231–48.

Goslin, L. N. and B. Barge. 1986. 'Entrepreneurial Qualities Considered in Venture Capital Support.' *Frontiers of Entrepreneurship Research* 22(7): 102–28.

Grail Research. 2012. 'The Indian Startup Ecosystem: On the Cusp?' Available at http://www.grailresearch.com/pdf/ContenPodsPdf/Indian-Start-up-Ecosystem Summary.pdf.

Gujarati, D. N. 2012. *Basic Econometrics.* Noida: Tata McGraw-Hill Education.

Gupta, A. K. and J. H. Sapienza. 1992. 'Determinants of Venture Capital Firms' Preferences Regarding the Industry Diversity and Geographic Scope of their Investments.' *Journal of Business Venturing* 7(5): 347–62.

Hair, J. F. Jr., R. E. Anderson, R. L. Tatham, and W. C. Black. 2015. *Multivariate Data Analysis*, 7th edition. New York: Macmillan.

Hall, J. and C. W. Hofer. 1993. 'Venture Capitalists' Decision Criteria in New Venture Evaluation.' *Journal of Business Venturing* 8(1): 25–42.

Hege, U., F. Palomino, and A. Schwienbacher. 2003. 'Determinants of Venture Capital Performance: Europe and the United States'. Working paper, HEC School of Management.

Hellman, T. and M. Puri. 2000. 'The Interaction between Product Market and Financing Strategy: The Role of Venture Capital.' *Review of Financial Studies* 13(4): 959–84.

———. 2002. 'Venture Capital and the Professionalization of Start-up Firms: Empirical Evidence.' *The Journal of Finance* 57(1): 169–97.

Hennig, C. and T. F. Liao. 2013. 'How to Find an Appropriate Clustering for Mixed-type Variables with Application to Socio-Economic Stratification.' *Journal of the Royal Statistical Society: Series C (Applied Statistics)* 62(3): 309–69.

Henisz, W. J. and A. Delios. 2001. 'Uncertainty, Imitation, and Plant Location: Japanese Multinational Corporations, 1990–1996.' *Administrative Science Quarterly* 46(3): 443–75.

Henisz, W. J. and O. E. Williamson. 1999. 'Comparative Economic Organization: Within and Between Countries.' *Business and Politics* 1(3): 261–78.

Hopp, C. and F. Rieder. 2011. 'What Drives Venture Capital Syndication?' *Applied Economics* 43(23): 3089–102.

Hochberg, Y. V., A. Ljungqvist, and Y. Lu. 2007. 'Whom You Know Matters: Venture Capital Networks and Investment Performance.' *The Journal of Finance* 62(1): 251–301.

Hsu, D. H. 2007. 'Experienced Entrepreneurial Founders, Organizational Capital, and Venture Capital Funding.' *Research Policy* 36(5): 722–41.

India Venture Capital Association. 2011. 'Venture Capital and Private Equity in India.' Available at http://indiavca.org/pdf/IVCABainIndiaPrivateEquityReport2011.pdf (accessed on 1 July 2015).

INSEAD. 2012. 'Global Entrepreneurship Rankings.' Available at http://www.insead.edu/library/rankings/countryrankings.cfm (accessed on 12 February 2020).

Ivanov, V. I. and F. Xie. 2010. 'Do Corporate Venture Capitalists Add Value to Start-up Firms? Evidence from IPOs and Acquisitions of VC-Backed Companies.' *Financial Management* 39(1): 129–52.

Jaffe, A. B., M. Trajtenberg, and R. Henderson. 1992. 'Geographic Localization of Knowledge Spillovers as Evidenced by Patent Citations.' Working paper no. w3993, National Bureau of Economic Research.

Jain, B. A. 2001. 'Predictors of Performance of Venture Capitalist-Backed Organizations.' *Journal of Business Research* 52(3): 223–33.

Jones, Tim. 2017. 'Innovation Hot Spots: Countries vs. Cities'. Available at https://innovationmanagement.se/2017/03/27/innovation-hot-spots-countries-vs-cities/ (accessed on 11 February 2020).

Joshi, K. 2015. 'Economics of Venture Capital Industry in India: Macro Ecosystem and Micro Parameters.' Unpublished thesis at the Department of Management Studies, Indian Institute of Science, Bangalore, India.

———. 2016. 'Venture Capital Industry in India: Determinants of Successful Exits from Funded Companies.' *Consulting Ahead: The Journal of the Consultancy Development Centre* 10(2): 61–73.

————. 2018a. 'Emergence and Persistence of High-Tech Start-up Clusters: An Empirical Study of Six Indian Clusters.' *International Journal of Global Business and Competitiveness* 13(1): 15–34.

————. 2018b. 'Managing the Risks from High-Tech Investments in India: Differential Strategies of Foreign and Domestic Venture Capital Firms.' *Journal of Global Entrepreneurship Research* 8(1): 21.

————. 2018c. 'Managing Information Asymmetry Risks Using Deal Syndication and Domain Specialization: An Indian Context.' *Asian Journal of Innovation and Policy* 7(1): 150–77

————. 2019. 'Specialization and Syndication as Investment Strategies for Venture Capital Firms in India'. *International Journal for Entrepreneurial Venturing*. 11(6): 541–67.

Joshi, K. and D. Chandrashekar. 2018. 'IPO/M&A Exits by Venture Capital in India: Do Agency Risks Matter?' *Asian Journal of Innovation and Policy* 7(3).

Joshi, K. A. and M. H. Bala Subrahmanya. 2014. 'What Drives Venture Capital Fundraising in India: An Empirical Analysis of Systematic and Non-Systematic Factors.' In 2014 IEEE International Conference on Management of Innovation and Technology, 35–40, Singapore, 23–25 September 2014.

Joshi, K. and M. H. Bala Subrahmanya. 2015. 'Information Asymmetry Risks in Venture Capital Investments: Strategies of Transnational Venture Capital Firms in India.' *South Asian Journal of Management* 22(2): 36.

————. 2019. 'Information Asymmetry Risks in Venture Capital (VC) Investments: Strategies of Transnational VC Firms in India.' In *Transnational Entrepreneurship: Issues of SME Internalization in the Indian Context*, edited by M. J. Manimala, K. P. Wasdani, and A. Vijaygopal, 117–42. Singapore: Springer.

Joshi, K. and K. Satyanarayana. 2014. 'What Ecosystem Factors Impact the Growth of High-Tech Start-ups in India?' *Asian Journal of Innovation and Policy* 3(2): 216–44.

Jeng, L. A. and P. C. Wells. 2000. The Determinants of Venture Capital Funding: Evidence across Countries.' *Journal of Corporate Finance* 6(3): 241–89.

Johnson, R. A. and D. W. Wichern. 2008. *Applied Multivariate Statistical Analysis*, Vol. 4. Englewood Cliffs, NJ: Prentice Hall.

Joseph, K. J. 2009. 'Sectoral Innovation System in Developing Countries: The Case of ICT in India.' In *Handbook of Innovation Systems and Developing Countries: Building Domestic Capabilities in a Global Setting*, edited by B. Lundvall, K. J. Joseph, C. Chaminade, and J. Vang, 183–213. Cheltenham and Northampton: Edward Elgar.

Kaplan, S. N. and A. Schoar. 2005. 'Private Equity Performance: Returns, Persistence, and Capital Flows.' *The Journal of Finance* 60(4): 1791–823.

Kaplan, S. N. and P. Stromberg. 2000. 'Financial Contracting Theory Meets the Real World: An Empirical Analysis of Venture Capital Contracts.' Working paper no. w7660, National Bureau of Economic Research.

Kennedy, P. 1992. *A Guide to Econometrics*. Oxford: Blackwell.

Kenney, M. and U. von Burg. 1999. 'Technology, Entrepreneurship and Path Dependence: Industrial Clustering in Silicon Valley and Route 128.' *Industrial and Corporate Change* 8(1): 67–103.

Kenney, M., D. Breznitz, and M. Murphree. 2013. 'Coming Back Home after the Sun Rises: Returnee Entrepreneurs and Growth of High-Tech Industries.' *Research Policy* 42(2): 391–407.

Ketels, C. 2003. 'The Development of the Cluster Concept: Present Experiences and Further Developments.' Prepared for NRW Conference on Clusters, Duisberg, Germany, 5 December.

Khan, A. M. 1987. 'Assessing Venture Capital Investments with Noncompensatory Behavioral Decision Models.' *Journal of Business Venturing* 2(3): 193–205.

Langford, C. H., J. R. Wood and T. Ross. 2002. 'Origins and Structure of the Calgary Wireless Cluster.' Working Paper, University of Calgary.

Lerner, J. 1994. 'The Syndication of Venture Capital Investments.' *Financial Management* 23(3): 16–27.

———. 1995. 'Venture Capitalists and the Oversight of Private Firms.' *The Journal of Finance* 50(1): 301–18.

Lu, H., Y. Tan, and H. Huang. 2013. 'Why Do Venture Capital Firms Exist: An Institution-Based Rent-Seeking Perspective and Chinese Evidence.' *Asia Pacific Journal of Management* 30(3): 921–36.

MacIntoch, J. G. 1994. *Legal and Institutional Barriers to Financing Innovative Enterprise in Canada.* Monograph prepared for the Government and Competitiveness Project, School of Policy Studies Queen's University Discussion Paper (No. 94-10).

MacMillan, I. C., D. M. Kulow, and R. Khoylian. 1989. 'Venture Capitalists' Involvement in Their Investments: Extent and Performance'. *Journal of Business Venturing* 4(1): 27–47.

MacMillan, I. C., R. Siegel, and P. S. Narasimha. 1986. 'Criteria Used by Venture Capitalists to Evaluate New Venture Proposals. *Journal of Business Venturing* 1(1): 119–28.

Madhavan, R. and A. Iriyama. 2009. 'Understanding Global Flows of Venture Capital: Human Networks as the "Carrier Wave" of Globalization.' *Journal of International Business Studies* 40(8): 1241–59.

Maital, S., S. Ravid, D. V. R. Sesadri, and A. Dummanis. 2008. 'Toward a Grounded Theory of Effective Business Incubation.' *Vikalapa: The Journal for Decision Makers* 33(4): 1–13.

Manigart, S., A. Lockett, M. Meuleman, M. Wright, H. Landström, H. Bruining, P. Desbrières, and U. Hommel. 2006. 'Venture Capitalists' Decision to Syndicate.' *Entrepreneurship Theory and Practice* 30(2): 131–53.

Manigart, S., P. Joos, and D. de Vos. 1994. 'The Performance of Publicly Traded European Venture Capital Companies.' *The Journal of Entrepreneurial Finance* 3(2): 111–25.

Manigart, S., D. Waele, M. Wright, K. Robbie, P. Desbrieres, H. Sapienza, and A. Beekman. 2000. 'Venture Capitalists, Investment Appraisal and Accounting Information: A Comparative Study of the USA, UK, France, Belgium and Holland.' *European Financial Management* 6(3): 389–403.

———. (2002). 'The Determinants of the Required Returns in Venture Capital Investments: A Five-Country Study.' *Journal of Business Venturing* 17(4): 291–312.

Manning, S. 2008. 'Customizing Clusters: On the Role of Western Multinational Corporations in the Formation of Science and Engineering Clusters in Emerging Economies.' *Economic Development Quarterly* 22(4): 316–23.

Marquardt, D. W. 1970. 'Generalized Inverses, Ridge Regression, Biased Linear Estimation, and Nonlinear Estimation.' *Technometrics* 12(3): 591–612.

Mosey, S. and M. Wright. 2007. 'From Human Capital to Social Capital: A Longitudinal Study of Technology-Based Academic Entrepreneurs.' *Entrepreneurship Theory and Practice* 31(6): 909–35.

Mason, C. 2007. 'Venture Capital: A Geographical Perspective.' In *Handbook of Research on Venture Capital*, edited by H. Landström, 86–112. Cheltenham: Edward Elgar.

———. 2008. 'Entrepreneurial Dynamics and the Origin and Growth of High-Tech Clusters.' In *Handbook of Research on Innovation and Clusters: Cases and Policies*, edited by C. Karlsson, 33–55. Cheltenham and Northampton: Edward Elgar.

Megginson, W. L. and K. A. Weiss. 1991. 'Venture Capitalist Certification in Initial Public Offerings.' *The Journal of Finance* 46(3): 879–903.

Megginson, W. L. 2004. 'Toward a Global Model of Venture Capital?' *Journal of Applied Corporate Finance* 16(1): 89–107.

Ministry of Micro, Small and Medium Enterprises (Ministry of MSME). 2013. *Recommendations of the Inter-Ministerial Committee for Accelerating Manufacturing in Micro, Small and Medium Enterprises Sector.* New Delhi, India. Available at http://msme.gov.in/.

Nahata, R. 2008. 'Venture Capital Reputation and Investment Performance.' *Journal of Financial Economics* 90(2): 127–51.

Neck, H. M., G. D. Meyer, B. Cohen, and A. C. Corbett. 2004. 'An Entrepreneurial System View of New Venture Creation.' *Journal of Small Business Management* 42: 190–208.

Neter, J., W. Wasserman, and M. H. Kutner. 1989. *Applied Linear Regression Models.* Homewood, IL: Irwin.

Newbert, S. L. 2007. 'Empirical Research on the Resource-Based View of the Firm: An Assessment and Suggestions for Future Research.' *Strategic Management Journal* 28(2): 121–46.

Nikoskelainen, E. and M. Wright. 2007. 'The Impact of Corporate Governance Mechanisms on Value Increase in Leveraged Buyouts.' *Journal of Corporate Finance* 13(4): 511–37.

Nitani, M. and A. Riding. 2013. 'Fund Size and the Syndication of Venture Capital Investments.' *Venture Capital* 15(1): 53–75.

Norton, E. and B. H. Tenenbaum. 1993. 'Specialization versus Diversification as a Venture Capital Investment Strategy.' *Journal of Business Venturing* 8(5): 431–42.

Patibandla, M. and B. Petersen. 2002. 'Role of Transnational Corporations in the Evolution of a High-Tech Industry: The Case of India's Software Industry.' *World Development* 30(9): 1561–77.

Patzelt, H., D. zu Knyphausen-Aufseß, and H. T. Fischer. 2009. 'Upper Echelons and Portfolio Strategies of Venture Capital Firms.' *Journal of Business Venturing* 24(6): 558–72.

Pe'er, A. and I. Vertinsky. 2006. 'Determinants of Survival of De Novo Entrants in Clusters and Dispersal.' Available at SSRN 940477.

Peteraf, M. A. 1993. 'The Cornerstones of Competitive Advantage: A Resource-Based View.' *Strategic Management Journal* 14(3): 179–91.

Petty, J. S. and M. Gruber. 2011. '"In Pursuit of the Real Deal": A Longitudinal Study of VC Decision Making.' *Journal of Business Venturing* 26(2): 172–88.

Planning Commission. 2005. *Report of the Committee on Technology Innovation and Venture Capital.* New Delhi: Planning Commission, Government of India. Available at http://planningcommission.gov.in/reports/genrep/rep_vcr.pdf (accessed on 1 July 2015).

———. 2012. 'Creating a Vibrant Entrepreneurial Ecosystem for India'. In *Report of the Committee on Angel Investment and Early Stage Venture Capital.* New Delhi: Planning Commission, Government of India. Available at http://planningcommission.nic.in/reports/genrep/rep_eco2708.pdf (accessed on 1 July 2015).

Poterba, J. M. 1989. 'Venture Capital and Capital Gains Taxation.' Working paper no. w2832, National Bureau of Economic Research.

Preqin. 2014. *Global Private Equity Report.* Available at https://www.preqin.com/item/2014-preqin-global-private-equity-report/1/8194 (accessed on 1 July 2015).

Pruthi, S., M. Wright, and A. Lockett. 2003. 'Do Foreign and Domestic Venture Capital Firms Differ in Their Monitoring of Investees?' *Asia Pacific Journal of Management* 20(2): 175–204.

Pullen, J. P. 2013. 'Emerging Tech: 9 International Start-Up Hubs to Watch'. *Entrepreneur*, 7 May, *Business Daily*, USA.

PwC. 2012–13. 'Family Firm: The India Perspective'. Available at https://www.pwc.in/assets/pdfs/family-business-survey/family-business-survey-2013.pdf (accessed on 1 July 2015).

Qian, H., Z. J. Acs, and R. R. Stough. 2012. 'Regional Systems of Entrepreneurship: The Nexus of Human Capital, Knowledge and New Firm Formation.' *Journal of Economic Geography* 13(4): 559–87.

Rah, J., K. Jung, and J. Lee. 1994. 'Validation of the Venture Evaluation Model in Korea.' *Journal of Business Venturing* 9(6): 509–24.

Rastogi S. 2008. 'Venture Capital and Private Equity: An Impetus to Indian Economy.' *Halsbury's Laws.* Available at http://www.indiajuris.com/halsbury.pdf (accessed on 1 July 2015).

Ray, D. M. 1991. 'Venture Capital and Entrepreneurial Development in Singapore.' *International Small Business Journal* 10(1): 11–26.

Ray, D. M. and D. V. Turpin. 1993. 'Venture Capital in Japan.' *International Small Business Journal* 11(4): 39–56.

Rea, R. H. 1989. 'Factors Affecting Success and Failure of Seed Capital/Start-up Negotiations.' *Journal of Business Venturing* 4(2): 149–58.

Reynolds, P. D. 1993. 'The Role of Entrepreneurship in Economic Systems: Developed Market and Post-Socialist Economies.' Paper presented at the Second Freiberg Symposium on Economics, Freiberg, Germany, 9–11 September.

Reynolds, P. D. and D. J. Storey. 1993. *Local and Regional Characteristics Affecting Small Business Formation: A Cross-national Comparison.* Paris: OECD.

Robinson, R. B. 1988. Emerging Strategies in the Venture Capital Industry. *Journal of Business Venturing* 2(1): 53–77.

Romano, C. A., G. A. Tanewski, and K. X. Smyrnios. 2001. 'Capital Structure Decision Making: A Model for Family Business.' *Journal of Business Venturing* 16(3): 285–310.

Rosenthal, S. S. and W. C. Strange. 2005. 'The Geography of Entrepreneurship in the New York Metropolitan Area.' *Federal Reserve Bank of New York Economic Policy Review* 11(2): 29–54.

Rosenstein, J., A. V. Bruno, W. D. Bygrave, and N. T. Taylor. 1993. 'The CEO, Venture Capitalists, and the Board.' *Journal of Business Venturing* 8(2): 99–113.

Ruhnka, J. C. and J. E. Young. 1987. 'A Venture Capital Model of the Development Process for New Ventures.' *Journal of Business Venturing* 2(2): 167–84.

———. 1991. 'Some Hypotheses about Risk in Venture Capital Investing.' *Journal of Business Venturing* 6(2): 115–33.

Sahlman, W. A. 1988. 'Aspects of Financial Contracting in Venture Capital.' *Journal of Applied Corporate Finance.* 1(2): 23–36.

———. 1990. 'The Structure and Governance of Venture-capital Organizations.' *Journal of Financial Economics* 27(2): 473–521.

Sah, R. K. and J. E. Stiglitz. 1984). 'The Architecture of Economic Systems: Hierarchies and Polyarchies.' Working paper no. w1334, National Bureau of Economic Research.

Sapienza, H. J. 1992. 'When Do Venture Capitalists Add Value?' *Journal of Business Venturing* 7(1): 9–27.

Sapienza, H. J., S. Manigart, and W. Vermeir. 1996. 'Venture Capitalist Governance and Value Added in Four Countries.' *Journal of Business Venturing* 11(6): 439–69.

Sapienza, H. J., D. de Clercq, and W. R. Sandberg. 2005. 'Antecedents of International and Domestic Learning Effort.' *Journal of Business Venturing* 20(4): 437–57.

Saxenian, A. 1994. *Regional Networks: Industrial Adaptation in Silicon Valley and Route 128.* Cambridge, MA: Harvard University Press.

———. 2002. 'Transnational Communities and the Evolution of Global Production Networks: The Cases of Taiwan, China and India.' *Industry and Innovation* 9(3): 183–202.

———. 2006. 'International Mobility of Engineers and the Rise of Entrepreneurship in the Periphery.' No. 2006/142. Research Paper, UNU-WIDER, United Nations University.

Schertler, A. and T. Tykvová. 2011. 'Venture Capital and Internationalization.' *International Business Review* 20(4): 423–39.

Scholtens, B. 1999. 'Analytical Issues in External Financing Alternatives for SBEs.' *Small Business Economics* 12(2): 137–48.

Schwienbacher, A. 2005. 'An Empirical Analysis of Venture Capital Exits in Europe and the United States.' In EFA 2002 Berlin Meetings Discussion Paper.

———. 2009. 'Venture Capital Exits.' In *Venture Capital Exits: Companion to Venture Capital,* edited by D. Cumming. Wiley/Blackwell.

SEBI. 2015. 'Alternate Capital Raising Platform.' Available at http://www.sebi.gov.in/cms/sebi_data/attachdocs/1427713523817.pdf (accessed on 1 July 2015).

———. 2019. *Handbook of Statistics on Indian Securities Market, 2018.* Mumbai: SEBI.

SeedTable. 2013. 'Analyzing Startups Worldwide'. Available at http://www.seedtable.com/ (accessed on 1 July 2015).

Senor, D. and S. Singer. 2011. *Start-up Nation: The Story of Israel's Economic Miracle.* New York: Random House Digital.

Shane, S. and T. Stuart. 2002. 'Organizational Endowments and the Performance of University Start-ups.' *Management Science* 48(1): 154–70.

Shepherd, D. A. 1999. 'Venture Capitalists' Assessment of New Venture Survival.' *Management Science* 45(5): 621–32.

Sorenson, O. and T. E. Stuart. 2001. 'Syndication Networks and the Spatial Distribution of Venture Capital Investments.' *American Journal of Sociology* 106(6): 1546–88.

Stinchcombe, A. L. 1965. 'Social Structure and Organizations.' In *Handbook of Organizations*, edited by G. James, 142–93. Chicago: Rand McNally.

Stough, R. R., K. E. Haynes, and H.S. Campbell. 1998. 'Small Business Entrepreneurship in the High Technology Services Sector: An Assessment for the Edge Cities of the US National Capital Region.' *Small Business Economics* 10(1): 61–74.

Sudhira, H. S., T. V. Ramachandra, and M. H. Bala Subrahmanya. 2007. 'Bangalore.' *Cities* 24(5): 379–90.

Timmons, J. A. and S. Spinelli. 1994. *New Venture Creation: Entrepreneurship for the 21st Century*, Vol. 4. Burr Ridge, IL: Irwin.

Transparency International. 2014. 'Public Sector Corruption Index.' Available at http://www.transparency.org/cpi2014/regional_analysis (accessed1 July 2015).

Tyebjee, T. T. and A. V. Bruno. 1984. 'A Model of Venture Capitalist Investment Activity.' *Management Science* 30(9): 1051–66.

Van Pottelsberghe de la Potterie, B., and A. Romain. 2004. 'The Economic Impact of Venture Capital.' No. 2004, 18. Discussion Paper Series 1/Volkswirtschaftliches Forschungszentrum der Deutschen Bundesbank.

VC Circle. 2014. 'Series-A Funding to Perk Up; Consumer Internet Emerges Hot Favourite: VCCircle VC Survey 2014.' Available at http://www.vccircle.com/news/alternative-investment/2014/02/05/series-funding-perk-consumer-internet-emerges-hot-favourite (accessed on 1 July 2015).

Venture Intelligence. 2014. 'Database on Private Company Financials, Transactions & Valuations for India.' Available at http://www.ventureintelligence.com (accessed on 1 July 2015).

———. 2019. 'Database on Private Company Financials, Transactions and Valuations for India.' Available at http://www.ventureintelligence.com (accessed on 1 July 2015).

Upton, N. and W. Petty. 2000. 'Venture Capital Investment and US Family Business.' *Venture Capital: An International Journal of Entrepreneurial Finance* 2(1): 27–39.

Wasmer, E. and P. Weil. 2000. 'The Macroeconomics of Labor and Credit Market Imperfections.' Number 1, IZA Discussion Paper.

Wennberg, K. and G. Lindqvist. 2010. 'The Effect of Clusters on the Survival and Performance of New Firms.' *Small Business Economics* 34(3): 221–41.

World Bank. 2015. *Doing Business.* Available at http://www.doingbusiness.org/data/exploreeconomies/india (accessed on 1 July 2016).

Wright, M., A. Lockett, and S. Pruthi. 2002. 'Internationalization of Western Venture Capitalists into Emerging Markets: Risk Assessment and Information in India.' *Small Business Economics* 19(1): 13–29.

Wright, M. and K. Robbie. 1998. 'Venture Capital and Private Equity: A Review and Synthesis.' *Journal of Business Finance and Accounting* 25(5–6): 521–70.

Yosha, O. 1995. 'Information Disclosure Costs and the Choice of Financing Source.' *Journal of Financial Intermediation* 4(1): 3–20.

Zacharakis, A. L. and G. D. Meyer. 1998. 'A Lack of Insight: Do Venture Capitalists Really Understand Their Own Decision Process?' *Journal of Business Venturing* 13(1): 57–76.

Zacharakis, A. L. and D. A. Shepherd. 2001. 'The Nature of Information and Overconfidence on Venture Capitalists' Decision Making.' *Journal of Business Venturing* 16(4): 311–32.

Zarutskie, R. 2010. 'The Role of Top Management Team Human Capital in Venture Capital Markets: Evidence from First-time Funds.' *Journal of Business Venturing* 25(1): 155–72.

Zhang, W., J. Gao, S. White, and P. Vega. 2007. 'Venture Capital and the Financing of China's New Technology Firms.' In *China's Emergent Political Economy: Capitalism in the Dragon's Lair*, edited by C. A. McNally, Routledge Studies in the Growth Economies of Asia, 60–83. London: Routledge.

Index